INTO SIBERIA

INTO
SIBERIA

George Kennan's

Epic Journey Through

the Brutal, Frozen

Heart of Russia

GREGORY J. WALLANCE

ST. MARTIN'S PRESS
New York

Library of Congress Cataloging-in-Publication Data

Names: Wallance, Gregory J., author.
Title: Into Siberia : George Kennan's epic journey through the brutal,
    frozen heart of Russia / Gregory J. Wallance.
Description: First edition. | New York : St. Martin's Press, 2023. |
    Includes bibliographical references and index.
Identifiers: LCCN 2023016840 | ISBN 9781250280053 (hardcover) |
    ISBN 9781250280060 (ebook)
Subjects: LCSH: Kennan, George, 1845–1924—Influence. | Kennan,
    George, 1845–1924—Travel—Russia (Federation)—Siberia. |
    Kennan, George, 1845–1924. Siberia and the exile system. | Exiles—
    Russia (Federation)—Siberia. | Siberia (Russia)—Description and
    travel. | Americans—Russia (Federation)—Siberia. | Journalists—
    United States—Biography. | United States—Relations—Soviet
    Union. | Soviet Union—Relations—United States.
Classification: LCC DK755.K343 W35 2023 | DDC 910.92 [B]—dc23/
    eng/20230614
LC record available at https://lccn.loc.gov/2023016840

First Edition: 2023

10 9 8 7 6 5 4 3 2 1

To Alexei Navalny

Here was a world all its own, unlike anything else; here were laws unto themselves, ways of dressing unto themselves, manners and customs unto themselves, a house of the living dead . . .

> —*Notes from the House of the Dead* (*Notes from the Dead House*), Fyodor Dostoevsky's semiautobiographical account of the four years he spent in a prison fort in the Siberian town of Omsk[1]

Investigative journalism is the "journalism of outrage" . . . a form of storytelling that probes the boundaries of America's civic conscience.

> —*The Journalism of Outrage* by David I. Protess, et al.[2]

Contents

List of Maps

List of Photographs
and Illustrations

Chronology of Relevant Events
in Russia in the Nineteenth and
Early Twentieth Centuries

1825—Nicholas I becomes tsar on the death of Alexander I; Decembrist revolt

1855—Death of Nicholas I; Alexander II's reign begins

1859—Surrender of Imam Shamil; Russian conquest of the Caucasus largely complete

1861—Alexander II emancipates the serfs

1865–67—Russian-American Telegraph Expedition

1867—Russian-Alaska sold to the United States

1873–74—"Going to the People" movement

1877–78—"Trial of the 193" held

1878–81—Height of terrorist activity in nineteenth-century Russia

1881—Alexander II assassinated; his successor Alexander III institutes emergency powers

1885–86—George Kennan's Siberian exile investigation

1894—Alexander III dies; Nicholas II becomes tsar

1899—Publication of *Resurrection,* a novel by Leo Tolstoy

1904–05—Russo-Japanese War

1905—Failed revolution of 1905

1914—World War I begins

1917—Nicholas II abdicates; provisional government overthrown by Bolsheviks under Lenin

Author's Note

Russian names, including those of famous figures, such as Tsar Alexander II and Fyodor Dostoevsky, are given in their commonly Anglicized form. I have generally relied on George Kennan's English spelling of Russian words and the names of the Siberian cities, towns, and villages that he visited. Dates are from the Gregorian calendar, unless noted otherwise. The Julian calendar, used in Russia from 1700 until 1918, was between eleven and thirteen days behind the Gregorian calendar. The term "exile" can be confusing because it often referred to not just the Russian subjects involuntarily sent to Siberia but also to the wives and children who often voluntarily accompanied them. The involuntary exiles included both common law convicts and regime opponents. Exiled regime opponents, in turn, included both those convicted of state crimes, or political offenses, and those involuntarily sent to Siberia without a trial or conviction. Here, "political exiles," unless noted otherwise, refers to regime opponents exiled to Siberia whether or not convicted of an offense.

INTO SIBERIA

The Russian Empire in the last half of the nineteenth century

Introduction

In mid-June 1885, a four-wheeled, horse-drawn carriage called a *tarantas* entered a small forest clearing just east of the Ural Mountains in Russia. At the center of the clearing stood a twelve-foot-high brick pillar, which marked the Siberian frontier. The driver brought the three-horse team to a halt, calling out to his passengers, "Here is the boundary." Two Americans in tweed traveling suits climbed out of the carriage.

George Kennan, a forty-year-old journalist, walked around the pillar, which had a façade of crumbling white stucco. He was a thin, sinewy man who stood ramrod straight. He had dark, piercing eyes, black hair flecked with gray, a well-groomed handlebar mustache, and an ample supply of resourceful energy. He had come to Russia on assignment for a widely read American journal, *The Century Illustrated Monthly Magazine,* to investigate the Siberian exile system. His companion, George Frost, a burly forty-two-year-old Boston artist, pulled out a sketch pad. He was there to provide the illustrations for Kennan's articles. Standing before the pillar, Kennan, who considered himself a friend of Russia, could not have imagined that his findings would inflame the American public against the tsarist regime and shape enduring attitudes toward Russia.

Ghosts of convicted criminals haunted the clearing in the forest. In an earlier era, the convicts, bearded and gaunt after months of marching from European Russia, had been allowed by their guards a brief stop at the pillar. Some kissed the European side of the pillar while others pressed their tear-soaked faces to it. Convicts collapsed to their knees and buried their faces in the earth. Some hugged each other or dug up handfuls of dirt to take with them. A few scraped their names or inscriptions on the pillar. "Farewell life!" The exile convoy commander shouted an order to form ranks. With a clinking of their chains and shackles, the convicts assembled, crossed themselves, and resumed their march to the east.

Of those who survived to reach their Siberian destinations, few

The Siberian boundary pillar, 1885 (from *Siberia and the Exile System* 1:53)

managed to return to Mother Russia after their sentences ended, which is why convicts wept at the pillar. A few years before Kennan's investigation, the Russian government had completed a railroad line that transported convicts across European Russia and over the Ural Mountains, apparently without stopping at the boundary pillar. But since the Russian rail network did not yet penetrate far into Siberia, the convicts still had to march thousands of miles from the railhead to Siberian prisons, mines, and factories. Like their predecessors at the boundary pillar, few saw their homes again.

After contemplating the "grief consecrated pillar," as Kennan called it, he and Frost climbed back into their carriage and rode into Siberia, which was so immense that it could swallow Europe (excluding Russia) and the United States (including Alaska) and still have more than enough room for Texas. They were unfazed by the challenge of a long Siberian journey because they were fit men familiar with hardship and privation.

The following March, Kennan and Frost stumbled out of Siberia. Frost had suffered a nervous breakdown with paranoid delusions and needed medical treatment. Kennan's face was old and sunken and he had difficulty walking. His wife barely recognized him when they reunited in London.[3]

George Kennan is a little-known American whose achievements have been overshadowed by a much younger, distant cousin, the diplomat George Frost Kennan, who was the chief architect of America's Cold War containment strategy. The George Kennan of this story was an intrepid explorer, a leading American journalist, and after his Siberian exile investigation, a moral force whose writings and lectures about the inhumanity of the exile system compelled Russia to implement reforms.

Kennan went into Siberia twice. The first time was in 1865 when, as a member of a Western Union–backed venture called the

Russian-American Telegraph Expedition, he explored a route for a telegraph line through the subzero wilderness of northeastern Siberia. It was a classic young man's adventure filled with challenges and hardships and driven by Kennan's quest to prove his courage. Twenty years later he returned to Siberia with George Frost to investigate the exile system and found himself on a moral journey. By then he had become one of America's most prominent defenders of Russia and its centuries-old practice of banishing criminals and political dissidents to Siberia. Kennan, who spoke Russian fluently and was regarded as a leading expert on Russia, believed that a thorough, objective investigation would vindicate his contention that the exile system, while hardly without flaws, was more humane than penal systems in European countries. He also hoped that his articles about the Siberian exile system would make him rich and famous.[4]

Kennan and Frost traveled eight thousand miles in Siberia in horse-drawn carriages, river steamers, and sleighs and on horseback. They suffocated in sandstorms in the summer and endured winter temperatures of minus forty-five degrees Fahrenheit. They inspected dozens of prisons, observed the marching parties of exiled convicts, spoke with Siberian officials, and met with more than a hundred exiled opponents of the tsarist regime. Both men were plagued by disease, vermin that infested their clothing and luggage, the jolting and pounding of carriages without springs or seats (they had to sit on their luggage), and by the stress of police surveillance. Worst of all was the nervous strain caused by their unrelenting exposure to human suffering because the exile system, as Kennan discovered, in fact was a brutal instrument of the Russian Empire's exploitation of Siberia's vast natural resources and a means of suppressing and punishing dissent.

Kennan's investigation discredited his own defense of the exile system, as he was the first to admit, and changed him as a person. When he returned to the United States, his overarching goal was no longer wealth and fame but to end the suffering of the exiles and bring freedom to Russia. His concept of courage, his attitudes toward women, his views on the Russian government's oppression of its Jews had all changed. "What I saw heard and learned in Siberia stirred me to the very depths of my soul—opened to me a new world of human experience, and raised, in some respects, all my moral standards."[5]

And Kennan's investigation changed America. Today it is nearly impossible to conceive of the close diplomatic relations between Russia and the United States and the affection of Americans for Russia at the time of Kennan's investigation. Many Americans held the benign perception of Russia as a "distant friend" of the United States, a colorful but mysterious land filled with tragically romantic characters. Kennan's investigative reporting put an end to that. His articles for the *Century* magazine, a nearly one-thousand-page, two-volume book, *Siberia and the Exile System,* and a nine-year lecture tour about the exile system left Americans so appalled and angry at Russia's mistreatment of its citizens that the relationship between the two countries was never the same.

I was drawn to Kennan because of my own experience in the Soviet Union, which still used exile as a punishment, during the Cold War. I had gone there as a young lawyer to submit legal petitions to Soviet authorities on behalf of Jews who had been exiled to Siberia merely because they had publicly demanded the right to emigrate to Israel. I was fortunate to meet courageous dissidents, such as the physicist, human rights advocate, and Nobel Peace Prize–laureate Andrei D. Sakharov and his wife, Yelena G. Bonner, who sacrificed their careers, comfort, and liberty in a fight for freedoms that I had taken for granted until I crossed the Soviet border. Not long after I met them, Sakharov and Bonner were exiled to the Volga River city of Gorky, which was then closed to foreigners, for protesting the Russian invasion of Afghanistan in 1979.

What it means to live without freedom was driven home to Kennan when, during his investigation, he interviewed a former Siberian political exile in the presence of a Russian liberal, who was amazed by Kennan's horrified expression as he listened to the exile's tragic story. The liberal later explained to Kennan that for him the exile's story was no more surprising than "an account of the running-over of a man in the street. As I watched the play of expression in your face—as I was forced to look at the facts, for a moment, from your point of view—I felt again, to the very bottom of my soul, the difference between a free citizen and a citizen of Russia." That difference had a lasting impact on Kennan.

Refreshingly, in the nineteenth century, character mattered as much as personality does in our times. Kennan once explained the importance of character in his Siberian telegraph exploration, but his words also apply to his even more demanding investigation of the Siberian exile system and grueling years on the lecture circuit. "Man carries on, for months or years, an almost incessant fight with a hostile and pitiless environment. . . . In such a situation, personal character rises into absolute predominance; and success, when achieved, is due almost wholly to the courage, forethought, and steadfastness of the individual actor." Diplomat George Frost Kennan paid tribute to his older cousin's character when he observed that his formal education ended at high school. "He really was in the intellectual sense a self-made man. He always had to do it himself with very little money. It is quite amazing for a boy of his background."

Kennan was asked late in life where he went to college. "Russia," he replied.[6]

The Bell of Uglich

Among the first Siberian exiles was a six-hundred-and-fifty-pound cop-
per church bell.

In 1591, a nine-year-old epileptic boy named Dmitry was found
dead in the town of Uglich on the Volga River. He was the son of the
late Ivan the Terrible and heir apparent to the throne, and his throat
had been cut. The dead boy's mother suspected treachery by the tsare-
vich's regent, the ambitious Boris Godunov (an official report later
claimed that Dmitry had died from self-inflicted knife wounds during
an epileptic seizure). The bell in the cathedral was rung to summon
the town to revolt. Godunov's representative in Uglich tried to silence
the bell but the townspeople killed him and the bell kept ringing. Godunov's forces eventually put down the revolt, executed two hundred
Uglichans, flogged and cut off the noses of another one hundred, and
sent scores, in some cases, whole Uglichan families, to Siberia. The bell
was lowered to the ground.

Church bells have long had an unusual status in Russia where they
are credited with lifelike qualities. The bells have names like "Swan"

or "Bear" that reflect their tones (a cry or rumble), and some believe they have a soul and the capacity to suffer. Godunov's men lashed the treasonous bell twelve times and tore off its "tongue" (the clapper) and one of its "ears" (the metal loop from which the bell hung). The bell was then sentenced to permanent exile in Siberia. Amid lamentations in Uglich, the mutilated and silenced bell was pulled away on a sledge by exiled Uglichans under an armed escort. The Uglichans dragged the bell for a year through swamps and forests, across rivers on rafts, and over the Ural Mountains. The bell arrived at its place of exile in the Siberian town of Tobolsk, where officials registered the bell as "the first inanimate exile." Authorities told the residents of Tobolsk never to ring the Bell of Uglich, but they fitted the bell with a new clapper and hung it in a belfry, where it was regularly rung.

Over the following centuries, countless Russian subjects followed the Bell of Uglich into Siberian exile.[7]

1

The Frozen World from Which Even the Favor of the Creator Had Withdrawn

The Kamchatka Peninsula plunges down from the northeastern corner of Siberia into cold waters. The peninsula's east coast is on the Bering Sea and its western shore lies on the Sea of Okhotsk, which has been called "unruly."

In early October 1865, more than halfway up the peninsula's west coast, a party of nine men, their fur clothing coated with ice, stood on a high escarpment overlooking the Sea of Okhotsk. The party's leader was the twenty-year-old George Kennan. His clothes had been wet or frozen for two days and nights and he had spent the last fourteen hours on foot or horseback, only to arrive at this desolate place. Below him, one foam-streaked wave after another rolled out of mists of snowflakes and, driven by howling winds, smashed against tall black cliffs that stretched along a submerged beach. Gurgling sounds echoed up to the escarpment as waves flooded into caves carved by the sea into the base of the cliffs. Behind him loomed a snow-covered mountain range, which he and his exhausted men—Viushin, a Cossack; Nicolai Bragan, a guide; and six Kamchadal workers—had just struggled to cross on horseback, along with twenty packhorses and a few dogs.

Kennan and his men mounted their horses and in fading daylight rode down to the mouth of the Samanka River. They set up camp and stood watch for two of their expedition colleagues, who were sailing up the coast in a whaleboat loaded with the expedition's heavy baggage and provisions. Once reunited, the expedition planned to continue north and, after clearing the Kamchatka Peninsula, begin exploring a route for a Siberian telegraph line. Kennan's orders were to wait two days for the whaleboat and, if it failed to appear, return over the mountains to the Kamchadal settlement of Lesnoy.

Two days came and went without the appearance of the whaleboat, which was unsurprising in view of the gale still pummeling the Sea of Okhotsk. The guide Bragan advised Kennan that, since they were almost out of food and heavy snow had fallen in the mountains, their best option was a go-for-broke thirty-mile dash down the beach at low tide to a ravine that offered an escape inland and a relatively easy trip back to Lesnoy. Kennan, preferring a reckless ride to starving in deep snowdrifts, agreed with him. But on learning of the plan, the swarthy, high-cheekboned Kamchadals killed and gutted one of their dogs and hung the carcass by the neck from the top of a pole. "Much as I pitied the poor dog thus ruthlessly slaughtered," Kennan later wrote, "I was glad to see the manifest improvement which it worked in the spirits of my superstitious comrades."

After Bragan judged that the outgoing tide had sufficiently exposed the beach, the party mounted their horses and, with the packhorses tied to the men's saddles by long lines, rode along the wet sand, chased by the remaining dogs. In five hours, waves would again crash into the black cliffs and if they were still on the beach the horses would drown and, unless they could cling to the cliffs, the men with them. The riders, skirting giant chunks of rock that had sheared away from the cliffs, made good progress for eighteen miles. Then the lead rider, the Cossack Viushin, abruptly reined in his horse. "Bears! Bears! There!" Black bears ambled in their direction on the beach ahead. Kennan, who had seen bears inland, could not fathom how these bears came to be on a beach, but that was beside the point. "The bears were there, and we must pass. It was a clear case of breakfast for one party or the other." The two dismounted and pulled out their rifles. Kennan slipped a fresh cartridge into his rifle and put a dozen in his pocket.[8]

A year earlier, in the autumn of 1864, George Kennan had gone home to Norwalk, Ohio, and announced to his family that he had left his job as a telegraph operator in a Western Union office in Cincinnati. He explained that he would soon be leaving for Russian-Alaska as a member of an expedition exploring a route for a telegraph line that would connect North America and Europe by way of the Bering Strait and Siberia. The announcement frightened his close-knit family because Kennan was in precarious physical and mental health after nearly two years of high stress, wartime telegraph work, and until now his most challenging outdoor experience had been boyhood camping trips. Kennan asked the family physician, Dr. Charles Morrill, to examine him and then vouch for his ability to survive the Russian-Alaskan wilds. The doctor looked him over and told Kennan's father, "You might as well let him go, Mr. Kennan. He can't do worse than die in Alaska, and he may live; but he's certain to die if you keep him in that Cincinnati telegraph office. He needs air, exercise, and change. He's nothing but a white bag of bones now."

The expedition planned to sail from New York City to Nicaragua, cross overland to the Pacific, and take a steamer up the west coast of the United States and Canada to Russian-Alaska. But, while still in Norwalk, Kennan contracted typhoid fever that left him barely able to walk. "I went to bed, caring little whether I should ever get up from it again. The expedition, of course, would sail without me, and that—so far as my future was concerned—would be the end of all things." Fortunately for Kennan, the ship's departure was delayed, which allowed him to recover and still have enough time to travel to New York City to join his team for the sailing. His mother knew something about the hazards her son would face because she had grown up in a pioneer family in the Ohio wilderness. She saw him off with a cheerful façade that he found more distressing than if she had sobbed. "I could see, behind it, the grief and suffering that she firmly controlled, in order to send me away hopeful, confident and happy."

The family doctor had been right. After sailing from New York City, Kennan's spirits rose and he put on weight; throughout his life he would prove most durable on adventures. During a stopover in San Francisco, the expedition leader offered Kennan the opportunity to join a different telegraph exploration party, which was leaving for Siberia. He readily accepted because Siberia might offer even more challenging adventures with which to prove to himself that he was not a coward, a fear that had haunted him since childhood. Kennan wrote letters home that he was going to Siberia instead of Russian-Alaska, ending a letter to his younger sister Hattie with "& now little sister good-by and may God keep you [and] all the dear ones at home until my return." From his family's perspective, Russian-Alaska at least was on the same continent as Norwalk, but Siberia might as well have been on the moon.

Kennan in the uniform of the Russian-American Telegraph Expedition, 1865 (courtesy Library of Congress, Prints and Photographs Division)

Kennan and his new team sailed from San Francisco in July 1865 on a Russian brig, the *Olga,* bound for the Kamchatka Peninsula, a wilderness of mountains, ravines, active volcanoes, and bears. Before sailing Kennan had been photographed in his brass-buttoned, blue expedition uniform, which resembled a Union Army uniform (second lieutenants on the semi-military telegraph expedition wore a shoulder strap marked with a silver snowshoe). The photograph shows an alert, dark-haired, clean-shaven young man on the eve of a great adventure.[9]

The idea of erecting a telegraph line through thousands of miles of Siberian wilderness would have provoked laughter a few years earlier because there appeared to be a much easier and shorter way to connect Europe and North America. In 1857, the Atlantic Telegraph Company had launched a flotilla to lay a telegraph cable across the Atlantic Ocean. Waves caused the cable to snap and part of it sank. It snapped again and sank on another try. In 1858, the cable was laid, worked for a few weeks, and then abruptly went dead, which ended the worldwide rejoicing. Another attempt was mounted after the Civil War but the cable snapped again.

In the belief that the Atlantic cable would never be successfully laid, the Western Union Telegraph Company, a competitor of the Atlantic Telegraph Company, committed to the Siberian route even though it was the long way around. The undertaking, at least in hindsight, seems gloriously mad, but American optimism and the profit motive are forces of nature. Just as a start, Western Union had to complete a thousand-mile telegraph line along the Pacific coast from San Francisco to New Westminster in British Columbia. Next, it had to erect more than two thousand miles of line through British Columbia and Russian-Alaska. Laying an undersea cable across the comparatively narrow Bering Strait and Anadyr Gulf may have been the easiest part.[10]

Then Western Union had to put up a two-thousand-mile line through Siberia to the Chinese border at the Amur River using indigenous Siberian workers to cut down enough trees to erect tens of thousands of telegraph poles, which would then be strung with telegraph wire

Kennan's journey as a member of the Russian-American Telegraph Expedition,
1865–1868 (from *Tent Life in Siberia*)

transported across the Pacific by the expedition's fleet. Finally, the five-
thousand-mile, two-continent Western Union line would be joined
to a yet-to-be-completed line extending seven thousand miles from
the Amur River to St. Petersburg and Moscow, which were already
connected by telegraph lines to European cities. Russia committed to
finish the Amur–St. Petersburg line, gave Western Union the right to

erect its line through Russian-Alaska and northeastern Siberia, and promised to provide logistical support to the exploration parties. A flotilla of two dozen ships, including naval vessels from both Russia and the United States, would provide ocean transportation for men and telegraph equipment.

The Russian-American Telegraph Expedition was a high point in decades of generally warm relations between the two countries. In 1861, Tsar Alexander II had assured President Lincoln that he could count on Russia's "most cordial sympathy . . . during the important crisis which it is passing through at present," which made Russia the only major European country to openly support the Union in the Civil War. Secretary of State William H. Seward emphasized to American diplomats in St. Petersburg that Russia "has our friendship, in every case, in preference to any other European power." In a seeming congruence of expanding personal liberty in both countries, in 1861, Tsar Alexander II freed the privately owned Russian serfs and two years later, President Lincoln issued the Emancipation Proclamation. In 1863, a Russian Navy squadron visited New York City, which held a parade down Fifth Avenue for the Russian sailors that featured a band playing "God Save the Tsar" and a huge Russian flag flying over Tiffany's.[11]

On August 20, 1865, the *Olga* anchored off Petropavlovsk, a settlement of several hundred on Avacha Bay on the Bering Sea coast of southern Kamchatka. Kennan glimpsed two majestic volcanic peaks rising above a snowy mountain range. "You see before you my country—the great Russian Empire!" cried Serge Abaza, the leader of the Siberian telegraph expedition. Abaza, who had worked for Western Union for the past ten years, was a flamboyant engineer from an aristocratic Russian family. His team addressed him as "Major Abaza," his expedition rank. Kennan's rank was quartermaster and secretary; later he was promoted to lieutenant.

The noisy lowering of the *Olga*'s anchor chain attracted the attention of little children in Petropavlovsk, who darted outside and then ran back into their log houses to announce the ship's arrival. The settlement's canine population also took notice. "Seventy-five or a hundred half-wild dogs broke out suddenly in a terrific chorus of howls in honour of our arrival." The captain's boat rowed Abaza and Kennan to the settlement. As the boat pulled away from the *Olga,* the second mate, who had taken a liking to Kennan, called out in broken English, "Oh. Mr. Kinney! Who's a g'un to cook for ye, and ye can't get no potatusses." Kennan assured him that his team could cook for themselves and anyway, there were always roots. "Poor Mr. Kinney! Poor Mr. Kinney!" the second mate said for days afterward. Kennan later watched the *Olga* pull up its anchor and sail away. "The *Olga* was gone, and the last tie which connected us with the civilized world seemed severed."

The green onion dome of a Russian Orthodox church rose above Petropavlovsk, where Russian peasants mixed with indigenous Kamchadal villagers clad in animal skins. They had been dropped at Petropavlovsk, and not closer to their route of exploration at the northern end of the Sea of Okhotsk, because the *Olga* had to continue south to land another team of explorers near the Russian-Chinese border. In the settlement Maj. Abaza hired a Cossack "orderly," Viushin, and recruited a young American fur trapper living in Petropavlovsk, James Dodd, who became Kennan's closest friend in Siberia. Dodd, who was from New Jersey, had been trapping in Kamchatka for the past seven years, spoke Russian, and knew the customs of the Kamchatka tribes.[12]

Kennan's team had been ordered to obtain information about the climate, soil, timber, and inhabitants of northeastern Siberia and "to locate, in a general way, a route for the proposed line." But first they had to travel to the northern end of Kamchatka, which is about the overall size of Sweden, before they could begin their exploration. Kamchadals poled and paddled Kennan and his teammates in two small whaleboats up the Avacha River, whose banks were lined with alpine roses and black Kamchatkan lilies. Each night the party set up camp on a sandbar where they cooked and ate their dinner, smoked, and talked around the fire, and went to sleep listening to the sounds of night birds on the river. The first days of travel in Kamchatka were the magical exploration Kennan had long dreamed about. "I cannot remember any journey in my whole life which gave me more enjoyment at the time."[13]

The Russian government had sent a Cossack courier ahead of the party to arrange for provisions, accommodations, and transportation on the successive legs of the team's journey up the Kamchatka Peninsula. Fresh horses awaited them at the Kamchadal river settlement of Okuta, where a pungent odor arose from salmon drying on wooden frames. At the center of the settlement was a log church painted deep red with a green iron roof and two blue onion domes decorated with golden stars. The inhabitants of Okuta and the other settlements on their route greeted the explorers like celebrities. "I believe they would have carried us on their shoulders if we would have permitted it," Kennan wrote in his journal. At Sherom they left their horses behind and boarded a raft assembled from three dugout canoes that the villagers had tied together with poles and sealskin thongs and then covered with a wooden platform topped with newly cut hay. The explorers pitched a tent on the platform, stacked their rifles and revolvers around the tentpole, and lay on bearskins as the Kamchadals paddled them north up the Kamchatka River. Eleven days after leaving Petropavlovsk, the party reached the village of Kluchei, which lay within sight of the smoking Kluchefskoi volcano.

The plan was to continue west on the Yolofka River and, with the aid of a local guide, Nicolai Bragan, cross the central Kamchatkan mountain range on horseback through the Yolofka Pass to the Sea of Okhotsk, and then, staying close to the coast, travel north through the mountains. But local Kamchadals firmly advised that fall storms had turned mountain streams into surging rivers that horses with heavy packs could not cross. Maj. Abaza proceeded anyway but rode south of the mountains through low, wooded hills to the Sea of Okhotsk, where he divided the team into a sea party and a land party. Despite lack of wilderness experience, Kennan had performed well in Kamchatka. Abaza assigned him to lead the land party, which included Bragan, Viushin, the Kamchadals, and twenty horses carrying light packs, north through the mountains to their rendezvous point at the mouth of the Samanka River. Abaza and Dodd purchased a whaleboat from villagers and sailed up the peninsula's west coast with the expedition's heavy baggage and provisions.

Kennan led his party away from the coast and into the mountains, where the horses floundered in deep snowdrifts and their riders had to dismount and half pull them up. Exposed rocks in windblown stretches cut open the men's sealskin boots. The party struggled through a whiteout, which lifted to reveal a black, wraithlike volcano that vanished into stinging, wind-driven snow. Kennan's clothing froze and he lost feeling in his hands. He thought of the admonition of the English writer Izaak Walton that every misery one misses is a new blessing, but, as he later reflected in his journal, "When you don't miss any miseries but encounter every one, there is very little to be thankful for." They made the crest but on the descent the party wandered aimlessly for hours until Kennan realized that their guide, Bragan, had gotten them lost. Using his compass, Kennan brought his party to the Sea of Okhotsk, where they waited in vain for the whaleboat, and then rode for their lives along the beach until bears blocked the way.[14]

Viushin and Kennan stayed low behind rocks but could not get a clear shot at the bears. Viushin stood, took aim, and started laughing. "They are people." Two Kamchadals, in soaked fur coats and pants, approached Kennan and Viushin, shouting in Russian not to shoot. The Kamchadals bowed ceremoniously and one handed Kennan a note from Maj. Abaza. Bad weather had driven their whaleboat farther north, where Maj. Abaza and Dodd went ashore and made their way to Lesnoy and from there sent the Kamchadals to find Kennan's party. Kennan gave packhorses to the two Kamchadals and the party resumed its race along the beach. The horses were splashing through water when they reached the ravine.

In Lesnoy, Kennan happily reunited with his teammates, but the expedition was in bad shape. Maj. Abaza was ill and half of the Kamchadals were unfit for further work. The expedition had not even gotten off the Kamchatka Peninsula to begin surveying a telegraph route and now they had to wait in Lesnoy until the mountains could be crossed by dog sleigh. For Kennan, though, it was a satisfying moment. Unlike the Kamchadals who had lived their lives in a wilderness, he was in good health; and, as he wrote in his journal, "After the most disastrous expedition I have now learned how much suffering, how much hunger, how much cold wet fatigue I can stand without breaking down."

Maj. Abaza and the Kamchadals recovered, the streams froze, and enough snow fell to support sleighs. They traveled north through the mountains in a caravan of eighteen men riding on sixteen sleighs pulled by two hundred dogs. Their route took them into the land of the "wandering" Koryaks, nomadic anarchists who put up a spirited but ultimately losing fight against the Russian conquerors of Siberia.[15]

In 1558, Ivan the Terrible rewarded the Stroganov family for its loyal service to the throne with a lease on vast tracts of land east of the town of Perm in the Ural Mountains, which was then the Russian frontier. According to legend, Mongols had executed an ancestor of the Stroganov family by removing his flesh layer by layer, leaving only bones, tendons, and ligaments. His defiant widow adopted the name Stroganov, based on the Russian verb *strogat,* which means "to peel." The Stroganovs built fortified posts and settlements as the first line of Russia's eastern defenses. From that staging area the conquest of Siberia was carried out by a varying mix of government officials, Russian soldiers, Cossacks from both Russia and Ukraine, and the hunters and trappers called the *promyshlenniki,* a word that means "men who work for themselves."

The *promyshlenniki* were lured by "soft gold," including the pelts of red foxes, ermines, and beavers but it was the sable, a shy, twenty-inch species of marten that they lived and lusted for. The lustrous pelts of the brown-hued sables were highly valued in western Russia and Europe, but as much for their status as a symbol of wealth and power as for warmth in cold weather. The *promyshlenniki* were, according to historian Janet Hartley, "the true pioneers who opened up Siberia and made its colonisation possible." At the height of the sable rush in the seventeenth century, the Siberian sable harvest annually sent between two and three hundred thousand sable pelts to European Russia.

Siberia's few hundred thousand indigenous peoples, who had only primitive weapons, were no match for the rapacious invaders, who vaulted from one great Siberian river basin to another. The invaders pushed back the Siberian frontier at the rate of a thousand miles a decade until they reached the Bering Strait. By 1650 they had conquered a vast territory, equal to about 9 percent of the earth's land surface, that stretched from the Urals to the Pacific and the Amur River to the Arctic. The Koryaks fought the Russian invaders on the Kamchatka Peninsula with stolen or captured firearms before succumbing early in the eighteenth century. As they had done to other indigenous Siberians, the Russians imposed on the Koryaks an annual sable quota, which they enforced by torturing and hanging the Koryak men and abducting their children if the quota was not met. Indigenous women were the other prize sought by the conquerors, who forced them into sexual and domestic slavery. Only the Chukchis in the far reaches of northeastern Siberia, where there were few sables, escaped subjugation. The conquest of Siberia was highly rewarding to the throne. In the mid-seventeenth century taxes on fur pelts generated one-third of the state's income.

By the time Kennan arrived in Siberia, the sable rush days were largely over because relatively few sables were left to trap and the frontier forts had grown into settlements and towns. Unlike the settled Koryaks living in villages along the sea coast, the wandering Koryaks still lived a nomadic life because their food, clothing, and transportation depended on herds of thousands of reindeer whose grazing rapidly depleted all grass and moss within miles of an encampment.[16]

To Kennan the approach of the expedition's sixteen sleigh teams to their first Koryak encampment, "resembled a midnight attack of Comanches upon a hostile camp, rather than the peaceful arrival of three or four American travelers." The party's two hundred dogs smelled the reindeer and began barking and, despite the drivers' snow brakes, dragging the sleighs ahead, which stampeded thousands of reindeer into the night. Although they went to considerable trouble to round up their scattered herd in the dark, the Koryaks hospitably invited the foreigners to dinner in a yurt.

The expedition continued north, stopping in Koryak encampments where, in exchange for tobacco and beads, Kennan and his companions ate and slept in smoky yurts, lying next to reindeer carcasses and piles of dried fish. Their hosts lectured them on the most efficient ways to kill an old or sick man or woman with a spear or knife, an expertise developed because the aged and afflicted were an intolerable burden on the nomadic lives of the wandering Koryaks. Kennan tried driving a sleigh, which he thought would be "as easy as losing money in California mining stocks," but the sleigh overturned and he was shot "like a huge living meteor through the air" into a deep snowdrift. He eventually learned to do it.

The temperature fell to minus twenty-five degrees Fahrenheit and the men frequently had to run next to their sleighs to maintain circulation in their feet. Frost circled their eyes and at the end of a day's travel beards had to be separated from fur hoods with a knife. The expedition finally cleared the Kamchatka Peninsula, made the hard turn west, and rounded the northern end of the Sea of Okhotsk. On November 25, they sighted the red church steeple of Gizhiga. Kennan had been traveling for three months, enduring intense cold and wearing the same clothes for weeks. He was grimy and smoky from the Koryak yurts and the skin was peeling from his face. "No one who has not experienced this can possibly understand with what joyful hearts we welcomed that red church steeple, and the civilization of which it was a sign." The team planned to rest and refit in Gizhiga, which had begun its existence as a Russian garrison in a chain of garrisons that protected lines of communications between fur trading centers in northeastern Siberia. Now it was a backwater settlement of log houses on the empire's periphery. In winter the only way in or out was by dog sleigh because the settlement's river harbor was choked by ice.[17]

Hearing the Americans' madly barking dogs, the population turned out to cheer as the expedition's sleighs careened into the settlement. The Americans had barely climbed off their sleighs when the nervous little Russian *ispravnik,* the equivalent of a mayor, greeted them like a marooned man. "Are you just from America? How did you cross the tundra? Any news from St. Petersburg? You must come and dine with me." Kennan and his companions used the mayor's home to change out of their furs and into their telegraph company uniforms. After a pre-dinner brandy they enjoyed a feast. "Yesterday we sat on the ground in a Koryak tent and ate reindeer meat out of a wooden trough with our fingers, and today we dined with the Russian governor, in a luxurious house, upon venison cutlets, plum pudding, and champagne." They brought the news-starved mayor up to date on world events, at least as of the previous summer when they last heard any, including the assassination of President Lincoln.

Two other American telegraph exploration teams, led by Union Army veterans of the Civil War, had landed in Siberia, one in the north and the other far to the south of Gizhiga. With the dual objective of finding a route for the telegraph line and linking up with those teams, Maj. Abaza again divided his men. His team would explore a telegraph route from Gizhiga five hundred miles south to the settlement of Okhotsk. Along the way Abaza hoped to find the team led by Richard J. Bush and James A. Mahood, which had landed at the Amur River on the Chinese border and was exploring to the north. Abaza ordered Kennan and Dodd to travel north and find a route for the telegraph between Gizhiga and the indigenous settlement of Anadyrsk near the Arctic Circle. On that journey Kennan and Dodd might encounter Collins J. MacRae and A. S. Arnold, whose team had been dropped at the mouth of the Anadyr River on the Bering Sea, and was exploring to the south. Collectively, the Russian-American telegraph teams were operating along an arc that stretched nearly two thousand miles along the Russian Pacific coast from below the Arctic Circle to the Chinese border.

Kennan estimated that the two-hundred-and-fifty-mile journey to Anadyrsk would take twenty to thirty days, depending on the weather. The little available information suggested that both trees and the indigenous workers to cut them into telegraph poles would be scarce on this route. "We were 'in for it,' however, now, and our first duty was obviously to go through the country, ascertain its extent and nature, and find out what facilities, if any, it afforded for the construction of our line." On the morning of December 13, 1865, Kennan and Dodd assembled eight drivers, eight heavily loaded sleighs, and almost one hundred impatiently barking dogs. The temperature was minus thirty-one degrees Fahrenheit. "God bless you boys!" Maj. Abaza said to Kennan and Dodd and the sleigh teams were off, churning up clouds of snow. At the edge of the settlement the grizzled, white-haired leader of the Gizhiga Cossacks came out of his small log home and waved his fur hat. They passed by groves of trees where magpies sat on the branches with their feathers flared around their heads. Kennan thought that even the magpies had been surprised by the severe cold.[18]

The scenery grew "strange, weird, arctic." In the daytime, which lasted only a few hours, they had their shadows for company, a long line of upside-down, dark dog sleighs that, due to the angle and position of the sun, appeared to be racing ahead of them ten feet above the snow. "This curious phenomenon lasted only a moment, but it was succeeded by others equally strange until we lost faith in our eyesight entirely." Although it was dark by midafternoon, the men sometimes had to keep traveling for hours until they found trees and could build a huge fire. Kennan and Dodd ate their dinner and then stretched out on their bearskins by the fire, talking, smoking, drinking tea, and occasionally singing American songs for the amusement of the drivers.

One night Kennan woke up from cold feet and raised his head out of his fur bag. In the glittery starlight he could make out the shapeless forms of the drivers lying in their sleeping bags around the smoldering embers of the fire, the silhouettes of the loaded sleighs, and the dogs curled up like hairy mounds scattered in the snow. He found the silence so intense as to be oppressive until the mournful howl of a dog, which other dogs soon took up, distracted his attention from the blood throbbing in his ears. The shimmering curtains of an aurora borealis lit up the snowy landscape. Kennan tucked his head back into his fur bag and fell asleep until dawn brightened the sky, the dogs began stirring, and the drivers left their sleeping bags to build a fire and boil water for tea.[19]

A week after leaving Gizhiga, they reached the settlement of Shestakova and heard startling news from the north, which had been passed south from one band of Chukchis to another. A party of Americans had been stranded near the mouth of the Anadyr River and were living in a shelter constructed from driftwood. Even though the location was far from where the Anadyr River party under MacRae and Arnold should have been by now, Kennan wondered, "What could Americans be doing there if they did not belong to our expedition?" He and Dodd discussed whether to go on a rescue mission even though Maj. Abaza had ordered them not to explore the Anadyr River this season. They decided that, when they reached the settlement of Anadyrsk, they would obtain more dog sleighs, drivers, and provisions and search for the trapped party.

The landscape beyond Shestakova was so bleak that Kennan could describe it in only two words—"snow and sky"—and the scarcity of trees from which to cut poles left him despairing for the future of the telegraph line. A storm blew up with winds so furious that the dogs refused to go on so the party arranged the sleighs in a semicircle as a wind barrier. Men and dogs huddled behind the sleighs for two days until the storm abated. New Year's Eve 1865 found Kennan eating dinner by a ten-foot-high fire at the foot of an isolated mountain. Despite the fire, at minus fifty-three degrees Fahrenheit, the tin knives and spoons were so cold that they burned his bare hand, his hot soup froze before he could finish it, and his eyelids partly froze together. "Words can give no idea of it," he wrote in his journal.

The settlement of Anadyrsk was made up of several Russian and indigenous villages with a total population of about two hundred. Just before Kennan and Dodd arrived, a band of nomadic Chukchis reported to the villagers that they had seen a smoking metal tube poking above the snow near the mouth of the Anadyr River. When he heard of the Chukchis' account, Kennan realized that they had seen a stovepipe from a hut buried by snow. "This fact alone convinced us beyond a doubt that there were Americans living somewhere on the coast of the Bering Sea." They faced another long dog sleigh trip just to reach the general vicinity of the stovepipe based on the Chukchis' description; unless their sleighs practically drove on top of it, the stovepipe could be easily missed. "It would be far worse than the proverbial search for a needle in a haystack."[20]

Much of the settlement turned out to see them off. The indigenous drivers harnessed one hundred and twenty-five dogs to eleven sleighs piled with long Siberian snowshoes, shovels, axes, rifles, and food for both men and dogs. Once in their harnesses, the dogs, who were far more eager to start out than their masters, leaped, barked, and strained to pull the sleighs, which were still anchored in the snow. A local priest offered his blessings and they set out. After eleven days of hard sleighing, Kennan found himself in the most disturbing environment he had yet encountered. On the vast tundra the winds had blown the snow into wavelike ridges. At night the temperature stayed close to minus fifty degrees Fahrenheit. The lurid glare of a swollen, red moon, which kept changing its shape, highlighted the unearthly desolation around them. By daylight or moonlight, Kennan could detect no trace of life, not a tree or a bush, and no sign of God.[21]

Throughout his life Kennan had a fraught relationship with organized religion and religious theology. His severe Presbyterian upbringing included family prayers, Bible studies, and rigid observance of the Sabbath. As a boy he dreaded the approach of Sunday "as I dreaded nothing else in life." Sitting in the Norwalk Presbyterian Church on a hard seat too high for his feet to reach the floor, he found it impossible to stay awake during the pastor's long sermons. His mother's response was to put her hand gently on his arm and, when he opened his eyes, "give me a pained, reproachful look that kept me awake for another ten minutes." Kennan's first religious doubts, as to "man's place in Nature and the adequacy of the Bible as an explanation for the Cosmos," arose in the spring of 1865, when he had spent time in California before his Pacific crossing to the Kamchatka Peninsula. A biologist in Sacramento introduced him to the microscope and the world of "the infinitely small," from the tiny stream of blood in the membrane of a frog's foot to the prism of colors in a butterfly's wing.

One slide contained microscopic shells pulled from the bottom of the Bering Sea by the lead line of a ship. To Kennan's naked eye, on the slide the shells looked only like dust but peering through the lens, he saw stunning colors and extravagant forms. "What was the object of God," Kennan asked himself, "in creating these beautiful things to lie for uncounted ages at the bottom of the Bering Sea? Was it merely in order that I, after thousands of years, should put a few of them on the slide of a microscope and be astonished by their delicacy and beauty?" He could not accept that. Rather, "God must have created living organisms in the bottom of the sea and given them beauty of form and color for some reason unrelated in any way to the existence of man. And if part of the Cosmos had been brought into being without reference to man, why not all of it?"[22]

Now, crossing the interminable tundra in search of a stovepipe, "We seemed to have entered upon some frozen abandoned world, where all the ordinary laws and phenomena of Nature were suspended, where animal and vegetable life were extinct, and from which even the favour of the Creator had been withdrawn." Kennan felt that he had forsaken his own existence.

Day after day the eye rests upon the same illimitable expanse
of storm-drifted snow, and night after night the traveler camps
in an utter solitude, over which seems to brood the mournful

silence of universal death. I do not know how to describe in words the impression of sadness, loneliness, and isolation from all human interests, which these great barren plains make upon the imagination. The world which you have left, with all its cares, strife, and busy activity, fades away into the unreal imagery of a dream; and you seem removed to an infinite distance from all the interest and occupations of your previous life.

The tundra raised the same doubts as the microscopic shells. If God had deserted the tundra or had never been there, then might the same be true about the rest of the universe? His time on the tundra would lead Kennan to abandon organized religion as an intellectual framework in which to live his life and begin a quest for what he would call a "working theory of life on new foundations and with different materials." As he put it many years later, he discovered in Siberia that there is "no pity, love, justice, or mercy in all the universe outside the heart of man."[23]

The party, stopping only once at sunrise to rest the dogs, traveled another twenty-four hours before reaching the stretch of the Anadyr River where they hoped to find the buried hut. Dodd was on the verge of falling asleep, which could be a death sentence in those temperatures. It dawned on Kennan that in their state of frigid exhaustion, with the nearest trees now dozens of miles behind them and the paws of the dogs cracking open and bleeding into the snow, the Anadyr River party and the buried hut might be their rescue and not the other way around.

Kennan ordered the main body of the party to stop, while the lead drivers searched for a protruding stovepipe and unsuccessfully dug in the snow on the riverbank for driftwood. The exhausted drivers with him "sat silently upon their sledges as if they expected nothing and hoped for nothing." He faced a difficult choice. He could abandon the search and make a sprint with his bleeding dogs for the nearest trees where, if they made it that far, they could build a fire. Or he could keep searching for the buried shelter and hope that, if they found it, the Americans were still alive and, even if not, the stove in their shelter had fuel. Otherwise, they faced the unpleasant prospect of camping that night without a fire unless they could find driftwood. He continued the search.

Encased in two thick fur coats, with both black bearskin-trimmed hoods drawn tightly over his head, and a squirrel-skin mask frozen to his face, Kennan heard faint cries from the lead sleighs. He threw back his hoods and heard more cries. His dogs perked up their ears and he let them charge forward to where advance drivers had gathered on the riverbank around an overturned whaleboat partly buried in the snow. As Kennan brushed frost from his eyelashes with his mittens, cries farther down the river heralded another discovery. "Here it is!" When Kennan arrived, he found a stovepipe protruding from a snow-drift. "Thank God," he whispered to himself. "Thank God."

Kennan shouted into the stovepipe. "Halloo the house!"

From under his feet came the startled response from an American. "Who's there?"

It was the Anadyr River party.[24]

2

As Miserable as a
Young Boy Can Be

When he was fourteen, George Kennan feared that an accident had ruined his dream of becoming an explorer. That dream, and his passion for the new technology of the telegraph, had occupied much of his boyhood in Norwalk, Ohio. At the middle of the nineteenth century, Norwalk was a family community with a population of around two thousand. The children of Norwalk roamed the town when they were not in school or doing chores. They played hide-and-seek around the distillery with its long rows of whisky barrels, in the summer they burrowed like rabbits in the sandbanks along Norwalk Creek (their tunnels frequently collapsed on them), and in the winter they sledded down its banks and skated on the ice.

The accident didn't happen to George Kennan but to a boyhood friend. One summer afternoon, when the two were together, Kennan's friend got his hand caught in the gears of working machinery. His arm was crushed before the machinery could be stopped. In agony the boy was taken to a surgeon's office, and, out of curiosity, Kennan followed. He peered through a window next to the operating table to watch the

surgeon work on his friend's arm, which had to be amputated at the
shoulder. The surgeon suddenly lost his grip on the forceps clamping
the end of a severed artery and a jet of bright red blood splashed against
the inside of the glass pane where Kennan had pressed his face close.
"The effect, upon me, was a sensation that I had never felt before in
all my boyish life—a sensation of deadly nausea, faintness and over-
whelming fear."

Kennan was so traumatized that at first he couldn't think clearly
about the episode, but his shock soon gave way to self-doubt. Throughout American history, insecurity about their courage and manhood
has been a common experience of adolescent boys and young men,
and so has finding a way to prove that they possess these traits. For
George Kennan, the failure to pass a test of his courage was shattering.
"I began to be tortured by a vague suspicion that I was lacking in what
we now call 'nerve'—that I was afraid of some things, perhaps of all
things, that involved suffering or peril." He lost "half my self-respect
and was about as miserable as a young boy of that age can be. . . . With
the boyish visions I then had of travel and exploration, it was a whole
spiritual tragedy."

To prove to himself that he had courage Kennan went looking for
danger, which was not easy to find in Norwalk, now more than a generation removed from its frontier days. He sat alone in the cemetery at
night. He climbed the bell tower of a church and, five stories above the
ground, walked along its six-inch-wide stone coping. At best, Kennan
was only partially reassured. He was caught in the exhausting contra-
diction between his ideals, especially his "high ideal of intrepid manhood" and his fear that he was hopelessly weak and a coward. He had
to listen to an inner voice constantly ask a question that he could not
answer. "Of what use is it for you to think of exploration and wild life
in wild countries, if the first time your courage or fortitude is put to
the test you get faint and sick?"[25]

Kennan's dream of becoming an explorer may have been inspired
by his mother's tales of life in the Ohio wilderness. In 1818, Zebediah

Morse, his three brothers, and their families set out for Ohio from upstate New York. They were small plot farmers who, dreaming of becoming "lords of the soil," had acquired fertile land south of Lake Erie. Zebediah's daughter, seven-year-old Mary Ann and the future mother of George Kennan, never forgot the sad farewells to their friends and neighbors. The families went by wagon to Buffalo, crossed Lake Erie to Ohio on a schooner, and then rode on a wagon through virgin forests to the town of Norwalk, where a few families had already settled.

A simple rule governed pioneers like the Morse families in a primeval forest: work hard or starve to death. They cleared land, built log cabins, planted corn, and burned the piles of unneeded felled trees in great fires that darkened the sky with smoke. The Morse families did well and had no regrets. Mary Ann's father marveled that, unlike his puny corn in New York, the stalks of his Ohio corn were "so tall I cannot even hang my hat on them." More log cabins went up as new settlers arrived, livestock was acquired, frame houses replaced the cabins, the Native Americans were driven off despite their treaty rights, and a circuit-riding preacher came to Norwalk on Sundays to hold services.[26]

Mortality among children on the Ohio frontier was high. Simply wandering off and getting lost in the forest could mean death for a child. The cheerful trill of a whippoorwill could be heard in the eerily still trees, but so could the doleful howl of a wolf. Mary Ann attended a funeral for a little girl her own age who was the first person to be buried in the cemetery behind the Episcopal Church. The gravestone inscription read: "I am the first come here to lie. Children and youth prepare to die."

Mary Ann was mentally and physically strong enough to survive illnesses, dangers, and frontier hardships. Once she had finished her chores she played by herself in the thick, gnarly, surface roots of the great trees because she had no playmates within miles and her brothers were out in the fields. Late in life she recalled that "I think I must have had a great love for nature in her wild, uncultivated state, for I never remember to have been lonely in those childish years, but looked up to the sky, where I felt God saw me, and all my actions." To Mary Ann nature and God were the same. Many years later, after experiencing the desolate, wind-swept Siberian tundra, George Kennan deeply dismayed his mother by questioning her beliefs.

At age seventeen, Mary Ann enrolled in the new Norwalk Academy. The first principal, an Episcopal clergyman, apparently found Norwalk uncongenial and left after a year. The trustees wrote to a young teacher and college graduate named John Kennan in Herkimer, New York, and offered him the vacant post. He arrived in 1828, and the following year, he and Mary Ann married. Their son George was born on February 16, 1845, the fifth of six children. He had one brother, John, who was thirteen years older; two older sisters, Mary Jane (Jennie), Ellen (Nellie); and a younger sister, Harriet (Hattie). Another sister did not survive infancy.[27]

Kennan grew up riding horses, hunting, fishing, and playing "two-old-cat," a forerunner of baseball. He was an avid reader of boy classics like *Robinson Crusoe* and *Swiss Family Robinson* but by age eleven he was reading everything from *The Iliad* and *The Odyssey* to any poems he could find about the beauty and wonder of the natural world. He read his mother's favorite, *The Lady of the Lake* by Sir Walter Scott, while sitting on the upper branch of a tree. Kennan's father took him for walks in a nearby patch of surviving primeval woods, known as the "Big Woods," which to the young boy was a wild land of mysterious sights and sounds, from the *kut kuts* of partridges to the bear tracks on a creek bank.

At age eight, after much begging by Kennan, his father permitted him to get up early in the morning, go to the Big Woods, cook his breakfast, and return in time for school. He enlisted a boyhood chum to go with him, explaining that, wholly consistent with his father's terms, he planned to leave at twelve-thirty in the morning. At the arranged time, the two boys crept out of their homes and set out with a lantern, blankets, provisions, and a spring-loaded, tin-barreled gun that shot small, round stones. They found a dry place to camp, slept until the sun came up, and then built a fire. After a satisfying, hot breakfast, they managed to be in their seats in the red schoolhouse on the Monroeville Road by nine. That camping trip, he later recalled, meant more to him then "than a whole arctic campaign would be now. It was my first venture into the great field of the untried and the tastes and inclinations that prompted it were to influence all of my subsequent life."[28]

The telegraph was Kennan's other boyhood enthusiasm. In 1844, Samuel F. B. Morse, who happened to be a relative of his mother, had transmitted the now-famous message "WHAT HATH GOD WROUGHT" on a telegraph line between Washington and Baltimore. Most Americans thought the telegraph was an amusing novelty, perhaps good for holding long-distance chess tournaments but with no real relevance to their lives. But once businessmen recognized the profit potential in near-instantaneous communication, in a remarkably short time they spun a web of telegraph lines around the country. By 1850, some twenty companies operated twelve thousand miles of telegraph lines, with several times that many miles of line under, or about to start, construction. The young industry created a new technological class of managers, office workers, and telegraph operators, and even became a source of respectable employment for women, who sometimes earned the same salaries as men.

Kennan's father, who had given up teaching for the law, gave up the law to become the manager of the telegraph office in Norwalk for the Speed & O'Reilly line, which connected Cleveland and Toledo. George Kennan spent hours in his father's office, where he learned Morse code on a machine with a "camel-back" key whose bulging knob he had to grasp between his small thumb and first two fingers. As a present on his sixth birthday, he was allowed to send a commercial message from the telegraph office to Cleveland. The message went through without the Cleveland operator having to interrupt the transmission and ask to have part of the message resent. Kennan was "very proud of the fact that the operator there received it without a 'break.'"

In the early days of the telegraph, the receiving apparatus used a stylus to make indentations on a winding paper tape that corresponded to the incoming dots and dashes. Operators then translated the impressions on the tape into letters and words. At slower transmission speeds, the young Kennan could even read by sound, which meant listening to the clicks of the incoming transmission and writing down the message without aid of the stylus and paper tape. Most operators, including Kennan's father, could not do that until the invention in the late 1850s of the "sounder," which amplified the sound of the incoming dots and dashes and made it easier for operators to transcribe them directly.[29]

In 1856, when he was eleven years old, Kennan entered the Norwalk High School. After less than two years of studies, he had to drop out to earn money to help support his family, which was in financial trouble because his father's investments had fared badly. In his unpublished autobiography, Kennan is mildly critical of his father for first becoming a schoolteacher and then a lawyer instead of developing his aptitude for applied science. "The result was the spoiling of a first-rate mechanic, inventor or civil engineer, in the making of an indifferent lawyer." But Kennan nowhere reproaches him for his bad investments or the loss of his high school studies and only matter-of-factly notes that "it became necessary for me to seek money-making employment."[30]

He became a messenger-boy and trainee in a railroad company telegraph depot in Norwalk, working in a different office than his father's. He was promoted to the position of telegraph operator and manager at a salary of twenty-five dollars a month. In nineteenth-century America, children did menial and exhausting work in factories, farms, textile mills, and mines. Industrialists regarded the ideal machine as one so simple that a child could operate it. It was rare to give a young boy like George Kennan a serious responsibility like the signaling of trains.

As a train came through Norwalk, small boys peered through the depot's windows to watch Kennan busily work his instrument to alert a central dispatcher of the train's passing. The dispatcher then sent orders to the telegraph depot ahead of the train to give to its engineer: speed up, slow down (to arrive on schedule), halt at a siding, or make an unscheduled stop to pick up freight or passengers. At the depot ahead, a hapless employee went out to the side of the tracks and held out a five-foot pole with a large wire hoop, to which the dispatcher's written order was attached. As the steam-whistling, smoke-belching train barreled toward the "hooper," the brakeman reached down and, unless the hooper flinched, grabbed the wire hoop.[31]

Initially Kennan functioned in a state of panic. "The excitement and responsibility of taking and transmitting orders upon which depended the safety of trains and passengers were a severe trial, at first, to my inexperienced nerves." But he made no serious mistakes and "gradually acquired self-confidence, as the routine of railroad business became familiar to me." Once he set up a field telegraph office at the scene of a train wreck, and on one local election night he helped his father receive the telegraphed tallies and announce them to an excited gathering.

The job of telegraph operator carried significant status, but when he was fifteen Kennan decided that the work was too hard and confining, offered too few rewards other than a decent salary, and did not aid in the development of "one's best faculties." Since he had few good alternatives without a higher education, Kennan resolved to attend college. His plan was to work his way through college, although he could not be sure whether his family's financial needs would ultimately make that impractical. "That, however, was only a possibility, and I determined to make a beginning." In 1860, he began studying Latin and mathematics in his spare time and meeting at night with the local school superintendent for tutoring. Kennan never attended college because the Rebellion, as it was called in Norwalk, broke out in 1861 and "turned all my thoughts, hopes and ambitions into a new channel."

He was elated by the martial electricity in the air. "Patriotic by inheritance and training, and naturally adventurous, I was completely carried away by a desire to take part in the momentous struggle." But he was too young to enlist without his father's permission, which John Kennan was unwilling to give. He could only watch as friends joined the 55th

Ohio Regiment, which mustered out in Norwalk in the early days of the war. In a festive atmosphere the ladies of Norwalk offered coffee, pies, and sweet cakes to the young soldiers of the 55th in their light blue trousers, dark blue jackets, and forage caps. Trains left Norwalk taking boys, who not long ago had been playing two-old-cat, to be cut down on battlefields from Second Bull Run to the Carolinas campaign.[32]

Still anxious to prove his courage, George Kennan sought the equally dangerous position as a field operator in the newly formed United States Military Telegraph Corps. Despite the word "Military," the Corps was a civilian unit whose superintendent reported to the secretary of war. By the end of the war, the Corps had built fifteen thousand miles of telegraph lines and transmitted over six million telegraph messages, which gave the Union a significant communications advantage over the Confederacy with its more limited telegraphic resources. President Lincoln was among the first to grasp the capacity of the telegraph to give him command and control from Washington over his forces in the field, a power no political leader had previously possessed without being on the battlefield.

Throughout the war Lincoln haunted the War Department's telegraph office. He personally sent nearly one thousand telegrams to his commanders, some asking about troop dispositions in ongoing battles. "What became of our forces which held the bridge till twenty minutes ago, as you say?" Lincoln telegraphed during one battle. The incoming telegrams filled the telegraph office with blood and gore. "The wounded & killed is immense," a field operator telegraphed to the War Department, where Lincoln paced anxiously during the Battle of Fredericksburg in 1862. "The battle rages furiously. Can hardly hear my instrument."

From the War Department a vast network of telegraph wires stretched to every theatre of the war and onto battlefields. Before a battle, field operators weighed down with telegraphs, relays, and sounders; mules loaded with rolls of telegraph wire; and covered wagons crammed with nitric acid batteries, moved into position. They set up their instruments on hard-tack boxes beneath tent flys, and in just hours men had strung five or six miles of wire along poles, fence posts and tree branches, and sometimes over rivers to connect brigades or divisions with the commanding generals. A field operator once held the ends of a severed wire together in his bare hands and read a transmission from his tongue, which felt the shocks of the incoming dots and dashes.[33]

Field operators were shot, blown up by artillery shells, and, when captured by Confederates, at risk of being executed as spies since they wore no military uniforms. Kennan could not entirely convince himself that he had the courage to be a field operator, but his doubts only made him more anxious to put his nerve to a supreme test. "Had I not camped out many a night—or at least many a morning—in the Big Woods?" he asked himself. "And was I not quite as familiar with firearms as most of the volunteers who were then going to the front?" He wrote Anson Stager, the superintendent of the Military Telegraph Corps, whom Kennan had met before the war when Stager was a senior Western Union official, asking to join as a field operator. Stager was too busy to respond and instead Kennan received a letter from another official advising him to defer joining the Corps and "wait and see what would happen."

Kennan spent 1861 in the Norwalk telegraph office, frustrated at not being in the war. The next year he found a position in the telegraph office in Wheeling in the soon-to-be new state of West Virginia, which had seceded from Virginia when Virginia seceded from the Union. The telegraph office was dark and depressing; the air in Wheeling, a coal mining town, was foul-smelling from the smoke and odor of bituminous coal; and he was homesick. Kennan felt as though he was suffocating in an underground prison cell. He telegraphed an aide to Stager begging "to be transferred to some other post where the environment would be more inspiriting" and was sent to a telegraph office in Columbus, Ohio, where the air was breathable, and his spirits recovered. In August 1863, he was assigned to Western Union's Cincinnati office, which, like other offices of the major private telegraph companies, had become an auxiliary operation of the Military Telegraph Corps. The Cincinnati office handled voluminous traffic between eastern, midwestern, and border states and Washington.

Kennan and a dozen or so other operators sat in armchairs at tables with instruments mounted on walnut bases. Wires came out of the walls and from under window casings, snaked along the floor, and crisscrossed the tables to connect to the instruments. The air had an unpleasant, pungent smell from the chemicals in the batteries that generated electricity. Each receiving operator had to mentally screen out the constant click, click, clickety-clack of the other instruments to hear his own. The shifts were so irregular that Kennan sometimes worked day and night shifts in succession; once he slept only ten hours out of seventy-two. Dinners often consisted of black coffee and greasy pie brought around midnight by a "night-lunch" peddler.

After battles, the lines went "red hot," in the operators' vernacular. Kennan worked all night to transcribe or send, in priority order, military dispatches, some written in code, and press reports from the battlefield. "Any news?" demanded operators in the east and west. "Give us news. We must have news!" Newspaper reporters sometimes bribed operators to give their bulletins priority. Messages also came pouring in from family members. "How is my son?" "My brother?" "My husband?" "My father?" Desperate messages went the other way, too. After the Battle of Shiloh in 1862, the Union Army, short of hospital beds, set up cots in the back of an empty store in Savannah, Tennessee, where a field telegraph office was operating in the front. The operators could barely hear their instruments because of the moaning and crying of the wounded, some of whom managed to write down farewell messages before they died for the operators to transmit to loved ones.[34]

Only talented, young, physically and mentally fit operators could keep up with the relentless pace. The best operators, who thought of themselves as "knights of the key," achieved transmitting speeds of forty or even fifty words a minute, which required the senders to make hundreds of motions every sixty seconds with their wrists. Receiving was equally challenging. Kennan once set a Cincinnati office record by transcribing ninety incoming telegrams in fifty minutes. Much of the time he and his colleagues functioned in a state of exhaustion. Kennan wrote and sent telegrams to his family so often about his chills, headaches, fevers, aches, and fatigue that he apologized in one letter for dwelling on his health. "I was sorry you were at all alarmed about me. My only object in telegraphing that I was sick was to get some of you to write me." But he added, "I don't know what was the reason but [for two days] my face had a most ghastly appearance. Against a white background nothing of me was visible except eyes & hair." It was an attempt at humor but also a barely disguised plea for help that likely alarmed his family even more.

In 1864, Kennan was promoted to assistant chief operator in the Cincinnati office. The pay increase allowed him to send more money to his family, but the new responsibilities only worsened his nervous tension. Without access to the outdoors, the absence of human companionship other than his equally exhausted colleagues, and often having to eat a piece of pie for dinner with one hand while transcribing with the other, "I lost all my buoyancy of spirit and most of my hopefulness." On a visit to the Cincinnati office, Anson Stager, who had a high regard for Kennan's abilities and considered him one of his best operators, expressed concern at his pale appearance but only said he would do his best to send more good operators to the Cincinnati office.[35]

While browsing in a Cincinnati bookstore Kennan came across *Out-Door Papers* by Thomas Wentworth Higginson, a Unitarian minister, editor, and prolific writer who had been wounded leading the First South Carolina Volunteers, a Black regiment drawn from former enslaved men. Kennan could not put the book down because, in a state of physical fatigue, his fear that he was a coward had returned to torment him and Higginson's thesis was that courage, like other skills, can be developed by almost anyone. "Once rouse the enthusiasm of the will, and courage can be systematically disciplined." Higginson quoted Emerson's maxim, "Always do what you are afraid to do," and then issued a challenge that Kennan took personally. "Are you afraid to swim that river? then swim it. Are you afraid to leap that fence? then leap it. Do you shrink from the dizzy height of yonder magnificent pine? then climb it." Kennan decided again to test his courage—or lack of it.

Cincinnati was known for its architecture, culture, and violence. Much of the violence was racial, driven by the fear of whites that Blacks, including enslaved people who had escaped across the Ohio River, would take their jobs as steamboat stevedores and roustabouts. In July 1862 whites attacked Black stevedores up and down the levee; a white mob attacked Bucktown, a Black neighborhood; Blacks from Bucktown responded by rampaging through an Irish neighborhood; and another white mob ambushed the all-Black crew of the steamboat *Magnolia*. Even without race as an excuse, mob violence was set off by religious conflicts, tensions with immigrants, and even the closing of a bank. On the levee, armed thieves, tough men thirsting for a fight, and belligerent drunks roamed neighborhoods with names like Rat Row. Operators and other workers in the Cincinnati telegraph office carried weapons with them when they reported for night shifts.[36]

Kennan began carrying a revolver but not for protection against trouble but because he was looking for it. If there was a "dark, narrow, cutthroat alley, down by the river, that I felt afraid to go through at that hour of the night, I clenched my teeth, cocked my revolver and went through it—sometimes twice in succession." Each morning, Kennan searched the police reports in the newspapers for murders and other violent crimes the day before, and then went to the scenes after his shift. He hung around prostitutes, as sex workers were known then, and frequented seedy river saloons, where short-tempered, disagreeable men in bowler hats, vests, and torn pants and carrying firearms and drank heavily.

One night Kennan saw robbers knock a man down with a slingshot. He pulled out his revolver and ran to the man's assistance, which scared the robbers away. On another night he watched a knife fight in a riverfront tavern, which ended when one man slit the other's throat. The scene was a ghastly reprise of the botched operation on Kennan's boyhood friend, but this time Kennan did not experience faintness, nausea, or fear. "In less than three months I had completely satisfied myself that while I did shrink from certain things, I was not so much afraid of any sort of danger that I could not encounter it with courage and self-possession if I willed to do so. Then I began to feel better." Doubts about his courage, however, still lingered.[37]

Kennan reapplied to Stager for a position as a field operator in the Military Telegraph Corps. Capable operators were needed more in the big city telegraph offices, responded Stager, than in the field. Kennan answered with a letter of resignation, which explained that he was breaking down mentally and physically under the strain of overwork and office confinement. He had "to get out by the first avenue of escape that presented itself." Stager urged Kennan to be patient. Kennan remained in the Cincinnati telegraph office through the summer of 1864 "failing constantly in health and drooping in spirits, until I feared that I should be good for nothing in the field, even if I finally did succeed in breaking away."

Then, reading a newspaper account of the formation by Western Union of a joint American and Russian enterprise to build a telegraph line through Russian-Alaska and Siberia, he immediately wrote a letter to Stager pleading "to let me go in some capacity, with one of the exploring parties of this new company." Stager was in a position to persuade Western Union to grant Kennan's wish. The next day, an office boy came over to Kennan and informed him that Stager wanted him "at the Cleveland wire." Kennan went over to the Cleveland telegraph and sent a message that he was ready to receive: "I, i, G.K."

A message came in from Stager, whom Kennan apparently had worn down. "Good morning, Kennan. Can you get ready to go to Alaska in two weeks?"

"I can get ready in two hours," Kennan telegraphed back, his heart pounding.[38]

3

I Have the Satisfaction of
Knowing That I Have Not
Failed in Anything

"Where's the door?" Kennan shouted down the stovepipe of the buried hut. The voice beneath the snow called out that the entrance was on the "southeast corner," which was not much help. "In the first place we did not know which way south-east was, and in the second a snow-drift could not properly be described as having a corner." As Kennan searched for an entrance, he inadvertently stepped on reindeer skins and sticks covering a deep trench in the snow. The reindeer-skin roof gave way and he fell into the trench, which had been dug to the hut's doorway. An American came into the trench from the hut but shrank back because he momentarily mistook Kennan, with his bearskin-trimmed hoods, squirrel-skin mask, and a silhouette ballooned by two fur coats, for a menacing animal. When the American realized it was a man, he helped the visitor into the hut where Kennan nearly fainted because it was more than one hundred degrees warmer inside than outside. He concealed his dizziness because he did not want to show "womanish weakness" to a group of fellow Americans.[39]

Once the three trapped men understood that a fellow expedition member was underneath all the fur, "never was there, however, such rejoicing as that which then took place in that little underground cellar." While the drivers sat together and drank hot tea, the three men explained to Kennan and Dodd what had happened to them. Originally, five men had been landed at the mouth of the Anadyr River and started exploring by whaleboat. They expected to reach a settlement upriver, but an unexpectedly early winter froze the Anadyr, stranding them. They built a hut with driftwood from the riverbanks and kept from freezing to death with a stove and fuel left by the company ship. The Chukchis, who happened on the shelter before it was fully buried under snow, made occasional visits to drop off fresh reindeer meat. A month before Kennan's arrival, the team leaders, MacRae and Arnold, had gone off with a band of Chukchis who promised to guide them to a settlement and had not been heard from since.

After Kennan's party had rested for several days, the Americans and the drivers set out for Anadyrsk. For all Kennan knew, MacRae and Arnold had starved or frozen to death on the tundra, but even if they were alive, rescue was hopeless without some idea of their location. In Anadyrsk one night, Dodd went outside to tend to the dogs but suddenly returned shouting, "Come out, quick!" Kennan emerged to witness an aurora borealis like none he had seen before. "Of Bronze— and Blaze, The North—Tonight!" went the Emily Dickinson poem "Aurora," and it was true that frigid Siberian night.

Waves of bright phosphorescent light crashed out of the northern horizon, swelling into a flaming crimson curtain that turned into bright orange lightning, flashing across the night sky. The orange lightning dissolved into dancing bars of purple, scarlet, and green, which formed two great prismatic bridges "on which we almost expected to see, passing and repassing, the bright inhabitants of another world." The silent display left Kennan and his companions tensely awaiting a cataclysmic explosion that never came. The indigenous workers prayed or cried out, "God have mercy!" The celestial bridges slowly broke up and faded away. "Never had I even dreamed of such an aurora as *this,* and I am not ashamed to confess that its magnificence for a moment overawed and almost frightened me."[40]

Kennan and his team resumed their exploration. They mapped out a feasible route for the telegraph line along the forested tributaries of the Penzhina and Anadyr Rivers. The treeless areas on the route could be easily reached in warm weather by rafts carrying telegraph poles cut in the forests elsewhere. After a week and a half of sleighing and mapping, Kennan returned to Anadyrsk, where he was relieved to find MacRae and Arnold. Their Chukchi band had been in no hurry to reach Anadyrsk and the two Americans had spent hard months in the mountains subsisting on reindeer entrails. In April, the MacRae-Arnold and Kennan teams made their way south to Gizhiga, where they had a happy reunion with Maj. Abaza and the southern party of Mahood and Bush. The three teams gathered in a log house around a pine table with a samovar and spread out their maps. Between them, they had journeyed nearly ten thousand miles and found a viable route for the telegraph line from Anadyr Gulf in the north to the Amur River in the south. "As we reviewed our winter's work, we felt satisfied that the enterprise in which we were engaged, if not altogether an easy one, held out at least a fair prospect of success."[41]

By the spring of 1866, the exploration and route mapping phase of the expedition's work in Siberia was largely finished. Company ships crammed with telegraph wire and other equipment were scheduled to arrive by summer. Kennan and several of his teammates rented a small log cabin on the Gizhiga River, which flowed into the Sea of Okhotsk. They brought in a few tables and chairs, hung their maps on a wall, and settled in for a stretch of comfortable inactivity. The air warmed, the ice on the Gizhiga River began breaking up, and the days lengthened until only a brief dusk interrupted the sunlight. Sitting by a window, Kennan wrote letters to family and friends for the company ships to take back to the United States. He could hear the cries of wild geese flying overhead and the faint sounds of the waves on the rocky coast ten miles away.

One letter was to Dr. Charles Morrill, the family doctor in Norwalk who had persuaded his father to let him go on the telegraph expedition. In it Kennan summarized what he imagined to be his family's fears for his safety. His father worried that "I might volunteer to go on hazardous & difficult expeditions too fatiguing for my strength." His mother believed that "her wandering son [was] lying sick in some miserable hut in the wilderness without friends." His sister Jennie was concerned about "the danger that that 'delicate construction' of mine would give out." Only his sister Hattie, "with a little spark of pride in her brother's adventurousness would combat Father's views." Kennan urged Dr. Morrill to read his letter out loud to his family and "see if it isn't exactly what they have thought a hundred times."

Happily none of their gloomy anticipations were realized. I have been on one or two somewhat hazardous expeditions but good fortune and good health have never deserted me & I have the satisfaction of knowing that I have not failed in anything which I have undertaken. I think that the strength of my constitution is now triumphantly proved: I have a better opinion of it myself than I have ever had before since it had held out through the hardships we have had to experience & it won't do for Mother to base her fears any longer upon my delicate health & "want of vitality!!"[42]

As the snow melted, flowers and blueberry bushes appeared on the tundra, which became soft and saturated with water. Venturing out on it, Kennan found, was like walking on a giant soggy sponge. With the short summer came clouds of buzzing mosquitoes ready "to furnish musical entertainment to man and beast upon extremely reasonable terms." The reindeer fled the tundra for higher ground and the dogs and cattle in the settlements ran in mad, agonized circles. No matter how thoroughly Kennan wrapped himself in gauze and calico, the mosquitoes found an entry. "They persecute every living thing with a bloodthirsty eagerness that knows no rest and feels no pity. Escape is impossible and defense useless."

The summer wore on, but no ships appeared, leaving Kennan and his colleagues first baffled and then angry. It was as if the Siberian telegraph expedition "had dropped out of the great current of human affairs, as if our places in the distant busy world had been filled and our very existence forgotten." Kennan wrote his sister Hattie that "I have been waiting anxiously and impatiently three interminable months for the arrival of those—(imagine some forcible expletives) vessels of ours."

On August 14, 1866, Kennan was in the log house in Gizhiga drawing maps of the telegraph route when he heard booming sounds. A Cossack servant rushed into the house. "A cannon! A ship!" Kennan and Dodd canoed down the Gizhiga River to the sea, where they were joined by Maj. Abaza, who had taken up residence on the coast. A barque flying an American flag and a three-masted steamer with a Russian flag were anchored offshore. "Where have you been all summer?" Maj. Abaza asked the American captain of the barque, named the *Clara Bell,* when he came ashore. The captain explained that they had been delayed leaving San Francisco, but that he had brought the promised supplies and equipment. He informed them that work on the North American side was progressing satisfactorily and that preparations were underway to lay a cable across the Bering Strait.

Soon they were joined on the beach by American and Russian officers, a Russian government official, and even a correspondent from the *New York Herald,* a measure of the public interest in the progress of the Russian-American Telegraph Expedition. The spirits of the Americans in Gizhiga rose. "We congratulated ourselves on the improving prospects of the Siberian Division." Other company ships dropped off workmen and equipment, including telegraph wire, brackets, and insulators, at locations up and down the Siberian coast. Maj. Abaza set out for Yakutsk to buy three hundred Siberian ponies and hire six hundred workers to begin cutting trees and putting up telegraph poles.

Before leaving for Yakutsk, Maj. Abaza ordered Kennan, once

enough snow had fallen, to lead a search for a party of twenty-five men commanded by Richard J. Bush, who had been scheduled to land earlier that year far to the north at the mouth of the Anadyr River. Abaza was afraid that, like the company ships that finally arrived off Gizhiga, Bush's supply ship had been delayed, or might not even arrive, which could leave his party in danger of starving or freezing to death once winter set in.

In early November, Kennan loaded five sleighs with provisions for himself, his Cossack drivers, and their dogs and started north from Gizhiga. He decided not to take Dodd or any other Americans with him rather than interfere with their work on the telegraph line. This was his second rescue mission to the Anadyr River, as though a curse had been laid on any American telegraph explorers who ventured into that region.[43]

Along the Gulf of Penzhinsk, Kennan replaced his good-natured Cossacks with a half-dozen drivers recruited from Koryak settlements. Kennan liked and respected the indigenous peoples he had met in Siberia, especially the self-reliant, wandering Koryaks, and later he became a harsh critic of the US government's treatment of Native Americans. But he detested these settlement Koryaks, who had poor outdoor skills and spoke no English and whose "obstinacy and sullen stupidity kept me in a chronic state of ill-humor." Sometimes he had to brandish his pistol to keep them from frequently stopping on the trail. Before the journey was over, "I should have been glad to talk to an intelligent American dog." He missed Dodd.

He followed the same route to Anadyrsk that he taken the previous winter to rescue the MacRae-Arnold team. He and the Koryaks first stayed overnight in the indigenous villages but once past the villages they had to camp, which first meant finding a grove of trees whose wood could be used to build a fire. After dinner, the Koryaks squatted in a circle around the fire, drinking tea from mugs and horns. The nights were clear, calm, and so cold that sometimes the mercury in Kennan's thermometer, whose scale stopped at minus twenty-three degrees Fahrenheit, never left the bulb. Bundled in his fur sleeping bag near the fire Kennan wrote in his journal until he went to sleep. One night his fingers nearly froze because the party had too little wood to build an adequate fire. "It's no use," he managed to write before giving up. "I cannot hold the pencil."

Under Kennan's pressure and guidance, the Koryaks' performance improved. "I'm not sure they are wholly irredeemable yet," he wrote in his journal. "If I could travel with them a couple of weeks I would make pretty good travelers of them!" At the indigenous settlement of Penzhina, Kennan encountered a long-haired Russian priest who had traveled the one hundred and thirty miles from Anadyrsk to report a terrible famine. For unknown reasons, the previous summer the salmon had failed to migrate up the rivers, which deprived the indigenous peoples in Anadyrsk and the surrounding area of their main source of food. Many of them, and almost all their dogs, had starved to death, and the survivors were eating their boots. The priest told Kennan that he had seen Bush in July at the mouth of the Anadyr River, but, as to what had happened to him since then, "God only knew."

Kennan spent the night agonizing over whether to abandon his rescue mission since the Bush party by now likely had perished from starvation. By morning he had decided that he had to go north if there was even the faintest hope that Bush and his men were still alive. "Much as I dreaded another journey to the mouth of the Anadyr in midwinter, I saw no way of avoiding it." He again despaired whether, with no work apparently possible along the Anadyr River this winter, the telegraph line could be completed. Before leaving Penzhina, Kennan persuaded the chief of a nearby tribe of Koryaks to drive his reindeer herd to Anadyrsk and provide meat to whoever was left alive. He wrote two letters to be delivered to Gizhiga by a dog sleigh team. One reported the famine to the authorities and the other asked Dodd to send to Penzhina as many sleighs as he could with provisions, which Kennan

arranged to have taken to Anadyrsk once they arrived. He set out for
Anadyrsk, reassuring himself that "if I don't return the Major will send
an expedition after me when he comes [back to Gizhiga]."

Kennan's teams were within twenty miles of Anadyrsk when a violent storm forced them to halt before a low mountain range called the
Russkie Krebet. By nightfall the wind had partly slackened, but the
snow was still swirling around them when they began the ascent of a
ravine-like pass. At the summit, both men and dogs were gasping for
breath, and they stopped to rest. Had Kennan not stopped his team at
the summit of the Russkie Krebet, he might never have glimpsed the
line of dark objects swiftly traveling in the opposite direction over
the mountain's crest and starting down the pass he had just emerged
from. Kennan shouted, turned his sleigh teams around, and caught up.
They were dog teams.

"Who is it?" Kennan called out.

"Bush."

As with the discovery of the MacRae-Arnold party the previous
winter, it was not clear who was coming to whose salvation. "Never
was that voice more welcome. . . . I was lonely and disheartened by
constantly accumulating misfortunes, when suddenly at midnight, on
a desolate mountaintop, I met an old friend and comrade whom I had
almost given up as dead." That night the two parties set up camp on
the south side of the Russkie Krebet. Kennan and Bush spread out their
bearskins in front of a fire and Bush told his story. On the Anadyr River
over the summer, his party had been mauled by mosquitoes and run
low on food while waiting for company ships. A supply ship finally
arrived in October only to be wrecked by ice, which added another
twenty-two men to Bush's already hungry party. The Chukchis once
again came to the aid of stranded Americans on the Anadyr River by
providing them with reindeer meat, and several were taking Bush to
Gizhiga so he could organize a rescue of his men.

Kennan and Bush discussed their options until sunrise. By then
both men were covered by windblown snow. They reached no decision

other than to travel the short distance north to Anadyrsk to observe conditions there. After a few hours on the trail, they entered the first of the several villages that made up Anadyrsk. No one greeted them, no dogs barked, and the streets were covered by untracked snow. "It looked as if one-half of the inhabitants had died and the other half had gone to the funeral!" The next village was also lifeless. They found half-starved families in the other villages. Kennan decided to return south to Gizhiga because he had insufficient provisions to feed the trapped men and, since most of the dogs in the vicinity were dead, no means to organize a large-scale evacuation by dog sleigh. Bush remained behind in Anadyrsk with his Chukchis to await the supplies that Kennan had requested, which eventually reached the settlement. Bush delivered the supplies to his trapped men, but they would not be evacuated from the Anadyr River for many months.

On November 29, 1866, Kennan started his return trip south with his Koryak drivers. During the nights he dreamed of the tsar, his father, and people whose names and faces he had long forgotten. "A man has curious dreams in this country," he wrote in his journal, and swore to never again travel like that in Siberia. Later a Canadian telegraph explorer, whom Kennan regarded as especially capable, prepared to make a winter trip from the Okhotsk region to Gizhiga accompanied only by six indigenous workers who spoke no English. Kennan tried to talk him out of going without an English-speaking companion, but the Canadian went anyway. He made it to Gizhiga but by then he was insane and shortly shot himself with a rifle. He left a note that he had written on the trip about the "sad days for me, among a lot of savages" with whom he could not communicate.[44]

Despite the near-disasters and the delayed arrivals of the company ships, Kennan's fears about the telegraph line proved unfounded; in fact, it appeared on the verge of success. Maj. Abaza had deployed hundreds of workers and ponies from Yakutsk and more were on their way. In minus forty to minus sixty degrees Fahrenheit, telegraph parties on snowshoes steadily cut down trees, which often buried themselves three feet deep in the snow and had to be dug out. By early 1867, the expedition had hacked fifteen thousand telegraph poles out of the forests. Work had even resumed on the Anadyr River. As they worked the Americans sang a song of victory over the Atlantic cable set to a popular Civil War song.

In eighteen hundred and sixty-eight,
Hurrah! Hurrah!
In eighteen hundred and sixty-eight,
The cable will be in a miserable state,
and we'll all feel gay
When they use it to fish for whales.[45]

Kennan's spirits were also high, but letters mailed to expedition members from St. Petersburg reported that the Atlantic cable had been laid and, so far, was working. He wrote his father that "it will be a great blow to our enterprise if it continues to work well through the winter." In the spring Kennan was drawing a topographical map in the expedition's headquarters in Gizhiga when a worker rushed in. "Oh Mr. Kennan! Did you hear the cannon?" A ship had been sighted from the mouth of the Gizhiga River. Kennan and several companions started downriver in a light skiff and reached the sea that evening. The next morning they rowed out in a whaleboat to the ship, which was anchored about fifteen miles offshore. The captain of the ship, a whaler from New Bedford, Massachusetts, named the *Sea Breeze,* was startled by the men coming aboard in fur clothing.

"But what are you doing up in this God-forsaken country?" the *Sea Breeze* captain asked when he realized that they were white men. "Have you been shipwrecked?"

"No," answered Kennan, "we're up here trying to build a telegraph line."

"A telegraph line! Well, if that ain't the craziest thing I ever heard of. Who's going to telegraph from here?"

"How about the Atlantic cable?" Kennan impatiently asked. "Do you know anything about that?"

"Oh, yes, the cable is laid all right."

"Does it work?"

"Works like a snatch-tackle." The captain happily delivered the exciting news. "The 'Frisco papers are publishing every morning the London news of the day before."

Expecting smiles, but seeing grim expressions, the captain realized that the delight of the world might be the worst possible news to his visitors. He invited them for refreshments in his cabin, but Kennan and his men could barely go through the motions of polite conversation. They soon left the ship, carrying bananas, oranges, and sweet potatoes from Pacific islands, and whatever newspapers the captain had on board. Back on shore, Kennan and his men built a fire, roasted the sweet potatoes, and read through the newspapers. They learned that not only had the Atlantic cable been laid, but a cable lost in an earlier effort had been retrieved, repaired, and put into service. "I think this discouraged us more than anything else."

As they continued to sift through the newspapers, a man angrily slammed his fist into his knee. He had been reading the back pages of a months-old newspaper, which had been published around the time that Kennan had set out from Gizhiga to rescue Bush and his party. "Boys! The jig is up! Listen to this! 'In consequence of the success of the Atlantic cable, all work on the Russian-American telegraph line has been stopped and the enterprise abandoned.'" The man said bitterly, "Well, that seems to settle it. The cable has knocked us out."[46]

The failure in 1865 to lay the Atlantic cable hardly deterred the directors of the Atlantic Telegraph Company. With the bitter learning experience of the earlier failed attempts, the engineers improved both the cable's design and manufacture and made modifications to the gargantuan cable-laying ship, the *Great Eastern,* which sailed on June 30,

1866, from the Thames Estuary. Day after day, for the most part in calm waters, the *Great Eastern* steamed west, steadily paying out its cable. The ship anchored in late July in Trinity Bay, Newfoundland, in sight of the wildly cheering inhabitants of the flag-draped hamlet of Heart's Content. The *Great Eastern* trailed two thousand miles of undersea cable, which was spliced into undersea lines that ran to mainland Canada. "All well. Thank God, the cable is laid and is in perfect working order," went the telegraphed message from Heart's Content, which set off worldwide celebrations.[47]

With the benefit of hindsight, some newspapers criticized Western Union for spending millions of dollars based on the "mere conviction" that the Atlantic cable would never be successfully laid. For a time the Western Union directors insisted publicly that they would not abandon the overland route through Siberia, but they had every incentive to do just that. The month before the *Great Eastern* reached Heart's Content, Western Union had hedged its investment in the Russian-American telegraph line by merging with the American Telegraph Company, one of the backers of the Atlantic cable. If the cable was successfully laid, Western Union would receive a share of the profits. In effect, Western Union had put down a bet against its own men in the Siberian wilderness.

Almost as an afterthought, Western Union dispatched a company ship to Siberia, the *Onward,* which arrived off Gizhiga on July 15, 1867. "We have come up to carry all the employees home," said the captain. Kennan found it heartbreaking to close a project to which he had devoted nearly three years of his life and endured all possible hardships, but his thoughts were also of home. Maj. Abaza went by an overland route to St. Petersburg, where he hoped to persuade the Russian government to complete the line through Siberia. Kennan spent August cruising along the Siberian coast aboard the *Onward* to gather up the telegraph line working parties. In September the *Onward* put in at Okhotsk, where a letter from Maj. Abaza directed Kennan to come to St. Petersburg. The *Onward,* with almost all the American telegraph workers on board, prepared to sail to San Francisco. On the day of the *Onward*'s sailing, Kennan and Dodd were both on the edge of tears. "He could only wring my hand in silence."[48]

Kennan sold to Russian merchants the company's remaining equipment and supplies, which included brackets, glass insulators, tools, and baking powder, and gave away or abandoned what he could not sell. By late October enough snow had fallen for Kennan, an American telegraph operator named Price, and two Russian workers to start out from Okhotsk for St. Petersburg. The two Russians, who were only going as far as Irkutsk, left first with lighter dog sleighs to break the trail, soon followed by Kennan and Price in sleighs with the heavier baggage. A largely indigenous crowd gathered to watch Kennan leave. "God grant you a fortunate journey," shouted the fur-clad men, while the women, grateful for his gifts of baking powder, waved colorful handkerchiefs. A priest blessed Kennan and Price but the mayor was dubious.

"Are you all ready?"

Kennan said they were.

"Well, then, go with God."

The first leg, to Yakutsk, took Kennan and his companions through a wilderness of mountains and evergreen forests inhabited by the Tungus, a nomadic tribe. The Russian government paid the Tungus in tea and tobacco to set up camps at intervals between Okhotsk and Yakutsk to supply government mail carriers, and the occasional private traveler, with food and transportation. At their first stop at a camp, where wolfish-looking dogs gnawed on the severed heads of reindeer, the Tungus stocked Kennan's sleighs with reindeer meat, replaced their dogs with reindeer, and took over as drivers. On November 16, after twenty-three days of nonstop travel, Kennan sighted columns of smoke rising from the chimneys of Yakutsk and slept that night in a Russian merchant's house. "The sensation of lying without furs and between sheets in a civilized bed was so novel and extraordinary that I lay awake for an hour, trying experiments with that wonderful mattress."[49]

The Russian government had set up a remarkably well-organized transportation system that operated year-round in Siberia. Ten thousand horses, several thousand drivers, and seven thousand sleighs and horse-drawn carriages were stationed at more than three hundred and fifty post stations. Typically, post stations were the homes of local villagers who earned money by keeping and feeding the horses and furnishing lodging and food to both drivers and travelers. Unlike the American stagecoach network, the sleighs and carriages did not depart and arrive at fixed times. Depending on the season, the traveler simply bought or hired a sleigh or carriage, changed fatigued horses and drivers at the post stations, and went as slowly or rapidly as the condition of the roads and the traveler's physical endurance allowed. Kennan planned to travel day and night.

In Yakutsk, Kennan purchased two *pavoskas,* partly enclosed traveling sleighs resembling a "burlap-covered baby carriage on runners." He and Price put their luggage at the bottom of their sleigh's passenger compartment, which had no seats, spread on top of the luggage a seven-foot-long, two-person, wolfskin sleeping bag and soft feather pillows, and stowed their food under the driver's seat. After a farewell toast of vodka and champagne with their merchant host, Kennan, Price, and the two Russians, dressed head to foot in thick furs, climbed into their sleighs. The drivers snapped their whips, and, in clouds of snow kicked up by the three-horse teams each pulling a sleigh, they raced out of Yakutsk to the merry jingle of the large bells hung from the wooden arches suspended over the middle horses in each team. The primary purpose of a sleigh's bell was not musical but to warn other sleighs at night or in a snowstorm of its oncoming presence. A short distance past Yakutsk, the two sleighs descended a gentle slope and turned onto the frozen Lena River, which would be their road for nearly a thousand miles.

The Lena, one of the world's longest rivers, flows twenty-seven hundred miles north to the Arctic Ocean from its mountain pond source near Lake Baikal. Traveling upriver, the party stopped every two or three hours at post stations on the riverbanks to change horses. "Boys! Out the horses! Lively!" the drivers shouted as the sleighs pulled up to the post stations. Kennan crawled out of his warm fur bag and went into the station. He displayed a *padarozhnaya*, a travel pass he had purchased in Yakutsk that directed post station masters to provide his party with fresh horses and drivers and, if needed, food and lodging. The nights were clear and cold, sometimes minus forty or minus fifty degrees Fahrenheit, and the snow-covered ice was smooth and fast. Kennan lay in his fur bag listening to the jingling bell and watching the moonlit silhouette of the river's forested shoreline as it flew by.[50]

Small evergreen bushes had been placed on the frozen river to mark a safe route around naturally occurring openings in the ice called air holes, but five hundred miles up the river their overconfident driver strayed from the evergreen path and crashed into an air hole. Kennan was awakened by their driver's cursing, the frantic neighing of the horses, and water rushing into the compartment. Kennan and Price leaped to safety on the sleigh's ten-foot-long outrigger runners, which, by partly bridging the hole, had kept the sleigh from sliding under the ice. The mishap cost the life of one horse and delayed their journey by several days while the sleigh was repaired and their sleeping bag and luggage were thawed and dried in houses in the nearest village. After nearly two and a half years in the Siberian wilderness Kennan was unfazed, but when they were back on the river, he kept an eye on the evergreen bushes at night instead of sleeping.

The two sleighs left the Lena River and in early December entered Irkutsk, the capital of the region known as Eastern Siberia, a town of houses with colorfully painted window shutters and churches with golden and blue domes. Caravans of sleighs piled high with goods from Mongolia entered the southern end of the town and the sound of a regimental band drifted from a military barracks. The telegraph men were stunned at the sight of Irkutsk because "we had seen nothing that even remotely suggested a city in two and a half years." Kennan and Price were invited to balls, dinners, and the theatre. Rather than show up looking like fur trappers, the Americans prevailed on a tailor to clean and press their telegraph company uniforms. At one dance, young women, eager to hear an American speak Russian, approached Kennan but they began to "show symptoms of shock" after a few minutes of conversation. An Irkutsk official listening to the conversation later explained to Kennan that the Russian he had learned working on the telegraph line had a heavy dose of ill-mannered words.

On December 13, 1867, leaving their two Russian companions behind in Irkutsk, Kennan and Price set out in a single sleigh on the Great Siberian Post Road, a central Siberian road extending three thousand miles from the Ural Mountains to the Amur River. Their sleigh overtook and passed slow-moving westbound caravans of two hundred sleighs loaded with tea from China and convoys of Cossacks transporting gold from Siberia. From the opposite direction came marching exile parties of convicts on their way east to hard labor prisons and mines. Their circumstances would become of intense interest to Kennan when he returned to Siberia eighteen years later, but now he paid them not much more attention than he did the white Yakut ponies in the fields pawing at the snow to uncover grass. They crossed the Ural Mountains, and on January 7, 1868, Kennan reached Nizhny Novgorod, which was then the eastern end of the Russian rail network. Kennan and Price sold their sleigh and boarded a train. Two days later, having traveled nearly six thousand miles since leaving the Sea of Okhotsk and changed horses, reindeer, and dogs two hundred and sixty times, they stepped off the train in St. Petersburg to behold a dazzling, snow-dusted, golden-trimmed fairy tale of a city, part architectural confection, part Potemkin village.

Massive pink, green, and yellow stuccoed palaces lined iced-over canals and crosses atop church domes reached high into crisp blue skies. Rows of sawed-off fir trees marked safe pedestrian paths across the frozen, snow-covered Great Neva River, which was three quarters of a mile wide and the city's main waterway. Luxurious sleighs with merrily jingling silver and brass bells, gaily painted in red, gold, and silver, and drawn by spirited, groomed horses, paraded up and down the fashionable Nevski Prospect, the city's main boulevard, carrying dashing men in expensive overcoats and elegantly dressed women wearing sable or white fox fur hats. Russian soldiers marched back and forth on the great square of the huge Admiralty, which was topped by a tall golden spire that one visitor compared to "the mast of a golden ship planted on the roof of a Greek temple." The soldiers wore crisp uniforms with rifles slung over their shoulders and turned and halted with precision as though attached to each other by invisible wires. "I felt as if we had been suddenly transported from the barbarism of the Paleolithic age to the high civilization of a northern Babylon."[51]

Kennan's stay in St. Petersburg may have sealed his bond with Russia. From the start of his journey on the Kamchatka Peninsula, he had been greeted warmly and treated well by indigenous peoples and Russians alike; Kennan endeared himself to them, and, with the exception of the settled Kamchadals on his lonely trip north to rescue Bush's party, they to him. After almost two and a half years of rugged life in Siberia, where the most imposing buildings were log churches, the young American was awestruck and overwhelmed by the beauty, wealth, culture, and power of the capital. That was the impact Peter the Great intended his namesake city to have on visitors when he built it at the cost of so many lives—the estimates start at twenty-five thousand— that it is said St. Petersburg is "the city built on bones."

But just half a mile from the Nevski Prospect, the poor sold firewood, rags of clothing, and stolen goods to stay alive, and an estimated thirty thousand tons of feces filled the courtyards and cellars of the decrepit buildings of the destitute neighborhoods. St. Petersburg's mortality rate was the highest of any major European city and alcoholism was so rampant that adolescents died from alcohol poisoning. The city's grandeur obscured its darker life even from a careful observer like Kennan, or he saw it but didn't want to spoil the splendor by acknowledging the sordid. No mention of the seamy side of St. Petersburg appears in his account of his time in the city.[52]

Nor did he apparently note the building political instability in Russia. Two years earlier, Tsar Alexander II had been enjoying his habitual stroll on the flower-lined paths of the city's Summer Garden. Waiting for him with a double-barreled flintlock pistol was an unstable young man named Dmitry Karakozov, a former student and, according to investigators, a member of a suicide-assassination cell called "Hell." It isn't clear what social changes Karakozov was seeking for Russia, but evidently he was unimpressed by Alexander II's emancipation in 1861 of more than twenty million Russian serfs from servitude to the nobles and his reforms of the universities, the judiciary, and the local government. Karakozov raised his pistol, took aim, and missed. The would-be assassin was tortured, convicted of attempted tsaricide, and hung. Another unsuccessful assassination attempt was made the following year, and it was not the last. Alexander, who had softened repressive measures begun in the regime of his father, Nicholas I, ordered his government to crack down on subversive Russians. As Russia historian Edward Crankshaw observed, the regime's repressive measures only "ensured a steady supply of martyrs and, in consequence, a steady supply of disciples of these martyrs driven to desperate acts in protest."[53]

Kennan spent much of the winter of 1868 in St. Petersburg exploring the Imperial Library and the Hermitage, attending masked balls and concerts, participating in the sports of the winter carnival, and studying Russian. He enjoyed listening to Russian army veterans reminisce about fighting in the Caucasus Mountains where, after decades of war, Russia had defeated the fierce, Muslim mountaineers led by Imam Shamil, a brilliant but cruel tactician. Shamil's mother once displeased her son by relaying a plea from a war-weary tribe for permission to make peace with the Russians. He had his mother flogged (claiming Allah had instructed him to do it), but when she fainted after five lashes, he took her place and received her remaining lashes. Shamil's surrender

in 1859 largely ended the Caucasian Wars, although rebellious out-
breaks continued in Dagestan for decades and the Chechens fought
into the twenty-first century. Shamil was taken to St. Petersburg, where
his capture was hailed as proof of Russia's imperial success in bringing
civilization to the Caucasus. The tsar received him, high society feted
him at balls and the theatre, and adoring crowds wildly cheered him.
Willingly domesticated, Shamil pledged allegiance to the tsar, settled
on an estate, and near the end of his life was permitted to live in Mecca,
where he died.

The veterans told Kennan of the harsh beauty of the Caucasus
Mountains and of their respect for the fighting skills of the Muslim
tribes. Regimental bands played strange, wild music from the coast
of the Caspian Sea and shops in St. Petersburg sold swords with or-
nate golden or silver hilts. Authors and poets who had spent time
or served in the Caucasus, such as Pushkin and Lermontov, penned
works that romantically depicted the mountaineers as proud, tena-
cious warriors. "Their god is freedom their law is war," Lermontov
had written. Kennan began thinking about someday exploring the
Caucasus Mountains.[54]

He still hoped to return to Siberia because Maj. Abaza was ac-
tively lobbying the Russian government to complete construction of
the telegraph line on its own territory. Committed explorers and ad-
venturers are blessed with a short memory of suffering and Kennan's
recollection of minus fifty degrees Fahrenheit temperatures, exhaustion, and loneliness had faded. But the Russian government had no
interest in a Siberian telegraph line, in part because it had agreed to
sell Russian-Alaska to the United States. The *New York Herald*, noting
Alaska's extensive resources and the close relations between the two
countries, applauded the sale. "All see in it proof of friendship on the
part of the one-headed giant of the North towards the many-headed
giant of the West."

Kennan started for home and the completion of a global circumnavigation. The Russian-American telegraph line was never built, the

stock he had bought in the Western Union entity that owned the line was worthless, and he was owed about one thousand dollars in wages from his Siberia work with uncertain prospects for payment. But Kennan returned to the United States with a more precious commodity than stock or money. "In almost daily struggles with difficulties, dangers and sufferings of all kinds, I finally lost completely the fear of being afraid, which had poisoned so much of the happiness of my boyhood, and acquired a reasonable degree of confidence in my nerve."[55]

4

The Mountaineers
of the Caucasus

The spacious town that Kennan had roamed as a boy had shrunk in size. Norwalk Creek was a trickling rivulet. He visited the Big Woods, where he had first camped overnight, but nothing was big about it because Siberia had altered Kennan's sense of scale. "I seemed to be looking at a memory-picture through the wrong end of a telescope." It took a month before Norwalk began to look as it did when he left in 1864. Kennan eventually received his one thousand dollars in back pay from Western Union, but he had to spend much of it on his family's needs. He feared that he would have to begin "again at the [bottom] of the ladder," as he had written his father near the end of his time in Siberia. His skill set—setting up a winter camp or navigating across the tundra on a dog sleigh—was hardly in demand in Ohio. He could work in a telegraph office, but he had resolved not to do that again. He found a job selling schoolbooks, but the life of a traveling salesman was tedious, and he quit after a few months.

Without any clear idea of how to earn a living, Kennan decided to write about his Siberian adventures. He did not expect to make any money but simply wondered whether "I could put some of my Siberian experiences into a literary form that would satisfy my judgment." The finished article, "Camping Out in Siberia," satisfied him and he sent it to the publishing house of G. P. Putnam's Sons in New York City, which promptly ran his article in the September 1868 issue of *Putnam's Magazine*. Encouraged, Kennan submitted several more articles about Siberia, all of which the magazine published. George Palmer Putnam, a founder of the publishing house, wrote Kennan to suggest expanding the articles to a book. Kennan had not considered such an ambitious undertaking, but Putnam's enthusiasm and "the confidence I felt in his judgment" led him to reply that he would at least try. Kennan began work in the fall of 1869.[56]

He first read works by authors from Plutarch to Emerson to John Ruskin, the Victorian art critic and social revolutionary whose love of nature fascinated Kennan. He studied principles of composition. He practiced writing descriptions of the woods and fields around Norwalk. He wrote short sketches of the Siberian landscape based on his journals and memories. Finally, he was ready to write what would become *Tent Life in Siberia, and Adventures Among the Koraks and Other Tribes in Kamtchatka and Northern Asia*. He wrote only at night, when "my mind seemed to respond more quickly at that time than at any other to the calls I made upon it for sustained effort," and devoted the day to reading more great works. His habit was to write at his desk, stop to pace back and forth, and return to his desk until he needed to pace again. Kennan paced so relentlessly that he had to relocate to his father's telegraph office to spare his family the nightly sound of his footsteps. He smoked cigarettes, a habit he had picked up in Siberia, while writing.

He did not so much edit his first draft of four hundred pages as tame it into submission. He rewrote the draft at least three times and parts of it thirteen times, a challenging task using only pen and paper. He sometimes spent two hours on a single paragraph, which led his father to comment, "You'll spoil your descriptions, George and make them artificial if you work over them so." Kennan disagreed because writing was his personal quest for perfection. "When I began to write my book, I could get my ideas into something like literary form if I worked long enough over them . . . the more labor I put into my sentences the less labored and studied they seemed to become."

Acquaintances in Norwalk invited Kennan to give a lecture on his Siberian experience to help raise money for a local charity. "I had not the faintest idea whether I could make a successful public speech or not; but it would do no harm, I thought, to try." He wrote out a twelve-thousand-word lecture, rehearsed it before fifty or sixty farmers and their wives in a small rural church, and then appeared at the charity event to deliver a lecture on "Our Life in Siberia." He looked over the audience, which included many familiar faces, and nearly collapsed from stage fright but regained his composure and delivered a well-received lecture. Kennan began receiving speaking invitations from churches and lecture groups. A friend from Cincinnati offered to promote and manage his speaking engagements.[57]

At one of his first lectures away from Norwalk, at a hall in Richmond, Indiana, only five people, including a child, were in the audience when Kennan arrived. Two started to leave because, as they told him, "judging from the appearance of the hall, there isn't going to be any lecture." Kennan immediately took the stage, shed his coat, and began speaking to stop anyone from walking out. The next lecture, his manager promised, would make money. That lecture, at the Pike's Music Hall in Cincinnati, which seated two thousand, nearly ended his lecturing career. From the stage he was dismayed to see just a few dozen persons scattered in twos and threes around the vast hall. But half an hour into his talk, several young men entered the opera house and took seats at the press table. Kennan turned his attention to them as though he were making "a personal appeal for sympathy and appreciation." Afterward, the reporters suggested that he return to Cincinnati to repeat the lecture. Ten days later Kennan reappeared at the opera house, and this time, thanks to their favorable reviews, hundreds were in the seats.

Invitations came pouring in. In the 1869–70 lecture season Kennan spoke on at least fifty occasions in Ohio, Indiana, and Kentucky. Good speakers had been in demand ever since the 1820s when the Lyceum movement, a form of adult education, began bringing leading literary, scientific, political, and cultural figures to public forums in thousands of communities. The renowned lecturers, such as Elizabeth Cady Stanton, Ralph Waldo Emerson, and Frederick Douglass, commanded handsome fees. Kennan did not earn anywhere near what they made, but he did well enough financially and emerged as a star regional lecturer.

To spellbound audiences, he described the indigenous peoples of Siberia ("one half of the world does not know how the other half lives"), the search for the stovepipe on the Anadyr River, and the beauty of the aurora borealis, which always drew applause. In an early sign of his sense of theatre, halfway through his lectures Kennan donned an exquisitely embroidered reindeer-skin coat and a sable-fur hat and sang Russian songs "with excellent effect," reported one newspaper, "as the applause which followed testified." A reporter in Louisville, Kentucky, wrote that Kennan's lecture was the "most instructive and interesting of any that have been delivered in the city." At another Cincinnati lecture, a reporter noticed the hush in the hall because the audience was "unwilling to lose a single word that fell from the speaker's lips." One Ohio newspaper reported that "Kennan's delivery is capital" and presciently predicted that with a little more experience he "will make one of the most popular lecturers in the country." In his lectures, Kennan mentioned and defended the Siberian exile system, although he had seen little of it in northeast Siberia. Many young women, who had heard about the handsome young explorer, attended his lectures, but Kennan had his eye on another adventure and not romance.[58]

In June 1870, using his lecture earnings, he set sail from New York City for Russia without much more than a vague plan to travel through the savagely wild Caucasus Mountains, starting in Dagestan, which means "the mountainous land." It was adventure for the sake of adventure, which Kennan called "vagabonding." In St. Petersburg, Kennan went sightseeing, worked on his Russian language skills, and completed the last chapters of *Tent Life in Siberia*. Russian acquaintances warned him of the dangers that awaited him in the Caucasus, especially in the overwhelmingly Muslim Dagestan (still part of Russia). Dozens of languages were spoken in the region; at the time of Kennan's visit, there was little local government and Russian control was tenuous at best. A rough semblance of social stability in the mountains, as contradictory as it sounds, was maintained by the practice of blood feud.

Kennan made his way to Dagestan by Volga River boat to Astrakhan and southbound steamer along the western shore of the Caspian Sea. He seemed heedless of the risks, perhaps because he no longer doubted his courage. "I have not the slightest idea how I'm going to travel in the mountains. Horseback, in a cart or on foot, or when I shall eventually come out," he wrote his family, adding for their reassurance but also sounding a bit cocky, "I have full faith in my own resources and I know there isn't any danger."

According to Caucasus historian Charles King, in Greek mythology the Caucasus was "the far edge of the world where Prometheus the fire-stealer was exiled by the Gods." Kennan walked up to the edge and leaped.[59]

On September 11, 1870, he disembarked in Petrovskoe (now Makhach-kala, Dagestan's capital), a town of one-story, earth-and-clay houses with a population of several hundred. Heavily armed mountaineers strutted in the streets of Petrovskoe, and, reflecting the Persian Empire's age-old influence, Persian women discreetly went about their errands in long white veils with two holes for their eyes. Kennan's conversational Russian proved useless because barely anyone spoke it. Some mountaineers spoke a language so heavy on consonants and abrupt guttural stops that it sounded like clicks.

His first acquaintances in Petrovskoe were Jews. Kennan apparently had not encountered many before and seemed to regard the Petrovskoe Jews as exotic. "I find myself in Dagestan befriended by Jews!" he wrote his family. "They are good fellows at any rate." The mountain Jews of Dagestan, as they were known, had strayed from the well-trod Diaspora route from the Middle East to Europe and western Russia, wandered into Persia long enough to learn a Farsi-based language (still spoken by the few remaining mountain Jews), and then settled in the Caucasus Mountains. They joined what Kennan called the "surviving Robinson Crusoes of a score of ship-wrecked states and nationalities" living on a "mountainous island in the sea of human history." Kennan and his new Jewish friends played billiards, swam in the Caspian Sea, and visited a village where the dwellings were so cantilevered out from natural hillside terraces that some roads ended on roofs.

He said goodbye to the Jews and started inland to cross the mountains to the Black Sea. He may have been the first American to venture into Dagestan's interior. A Russian merchant gave him a ride in his carriage as far as Temir Khan Shura, a town of several thousand at the approaches to the main Caucasus Range. He stayed for several days to explore narrow mud-filled streets and shops that sold everything from European dry goods to screeching falcons. He made the acquaintance of a Russian-speaking man from the Lezgin tribe of South Dagestan who told Kennan of a mountain tribe that left its dead standing upright in their homes until the corpses disintegrated and collapsed to the floor. That was considered the moment of death and the remains were then buried. The word "curious" frequently appears in Kennan's journal, as in "Verily, this is a curious country."[60]

Kennan now faced the main Caucasus Range, a nearly eight-hundred-mile-long mountain barrier between the Caspian Sea and the Black Sea. He had no idea how to get across, but he learned that a nobleman, Prince Giorgi Davidovich Jorjadze, was departing shortly from Temir Khan Shura for his home in Kakhetia in Georgia, a route that would take him over the mountains. Kennan called on the prince, introduced himself as an American traveler, and asked permission to go with his party. The prince, a dignified man in his late fifties wearing a Persian kaftan with long sleeves, told him that the journey was beyond someone without mountain experience. Kennan summarized his exploration of the Kamchatka Peninsula and northeastern Siberia. The prince was less than enthusiastic at having this young American tag along with him, but in Dagestan hospitality was a virtue as prized as proficiency with weapons. The prince told Kennan to find heavy riding boots, a burka, and a pair of saddlebags and be ready to leave the next day.

Kennan searched through the town until he had the required gear, including a sheepskin burka, which is a heavy cape useful as a blanket at night or in stopping a knife thrust in a fight, but he had to abandon much of his luggage to make the trip. The next day, on a horse provided by the prince, Kennan rode in an entourage of twenty-five colorfully outfitted mountaineers and a contingent of interpreters. It was a stroke of good fortune for Kennan because Prince Jorjadze performed a role roughly akin to a circuit-riding judge in America. On his way to Georgia, the prince planned to stop in mountain villages to mediate disputes and even hold trials, which would give Kennan access to the communities at the heart of mountaineer society.[61]

They spent the first night at a house in the village of Dzhengutai where, on the veranda, young women dressed head-to-toe in brightly-colored Persian silks danced and sang for the entertainment of Prince Jorjadze and his dark-complexioned mountaineers, who wore long coats, called khalats, and leather boots with turned-up toes that narrowed to a point. Rows of cloth pouches, each holding a rifle cartridge, lined the front of their khalats. Silver-sheathed daggers, called kinjals, and long barreled pistols dangled from golden cloth belts around their waists. Their rifles hung on hooks on a wall. To a man, the weapons-draped mountaineers looked ready for a fight. Kennan felt out of place in his weaponless clothing—blue flannel shirt, English shooting jacket, and top boots.

He attracted the attention of the young women, who whispered and pointed at him. He was led by one to a three-legged milking stool, where he sat while another woman, holding a two-foot club, circled around him. "This young man has come from a far-off land to see our Dagestan," she sang as an interpreter translated for Kennan. "To observe our ways and our social customs and our mode of life. And to write them down, and perhaps to print them in that far-off land." At the end of each stanza other young women chanted, "Hi! Hi! Hi! An-nan-nan-nan-ni!"

"We must therefore show to this traveler how we always treat our friends," said the woman and smacked Kennan on the shoulder with the club. "Hi! Hi! Hi! An-nan-nan-nan-ni!" Kettle drums rolled, Prince Jorjadze clapped, and the mountaineers pulled out their pistols and fired into the air. The choruses, blows with the club, and pistol shots continued until the young woman handed the club to Kennan, who stood up. She sat down on the stool to await his retaliatory blows. Kennan diplomatically handed the club to a nearby mountaineer "and asked him to sing my song and avenge my injuries."[62]

Kennan traveled for two weeks with Prince Jorjadze and his entourage, who sang Dagestan war songs as they ascended and descended steep mountain valleys. "It is almost impossible to exaggerate the depth, narrowness, and gloominess of these valleys." He rode his horse on narrow, zigzagging paths cut into hillsides so steep that his right shoulder sometimes grazed a rock face while his left stirrup hung over a valley floor far below. On one descent he witnessed a rider dismount, sit down from dizziness, and cover his face in his hands. Suspecting that the prince was watching him, Kennan did his best to conceal his fear. He came to understand the wisdom of the prince's advice that "whatever happens, leave the reins alone. That is your only safety." Once, when his horse slipped on splinters of slate and appeared about to go over the edge, Kennan attempted to guide him. The horse shook his head furiously "as much to say, 'I know these mountain paths better than you do.' His judgment with regard to the best place to step was really remarkable." Kennan never had to dismount.

The prince resolved disputes ranging from minor offenses to murders by applying the unwritten, pre-Islamic, customary law called *adat*. The prince tutored the inquisitive Kennan on *adat*, which provided adaptable but sometimes nonsensical rules for everything from hospitality to the way blood feuds could be settled to the bizarre penalties for perjury. If a male witness swore on his marriage to tell the truth, one of the oldest and most sacred oaths in that society, but was found to have lied, he was required to divorce his wife. If he had several wives, the witness designated before testifying which wife to divorce should he be judged a perjurer. *Adat* also prescribed stoning as the punishment for unchaste women.[63]

The women of the mountain villages attracted Kennan's attention. "Women coarse-featured, dark-complexioned and not all handsome," he wrote in his journal. "Evidently degraded and brutalized by hard work." At sunrise, the women went into the fields, sometimes knitting as they walked, carrying their infants in baskets slung across their backs, and driving their cattle ahead of them. They worked all day in the fields and at sunset they returned, herding the cattle home and carrying both their infants and a giant bundle of wheat on their bent backs. "An idle woman in Dagestan would be a curiosity. I have never yet seen one who was not occupied with something." The men slept late, rising only after the sun had warmed the air, and congregated at the mosques, smoking and socializing until the noonday prayers. Kennan observed that the men did some work, such as plowing and sowing grain, but overall, he found a male-dominated society that depended on the near-enslavement of women. His journal offers no evidence, however, that he was personally moved or offended by the mistreatment of the women. He was a keen but apparently detached observer of their oppression.

The treatment of women in Dagestan has not changed all that much since Kennan's visit. Frith Maier, an adventurer and expert on the Caucasus, retraced part of Kennan's travels in Dagestan for her 2003 book *Vagabond Life*. She saw women walking on the roadside bent under giant bundles of straw and other women hauling water from the springs. When they were not working, women were largely confined to their homes and did not interact with men outside those in their families. Men still claimed the warrior tradition but less because of blood feuds, although they still exist, than as an excuse for their own idleness. One man justified the burdens on women by explaining to Maier that men "must be prepared at any moment to take up our weapons and defend our towns and families."[64]

In Bezhuta, a village of several hundred, Kennan watched mountaineer children at play. Laughing, they ran races, threw mud at each other, and whirled cats in the air by their tails and flung them into stone walls. One child, Kennan noted, had a "very bright intelligent face and I have no doubt that if he could be taken to America now and educated, he would make an able useful man." He decided that the principal difference between the average American and the average mountaineer was their circumstances. "One has advantages, education, culture, and the other has not. One grows up an intelligent, thinking reasoning human being and the other a mere wild animal."

Kennan admired the mountaineers for their bravery in fighting off invaders for centuries and he praised their personal characteristics, including love of music, hospitality, and generosity. But he did not think of the mountaineers as civilized in the manner of Americans and Britons and considered the Russian presence to be an enlightened one. Kennan was an able observer of life in Dagestan but his pro-Russian bias, an imperialist sensibility and, at least by today's standards, a touch of racism, blinded him to larger truths. The Russian conquest of the Caucasus was no more enlightened than its subjugation of Siberia. It was an exercise in glorifying Russia as a European-style imperialist nation under a self-congratulatory veneer of bringing civilization to the barbarians. As Fyodor Dostoevsky candidly wrote, "By capturing Asia our spirits and strength will lift . . . In Europe we were hangers-on whereas in Asia we will arrive as masters."[65]

Near the end of the journey to the prince's home in Kakhetia, the party rode above the tree line. The prince, who was ahead of Kennan, seemed to drift away from the mountain because a thick, cold mist had erased any distinction between the snow-covered paths and the sky. "There lies Kakhetia," said the prince, pointing downward through the fog, when they stopped at the summit to rest the horses. As they began descending, the fog lifted and far below Kennan could see the lush vineyards of the wine-growing region of Georgia. "The most magnificent picture I have ever seen." He stayed at Prince Jorjadze's stone-and-brick residence where he slept in a bed, instead of on tables or boards, drank tea and coffee, and lay on a divan smoking a pipe. After five lazy but boring days, he decided that he had not seen enough of the Caucasus, said farewell to the prince, and set out alone.[66]

Russian Army Capt. Cherkassof was lonesome in his mountain outpost in Chechnya, where he supervised the construction of a road into Dagestan. So he was delighted when the Russian-speaking young American appeared at his tent, introduced himself, and asked for a place to sleep. Since leaving Prince Jorjadze's home, Kennan had visited Tbilisi in Georgia and then traveled the Georgian military road, the historically central Caucasian corridor for trade and invasion. "Of course, you'll stay with me tonight. You're simply a godsend! I haven't seen an educated man in three months." They dined on lamb accompanied by bread, honey, grapes, and red Caucasian wine, and talked through the night about politics, literature, science, and art.

The next morning Kennan explained to Capt. Cherkassof his plan to travel through western and central Dagestan, return to Temir Khan Shura near the Caspian Sea (where he had first joined Prince Jorjadze and his entourage), and start home. This final leg of his trip would complete a circumnavigation through Dagestan, Georgia, and Chechnya, but he needed to cross the mountains to Temir Khan Shura before the snow fell. Kennan asked Capt. Cherkassof for help in obtaining a horse and an interpreter. His host immediately offered the horse but then thought for a while about choosing an interpreter.

"Suppose I give you my interpreter. I can spare him for two or three weeks. He's a tenth-century barbarian, of course, but you won't mind that."

"I'll take him."

Capt. Cherkassof snapped orders at an aide, who quickly left. A tall, rugged Dagestan mountaineer, perhaps fifty years of age, appeared in the tent. He wore a black *khalat* with a chest full of bullets in ammunition pouches. His eyes were blue and his hair was flecked with gray and white. He had dyed his beard and mustache a bright red and his forehead displayed a wide, white scar. An ornately decorated pistol and *kinjal* hung from his silver studded belt. "Akhmet," said Capt. Cherkassof, "this is a foreign traveler from the other side of the great ocean who is about to make a trip into Dagestan. He wants an interpreter. Will you go?"

"Why not go, if it is ordered?"

"Well, I order it."

On their first day together, Akhmet led Kennan up a zigzagging trail to an eight-thousand-foot ridge, where they dismounted to have lunch. Akhmet took bread, dried meat, and several hard-boiled eggs from his pockets and the lining of his lambswool hat. Kennan went to his saddlebags and brought out cheese, white bread, half a chicken, and a bottle of red wine, which had been given to him by Capt. Cherkassof's aide, and proposed that they share their food, which "immediately improved our social relations." Akhmet pointed out his birthplace in the distance and the mountain named Gunib where Imam Shamil had surrendered to the Russians.[67]

As they journeyed through a landscape of jagged mountains, deep gorges, terraced hills, and vineyards, and crossed high, rickety wooden bridges, Kennan made "progress toward intimacy" with Akhmet by demonstrating a sincere interest in mountaineer culture. In response to Kennan's questions, Akhmet pointed out more features of the landscape, sang a mountaineer song for Kennan, and explained that the thick pillow-like hats worn by Dagestan women originated in an effort to keep their husbands from breaking their skulls. Akhmet also gave Kennan a lesson in mountaineer hospitality ethics. He found places for them to stay overnight in mountainside villages, once by simply walking into the most affluent-looking house and making the two of them comfortable. But Kennan made the mistake in one village of offering money to their host, who immediately reached for his double-edged knife. Akhmet quickly intervened and calmed the host. As they rode away, Akhmet explained that, "It isn't safe to do that. In our Dagestan you can't offer money to a man in whose house you have been a guest. It is a deadly insult."

In some villages Akhmet was greeted like a returning favorite son. The villagers stopped what they were doing and came to shake his hand or, as in one village, press thumbs. In the village of Antzakhoul, in the midst of another jubilant reunion, Kennan asked Akhmet how he had come to know the villagers so well. Akhmet explained that, under the law of *adat,* the villagers had to give him refuge from his enemies, which could last for months or even years. "Many years ago when I was young I killed a man and had to flee to this village to escape his blood avengers."

"Why did you kill him?"

"He said a bad word to me. I drew my *kinjal.* Batz! and it was done."

"How many men have you happened to kill, Akhmet?"

"Fourteen, besides some Russians that I killed in battle. I don't know how many of them there were." It dawned on Kennan that, as Akhmet's companion, he had become associated in a wild, lawless land with a murderer.

Akhmet was equally curious about the customs in Kennan's land. "What do you do in your country when a man says a bad word to you?"

"Knock him down," Kennan explained, "or perhaps call the police; it depends on circumstances."

"Then you don't ever kill anybody; or go on raids, or protect your cattle, or avenge blood?"

"We are protected by the law."

"Yours must be a sheep's life."

Kennan built such a rapport with Akhmet that one night, while they stayed warm by a fire built from dried cow dung, Akhmet revealed to Kennan how one of his feuds had led to the worst humiliation of his life. He had killed a member of an especially fierce family, who would have hunted Akhmet for the rest of his days unless he made peace through a "blood adoption" ritual. The ceremony required Akhmet to kiss the bared breast of the victim's aged mother, a sacred gesture that would settle the family's grievances and commit Akhmet to fight for them. But the grieving mother wanted no part of the blood adoption, and as soon as Akhmet came into the family's home, she ferociously cursed and then physically attacked him. "She fought like a she-wolf," Akhmet explained, "and I was so ashamed and humiliated that I was ready to cut my own throat." The rest of the family decided that the blood adoption could be successfully completed without the breast-kissing, and he became a member of the dead man's family and fought in its feuds. Akhmet stopped talking and stared gloomily into the dying embers of the cow dung fire.

Kennan was baffled by the idea that Akhmet could become a fighter for an enemy family. But in a society lacking a central, unifying government and any semblance of law enforcement, as one historian of the Caucasus has explained, each family or village had to defend itself and needed as many warriors as possible. "The [Dagestan] highlanders engaged in blood feuds not because they were too stupid to see the negative consequences of escalating a dispute between two people into a dispute between two clans, but rather because in the absence of a police force, the threat of escalation was the best deterrent to any attack." Of course, when deterrence theory failed, the mountaineers' feuds were long and bloody.

By the time the two men parted in Temir Khan Shura, they were friends. Akhmet had decided that Kennan was trustworthy and a man of some intelligence and Kennan thought that Akhmet possessed "tact, consideration, and delicacy of feeling."[68]

From Temir Khan Shura, Kennan rode in a caravan of horse-drawn wagons, sitting on a bag of flour, to the Black Sea port of Poti. He left the caravan white from head to toe in flour and boarded a steamer bound for Constantinople. His fellow passengers included three hundred Muslim pilgrims returning from Mecca, some of whom became seasick. A cleric read a chapter from the Koran over one violently sick pilgrim, but it had no discernible effect. The cleric then wrote a Koranic verse on the inside of a saucer with pen and ink, poured water into the saucer, and with his finger mixed the ink and water. He gave the mixture to the ill pilgrim, who drank it, and ceased vomiting. Kennan, impressed, reflected on his youthful religious upbringing with amusement, regret, and a tinge of resentment. "If I could only have had the proverbs of Solomon, hymns and the Westminster catechism written on a big platter and washed off with a tumbler of water so that I could have swallowed them at a draught—how many tearful hours I should have been spared." From Constantinople, he went by deck passage to the mouth of the Danube River, traveled up the Danube in the hold of an Austrian steamship, and crossed the rest of Europe to England in third-class train and boat accommodations.

When George Kennan entered the Russian Empire six months earlier, he had with him a trunk and two valises. Now, he had only a few personal items and the clothes he wore, he was close to broke, and he was subsisting on bread and water. On Christmas Eve of 1870 his train reached Charing Cross station in London "with triumph in my heart and two shillings & sixpence in my pocket." Kennan wired home for money and took a cab for two shillings to the Euston Hotel. He bought a cigar with his remaining money and smoked it.[69]

5

The Making of a Journalist

Tent Life in Siberia was published to enthusiastic reviews and strong sales but the royalties were insufficient for Kennan to both support himself and provide money to his family. In mid-1871 his brother, John, now the president of the Union Bank in the sleepy village of Medina in upstate New York, offered him a job as the bank cashier, presumably as a stepping stone to a banking career. Kennan accepted and went to Medina, where he lived in his brother's house. Not long after arriving he wrote his mother that he was suffering from both a bowel ailment and the confinement of office work. "Working at a desk doesn't agree with me as well as knocking around in the mountains of the Caucasus." He wrote his sister Jennie that "if it were not for books, I don't believe that I could live in a town like this a week" and that "his true vocation [was] that of an explorer."

The attractive, eighteen-year-old Emiline Rathbone Weld was Kennan's rescue from the tedium of life in Medina. References to Emiline, whom Kennan and his family called "Lena," began appearing in letters to his family in 1872. She is a somewhat elusive figure in this narrative.

A search for information about her family and education in county his-
tories and old newspaper articles reveal little beyond that she had seven
brothers and sisters, one of whom died in infancy and two in their ado-
lescence; her parents were active in the local Episcopal Church; and one
of her school classmates married Grover Cleveland and became First
Lady of the United States. It's plausible, but conjectural, that Kennan
and Emiline were introduced to each other by her father, John Weld,
a prominent town figure who, as an owner of a local flour mill, may
have met Kennan through dealings with the Union Bank. Emiline had
a lifelong interest in literature and art, which would have given the two
a common bond, especially in a village like Medina.

What is not elusive is their devotion to each other. In an era that
supposedly "was afraid of sex," their correspondence offers a glimpse
into a passionate relationship. Kennan declared in one letter to Emiline
a few years after they met, but before they married, that "It seems a
long time since you last kissed me, since I felt the soft pressure of your
arms around my neck, and I long once more to be made happy by your
caresses. Sweetheart is it foolish? Perhaps. I don't care. I love you. Write
me often." And later, "I wish I could come home to you & be taken
in your arms & lay my head on your soft warm breast." But Emiline
destroyed perhaps even more intimate correspondence before Kennan's
papers went to the Library of Congress after his death. One imagines
that she had a faint smile while writing a note for Kennan's frustrated
biographers to someday read in the library's archives. "GK had a horror
of endearments being published, so altho we wrote daily, often 2 or 3
times daily, I have destroyed nearly all."[70]

A young couple in love needs money, and not just passion. Kennan's
salary as cashier was likely insufficient for them to marry and start a
family and, to make matters worse, Kennan's future at the Union Bank
of Medina was uncertain. The bank had become mired in a financial scandal that pushed his brother into a nervous breakdown, even
though he bore no responsibility. George and Emiline put off marriage, although the critical success of *Tent Life in Siberia* should have

reassured them that he would someday make a good living as a writer. The *New York Times* wrote that "the narrative manner of Mr. Kennan is full of animation and pleasantry." The *Nation* noted that, while Kennan often found himself in treacherous circumstances, "the humors of the occasion seemed to impress him more strongly than the dangers," and described his observations of Kamchatka and its indigenous peoples as a "valuable contribution" to science. The *Atlantic Monthly* told its readers that "to learn what hardship the human frame is capable of enduring . . . one must read 'Tent Life in Siberia' for himself." Equally favorable reviews appeared in other prominent American newspapers and in the *Pall Mall Gazette* in London. The American consul general in St. Petersburg wrote Kennan that many Russians had read and liked *Tent Life in Siberia*.[71]

Religious theology was Kennan's other preoccupation in Medina. He initially resumed a conventional relationship with the church by becoming the superintendent of a Presbyterian Sunday school. But the religious doubts that had emerged on the Siberian tundra, further provoked by his exposure to other religions in the Caucasus, began to torment him. He realized that if he was to have any peace of mind, as he wrote years later to a cousin, "I should have to re-examine the very foundations of my religious belief. So I went at it." As much the driven as the driver, Kennan began in his methodical fashion by first studying science, especially geology, paleontology, and astronomy. He then read the Old Testament and prodigious quantities of biblical commentary. "In fact, I read everything that was accessible on the subject."

After completing his self-assigned theological curriculum, he dismissed the entire biblical history of man. "While the Old Testament embodies the spiritual experiences of a gifted race, and as a record of that experience was very valuable, it also embodied the childish mythology of that race, and was wholly untrustworthy as a history of the beginning of the world and mankind." Kennan moved on to the New Testament, critically examining the Gospels and "all known facts that had any bearing on the life of Christ and the records of it." Questioning the faith in which he had been raised nearly caused him to abandon his examination of religion. "Perhaps it <u>was</u> sinful to doubt after all—perhaps I <u>had</u> been wrong in presuming even to question the mystery of God's dealings with man," he wrote a friend and confidant. "Would it not be better to stop thinking and wondering and speculating and simply believe?" But he persisted and, after a year of study, concluded that Christian theology was "a fictitious landscape painted on a drop curtain by sincere but ignorant theologians centuries ago."

Rather than abandon religion altogether, Kennan constructed an evidence-based "working theory of life" that, while not denying the existence of God, rejected the biblical God "of injustice, cruelty and revenge." Kennan understood the limits of his new philosophy, which hardly "illuminated the landscape or one hundredth part of it. What little it does show it shows truly." He had decided to "hold fast [to] what seemed to me to be *true,* let it lead where it would. No infidelity I felt sure could be worse than infidelity to my own convictions. If I guided my life by what seemed to be true, I was content to leave the rest with God."[72]

The process, he later wrote a cousin, caused him "great unhappiness, but I came to definite conclusions at last, and these conclusions have never been shaken." The unhappiness was shared by his family and especially his mother who, devastated by her son's withdrawal from the church, reproached him as a sinner. He never wavered, writing her that "I believe not what I would like to believe—not what it would be pleasant to believe—but what the evidence <u>compels</u> me to believe." None of his arguments assuaged his mother's anguish or, despite the strength of his new, hard-won convictions, relieved his own guilt over betraying his family's deep religious devotion.

In June 1876, around the time that his brother left the bank, Kennan quit his cashier's job and left for New York City to make a fresh start while Emiline remained in Medina. Even apart from the loss of his patron at the bank, by his own declaration he was unsuited to a career in banking. Kennan had just fifty dollars in his pocket and no job awaited him in New York. He was essentially gambling his and Emiline's prospects on the promise made by Samuel Clemens (Mark Twain): "Make your mark in New York, and you are a made man." Kennan's entrée to New York City was an invitation to speak at the American Geographical Society, which had been formed by prominent New Yorkers to aid Lady Jane Franklin, her dozen clairvoyants, and the British Navy in finding her husband, Sir John Franklin, whose expedition had disappeared while searching for a route through the Northwest Passage. Sir John was never found but having come into existence, the society dedicated itself to the advancement of geographical knowledge. Kennan's lecture topic was "Dog-sledge" travel in Kamchatka and northeastern Siberia. The lecture, which was well received, was a stepping stone for George Kennan, but less to outright success than to a frustrating glimpse of it.[73]

On the Saturday evening following his lecture, Kennan was admitted to the lower Fifth Avenue home of the society's president, Judge Charles Patrick Daly, a prominent state court judge, who had invited him for dinner. Kennan entered a large, gloomy front parlor whose windows were draped with heavy curtains. His count of the paintings on the parlor walls had reached forty-four when Judge Daly came in and escorted him to the dining room. Over a seven-course meal served with sherry, claret, and champagne, Judge Daly and his guests debated the nature of the forces that tend to invigorate civilization or destroy it. Nothing in Kennan's letter to Emiline about the evening suggests that the conversation touched on the ravages of a nationwide depression, which had left the Gilded Age considerably less gilded and one-quarter of the New York City workforce unemployed.

The depression had also ruined some members of the city's elite but their financial carnage was hardly evident at the Century Club, a handsome redbrick mansion close to Union Square, where Judge Daly took Kennan after dinner. The members of the city's important social clubs such as the Century were mainly white Protestant men, although the Union Club admitted a few prominent Jews. Club members considered themselves to be well-bred gentlemen who, as defined in a leading etiquette manual of the era, possessed "high moral character, a polished education, a perfect command of temper, delicate feeling, good habits, and a good bearing." Women were not admitted.

Kennan found himself in one of the Century Club's hardwood-paneled drawing rooms, whose walls were decorated with the heads of horned animals. The room was filled with self-satisfied, cigar-smoking men in black swallowtail coats, white cravats, and black patent leather shoes. Drinks were served, Kennan wrote Emiline, from "huge bowls half as big as washtubs where miniature translucent icebergs floated about in an Arctic Ocean of claret with bobbing strawberries and little circular islands of lemon." While a majority of its members engaged in trade and finance, the Century Club, which had begun as an "association of gentlemen engaged or interested in letters or the fine arts," had a healthy representation of artists, writers, and scientists. Judge Daly introduced Kennan to among others, the poet and travel writer Bayard Taylor, the geologist John Strong Newberry, and the American landscape painter Albert Bierstadt.[74]

The Century Club's portal to the city's leading mercantile, banking, political, literary, and artistic figures offered a tantalizing prospect to Kennan. "It would be a very great advantage to me in a dozen ways," he wrote Emiline, "if I could afford to become a member of either the Century Club or the Lotos." But Kennan did not have the social standing and connections to become a member of the Century Club and lacked the money to pay the initiation fee and annual dues of the more accessible, up-and-coming Lotos Club, half of whose membership had to be from the literary and artistic professions. "At present," he had to admit, without membership in at "least one good club it is hard to make the acquaintance of prominent literary men—or indeed prominent men of any kind."

Kennan's political outlook at the time would have been at home among the conservative businessmen and financiers in the clubs. In July 1877, Kennan was visiting Emiline in Medina when a strike by railroad workers threatened to prevent him from returning to New York City. He suggested in a letter to his mother that the authorities should put down the strikes with force if necessary. "If a mob refused to disperse after due notice, I would scatter them with grape[shot] and canister without pity and without hesitation." That the strikes were due to the terrible plight of the railroad workers in the depression appears to have escaped his attention.[75]

Kennan evidently had hoped to make a living in New York City from lecturing and writing but even in prosperous times that would have been challenging. His lectures on his Siberian and Caucasus adventures at prominent forums like Cooper Union did not generate significant fees. He unsuccessfully sought positions on the staffs of the *New York Times* and the *New York Tribune;* despite his connections to the American Geographical Society, he failed to obtain a job there. In the summer of 1877, Kennan took a mundane position with a life insurance company, but it paid a steady salary of one hundred dollars a month.

Russia, his youthful romantic flame, was never far from Kennan's mind in those years. He spent an evening with officers from a Russian warship, the *Svetlana,* which was on a port of call to New York City and gave a tour of the city to a Russian man he had just met. "I feel as if I ought to show him as much as I can while he stays," he wrote Emiline. "I have received so many kind attentions from Russians when in their country that I am in duty bound to treat a Russian well wherever I may meet him." He had a happy reunion with his best friend from the Siberian telegraph expedition, James Dodd, who was living in Jersey City. While visiting Dodd, Kennan attended Sunday service in a Russian Orthodox church, where he heard the "sonorous chanting of the old Slavonic liturgy—inhaled the spicy well remembered fragrance of Russian incense and imagined myself back in Siberia."[76]

The critical success of *Tent Life in Siberia* and his lectures on the

Caucasus enabled Kennan to establish himself as an authority on Russia. The *New York Tribune* published his letters defending Russia from attacks by, among others, the British press. Great Britain was obsessed with the threat to India from Russian ambitions in Central Asia, a diplomatic rivalry that a British officer had termed "the Great Game." The British officer lost his part of the game when he was later captured by an Uzbek emir, who threw him into a well filled with reptiles and cut off the skeletal head when the officer's remains were hauled up.

Kennan argued in one letter that Russia had no designs on India but was only interested in protecting its hard-won gains in Central Asia. Any danger of a conflict between the two powers, he suggested, could be deferred for five or even ten years if Britain simply accepted Russian expansion in Central Asia "as she must." The *Tribune's* editors highlighted this letter for their readers as offering "a clear light over the threatened conflict between Russia and Great Britain in Central Asia. There is scarcely a better authority in the United States on this particular subject."[77]

In his free time Kennan explored the city. He spent an afternoon at the studio of Albert Bierstadt, whom he had met at the Century Club, examining studies of Yosemite Valley, the Sierra Nevadas, and Native Americans. "They were wonderfully delicate and finished," he wrote Emiline. "I wish you might see them." He attended a séance, which was a popular pastime, where one medium writhed and moaned "as if she were undergoing a surgical operation of unusual severity with unusual fortitude." But nothing in New York City so intrigued George Kennan as his visit to a prayer meeting on Water Street.

"George," an artist friend said to him one day, "I want you to go with me tonight to Jerry McAuley's prayer meeting." When Kennan insisted that he did not go to prayer meetings, the friend said, "this isn't a common prayer meeting. It's Jerry McAuley's," and took him to the East River waterfront and a world far removed from the Century Club. Dirty, half-clothed children roamed the sidewalks; men with mean, florid faces hovered in the shadows of tenement and dance hall doorways; and an odor hinting of decomposing bodies rose from the openings and gaps in the streets.

On the benches inside the mission on Water Street sat the most hopeless group of Americans Kennan had ever seen. Following the hymns, Jerry McAuley, a tall, lean man about thirty-five years old, whose kind eyes held no trace of the years that he had spent in prison, came forward. "Why do you come to this prayer meeting? You come here because you're wretched and miserable. God didn't put you in the gutter—you went there of your own accord." He invited the assorted drunks, tramps, prostitutes, and criminals to stand up one by one and pledge to stop sinning, come to Christ, and start a new life. An elderly man with an exhausted face came forward. "I am a confirmed drunkard. I have spent for drink all that I had in the world. My wife died of a broken heart. I have sunk to the lowest depths of degradation. God help me!" He began sobbing and Jerry McAuley helped him back to his seat. One after another, men and women rose and flayed themselves until nothing was left but their raw, bleeding souls.

Their abject sincerity overwhelmed Kennan. "In less than ten minutes, I had forgotten who I was, how I came there, what I thought about religion, and what had been my attitude toward prayer-meetings . . . it was interesting and absorbing beyond anything that I had ever heard or witnessed." Kennan's fascination with the broken men and women at the prayer meeting, however, did not move him to act. He had brought a notebook with him to make notes for an article but never wrote about the deplorable New York City slums or joined any of the charities, church groups, or progressive organizations campaigning to clean up them up. His reaction might not have been all that different had he attended an especially moving performance of a Shakespearean tragedy.[78]

In the end, Kennan made his mark in Washington and not New York City. In 1878, Walter P. Phillips, the manager of the Washington office of the Associated Press, whom Kennan had met through the lecture bureau that booked both of their speaking engagements, approached him with a proposition. The Associated Press had been founded in 1846 by five New York City newspapers who pooled their resources to deliver news by horseback rider and stagecoach from the battlefronts of the Mexican-American War to a telegraph office in Richmond, Virginia. In 1876, a reporter named Mark Kellogg became the first of dozens of Associated Press correspondents to die while covering a story when he rode with Lt. Col. George Armstrong Custer and the 7th Cavalry into the Battle of the Little Bighorn.

Phillips asked Kennan to become the Associated Press reporter for the United States Supreme Court. Kennan initially declined, saying he had no legal experience. "Well, you could not know less than the man currently in that job," replied Phillips, "and you have the affirmative advantage that you know how to write." Kennan started work on a Monday, which was the day that the Supreme Court announced its opinions. "Ordinarily however they don't hand down more than 5 or 6 opinions," he wrote Emiline. "Today however they came down on me—a beginner—with 12—each one covering from 5 to 20 pages of foolscap." Kennan had just one day to read and write up summaries of the twelve decisions, which are typically dense legal documents that, other than the recitation of the facts of the case, might seem like Sanskrit to the uninitiated. By the evening he had produced a two-thousand-word article on the decisions. "It's safe to say," he wrote Emiline after a few days at the court, "that I haven't worked under such constant & severe pressure in 13 years."

The Supreme Court then sat in what is now known as the Old Senate Chamber, in the north wing of the US Capitol, a semicircular room previously occupied by the US Senate. Kennan worked at a velvet-covered table in the corner of the clerk's office, which had a fireplace and a window view across the Potomac River to Arlington Heights. He was well suited to work that required "quickness of apprehension, judgment, facility of condensation & brains generally."

The Supreme Court reporting brought out Kennan's competitive side. "Before I've been here 3 months," he wrote Emiline, "I'll give them better Supreme Court reports than they've ever had before." Walter Phillips later wrote that Kennan "was complimented on the accuracy of his work by every judge on the bench during the several years he was in the service of the Associated Press."[79]

Through a friend in Washington, Kennan joined a circle of bright, ambitious young government men who often gathered on weekends to drink tea, eat graham crackers, and engage in animated discussion and debate. Most had read *Tent Life in Siberia* and regarded Kennan as a celebrity, although one secretary to a congressman was disappointed that the wiry Kennan was not the "muscular, athletic type." Through this circle, Kennan met important Washington figures, including John W. Powell, the chief of the United States Geological Survey, and Gardiner G. Hubbard, who would later co-found the National Geographic Society.

It was a measure both of Kennan's ability to impress influential men and his love for reporting on the Supreme Court, that when Powell offered him a job with the Geological Survey and Hubbard tried to recruit him for an editorial position with *Science,* the new journal of the American Association for the Advancement of Science, he declined both offers. For the first time in his life, George Kennan had a full-time job suited to his intellect and ambitions and a salary that could support a family. He and Emiline were married on September 25, 1879. They initially lived in Walter Phillips's home on Q Street before moving into their own home.

Kennan's career at the Associated Press reached its zenith when President James A. Garfield entered a Washington train station on July 2, 1881, on his way to a summer vacation. Charles Guiteau, a delusional lawyer who had failed at most endeavors in his life, stepped behind the president and fired two bullets, one of which hit him in the back. In perhaps the most infamous case of presidential medical malpractice in American history, Garfield died seventy-nine days later from an infection caused by his physicians' failure to wash their hands and sterilize their instruments while they probed for the bullet. Kennan's coordination of the Associated Press's coverage for a riveted nation of the president's wounding and slow death led to his promotion as night manager for the Washington office with a full-time assistant and a half-dozen reporters to supervise. He was invited to join the recently founded Literary Society of Washington, whose membership was limited to prominent Washingtonians who regularly met for "literary and intellectual intercourse." In contrast to the New York City clubs, women were among the Literary Society's founders and active members. Professionally and socially, George Kennan had arrived, but only to experience a tragedy.[80]

In mid-1882 Emiline became pregnant but the birth the following year went badly. The baby died the same day and Emiline struggled to survive. It was a crisis for the entire Kennan family, who followed her ordeal through Kennan's letters and telegrams and sent back messages of support. "I can think of nothing else, but your dear Lena, my heart aches for you both," wrote Kennan's sister Jennie, "the tears are streaming down my face. . . . My constant prayer is that God will spare to you your darling one." Emiline lived but she needed multiple surgeries and a prolonged recovery period. "She bears her troubles and confinement as patiently and cheerfully as ever," Kennan wrote his father. At the suggestion of her physician, who believed that a sea voyage could aid her recovery, she and Kennan sailed to Great Britain once she was stronger. Eventually Emiline regained her health, but she could no longer have children. In an era when the primary role of women was to bear and raise children, she would instead devote much of her time and energy to her husband's career, but she would also emerge in her own right as a lecturer, social figure, and friend to prominent women.[81]

Kennan's mother expressed the hope that the tragedy would bring her son back to the church. "Have you and Lena decided on some church to attend regularly?" Mary Ann wrote Kennan after he and Emiline had returned from overseas. "You do not know how many tears I have shed over your departure from the faith and practice in which you were reared as a child and you bade so fair to become an eminent Christian man, one that would be a leader and guide to all over whom you had influence." Several years later, after more of his mother's anguished expressions of fear for his soul, Kennan typed out and sent his mother a lengthy explanation why his renunciation of the church and ecclesiastical doctrine and his reconception of God was not a sin that would send him to Hell.

> *My tendency, my dear mother, is the tendency of the age and it is upward not downward—upward in the direction of greater freedom, more charity and tolerance, and a higher nobler ideal of life and God . . . I am not afraid of the God that made me . . . He is above all a God of justice, and of justice I have no fear on this side [of] the grave or the other . . . I beseech you not to make yourself unhappy any longer over my spiritual condition. Have some faith in the love and the justice of the God in whom you believe . . . How dare you assume that God is less loving and merciful than you—his creature. When the great day of final reckoning comes—if such a day is ever to come for the dwellers on earth—it will be the <u>lives</u> of men that will count and not the doctrines they have professed to believe.*

Much later someone—most likely a member of the Kennan family—wrote an instruction on the first page of the typewritten document which, for unknown reasons, was never carried out before it went to the Library of Congress.

"To be burned—"[82]

6

It Will Really Be a Magnificent Trip

At the outset of the 1880s, the prospects for even better Russian-American relations, as historian Norman E. Saul observed, "appeared excellent." American trade with Russia, while not as robust as Germany's, was expanding; Russian interest in America had never been greater; and the United States now had several experts on Russia, including George Kennan. Almost every issue of *Harper's Weekly*, according to Saul, "had some sort of picture relating to Russia with an accompanying, descriptive text: scenes of holidays, celebrations, military maneuvers, weddings, peasant life, buildings, [the] Nevski Prospect, the Kremlin, [the] royal family, leading members of government etc." The photographs and illustrations revealed that the Russian elite "looked very much like white Americans." Informed Americans recognized the Russian government's harsh autocratic nature, but, as former President Ulysses S. Grant had told Alexander II on a visit to Russia in 1878, "although the two governments were very opposite in their character, the great majority of the American people were in sympathy with Russia, which good feeling he hoped would long continue." More reforms were expected under Alexander II's rule, including a national, representative "advisory" body.[83]

But events in Russia, often driven by young revolutionary women, were building to a climax that would put an end to reform in Russia, create controversy over the Siberian exile system in the United States, and change George Kennan's life.

As Russia historian Richard Pipes noted, Russia was "the last European country to deny its citizens any voice in government." The educated classes, whose learning and sophistication was equal to their counterparts elsewhere in Europe, pressed for change because Alexander II's reforms had left them both unsatisfied and emboldened. In 1874, thousands of university students put on peasant clothing and, in what they called the "Going to the People" movement, went into the countryside to explain to the Russian peasantry the necessity of overthrowing the tsar. The movement was in part an exercise in relieving the students' guilt over their advantaged lives at the expense of the peasants, whose impoverished lives had not been improved by their emancipation in 1861. "Like a bolt from the blue," wrote the nineteen-year-old daughter of a well-to-do family, "it hit me that I . . . was already an exploiter, and my mother and my uncle and all of my relatives were all greedy, mercenary exploiters." (She later plotted to kill the tsar.) As historian Orlando Figes observed, "nineteenth-century Russia had its 'sixties' movement, too."

The audacity of the attempt by the *narodniki*, as the students were known, to lead the peasants out of poverty and into a socialist utopia was exceeded only by their ignorance of the peasantry. Many peasants, suspicious and hostile to the students and their radical ideas—"How can we live without a tsar?"—reported them to the authorities. The students posed no significant threat to the regime, who nonetheless arrested hundreds of *narodniki*. They were charged with political offenses, such as possession of illegal literature, and scores died from disease or went mad in solitary confinement. Three years after their arrests, in August 1877, one hundred and ninety-three broken *narodniki* appeared before a special tribunal in what became known as the "Trial of the 193." In early 1878, in a blow to the regime, the tribunal acquitted nearly half of the defendants, most of whom the authorities promptly rearrested anyway.[84]

A group of young people gathered in a St. Petersburg apartment following the announcement of the verdicts in the Trial of the 193. Two women in their twenties were the center of attention. One was the lively Maria Kolenkina, who had bright blue eyes and curly blond hair. The other was the black-haired, moody Vera Zasulich, who had a pronounced disinterest in what the future held for her. As someone sang a mournful Ukrainian folk song, Vera rested her head on Maria's shoulder, which caused the others in the apartment to weep. In the morning, the two women planned to change the course of Russian history by assassinating important officials, and they had poor prospects for survival. Maria and Vera saw the assassinations, as well, as an opportunity to "vindicate the revolutionary credentials of their sex" because some of the men in their circle did not consider women to be true revolutionaries. That night Vera screamed in her sleep and Maria had to wake her up.

They set out the next morning, each carrying a revolver. Maria Kolenkina went to the residence of a prosecutor in the Trial of the 193, whom she had been assigned to kill, but she could not gain access even though she had bribed a servant to let her in. She went to the apartment of a friend and collapsed into his arms sobbing inconsolably. Vera Zasulich's target was the governor of St. Petersburg, F. F. Trepov, because he had recently ordered the flogging of an imprisoned student for failing to remove his cap in the governor's presence. Vera went to Trepov's office and asked to present him with a petition to allow her to work as a teacher. When Trepov appeared, Vera pulled out her revolver from underneath her cloak and managed to fire a shot before she was knocked to the ground by the governor's aides. The bullet hit Trepov but missed vital organs and he survived. Vera's jury trial for attempted murder was another judicial disaster for the regime. The jury, swayed by Vera's moving testimony about her rootless existence and her revulsion on hearing of the student's flogging—"It is a terrible thing to raise one's hand against a human being, but I felt I had to do it"—acquitted her. Vera evaded rearrest and Siberian exile by fleeing to Switzerland. After meeting her, Lenin wrote his wife, "There's a person as clear as crystal."[85]

A radical organization called the "People's Will" concluded that Zasulich's acquittal legitimized political violence and mounted a series of unsuccessful attempts to assassinate Tsar Alexander II. Women made up nearly a third of the Executive Committee of the People's Will and participated in all the failed assassination attempts, which included blowing up part of the Winter Palace in St. Petersburg. The regime's secret police decimated the leadership of the People's Will, but on Sunday, March 13, 1881, the survivors made another effort to fulfill their self-assigned task of regicide. Their leader was twenty-seven-year-old Sophia Perovskaya, a petite, blond, blue-eyed, steel-willed descendant of Peter the Great.

Under her direction a team of assassins took up positions along the road next to the Catherine Canal in St. Petersburg, where the tsar went for Sunday rides in his bulletproof carriage. At Sophia's signal one of

Sophia Perovskaya, who led the assassins of Alexander II, date unknown (courtesy Library of Congress, Prints and Photographs Division)

her assassins tossed a bomb at the passing carriage. The tsar was unhurt by the blast although his carriage was damaged. He got out, but instead of fleeing the scene, he unaccountably stayed to inspect the damage and the casualties among his guards and passersby. A second bomb exploded at his feet, and he bled to death before the day ended.[86]

Sophia and four others were arrested and put on trial. The People's Will publicly offered to renounce terrorism and disband if the government adopted universal suffrage, freedom of speech and the press, held elections, and amnestied Sophia and her accomplices. The regime had no interest in reforms or in freeing the assassins, who were convicted after a three-day trial and sentenced to be hanged. In her last letter to her mother, Sophia wrote that "I don't grieve over my fate at all and am facing it with utter calm. . . . I have lived according to my convictions; I could not oppose them. . . . My fate is not so deplorable, so please don't grieve over it."

On the day of the executions, the conspirators were paraded through St. Petersburg wearing placards with the word, "Tsaricide." Tens of thousands, many of whom had waited all night for a good view, watched the hangings. At the gallows, where drums beat incessantly and five nooses dangled, the calm Sophia kissed her accomplices, including her lover but not the man who had confessed and betrayed them, which gained him no leniency from the government. The deaths were slow because the executioner, who was drunk, had failed to provide a sufficient drop. He also misjudged the weight of one of the condemned, whose noose broke twice. Several men had to lift the barely conscious assassin into position to place two nooses around his neck for a third and finally successful hanging. The botched execution earned the executioner one hundred lashes.

The assassination did not ignite a popular uprising, but did accelerate Russia's downward spiral to eventual revolution and catastrophe. The fatal mistake of the privileged opposition, as historian Richard Pipes wrote, was failing to appreciate the instability of the tsarist regime and the "possibility that it might crash and bury them in its rubble."[87]

Alexander's assassination at first drew the United States and Russia even closer because of the still traumatic American memory of Lincoln's assassination. The US Senate passed a resolution of sympathy for Russia emphasizing the "relations of genuine friendship that have always existed between the people and governments of Russia and of the United States." Former president Grant recalled fond memories of his 1878 meeting with the late tsar. The *New York Times* ran an editorial attacking the "Nihilism" of the assassins as the "chief foe of the liberty of the Russian people." The Russian government reciprocated the sympathy when Charles Guiteau mortally wounded President Garfield a few months after Alexander's assassination.

But the policies of the new tsar, Alexander III, managed to blunt the American sympathy for Russia generated by his father's assassination. A foreign diplomat anonymously reported that the tsar and his advisers were preparing to "adopt rigorous repressive measures, having no example in Russian history." Among the measures was a decree allowing the regime, without a trial, to jail or exile to Siberia anyone whose presence in Russia was deemed "prejudicial to the public order" or "incompatible with public tranquility." A former head of the Department of the Police remarked that the decree caused the fate of the "entire population of Russia to become dependent on the personal opinions of the functionaries of the political police."

Simultaneously with political repression, Alexander III tolerated, if not encouraged, a wave of brutal pogroms against Jews in European Russia. In some places Russian soldiers, mobilized to restore order, joined the mob in ransacking Jewish homes and businesses, and raping Jewish women. As historian Edward Crankshaw observed, "it was under Alexander III, and thanks to Alexander III, that anti-Semitism in Russia became institutionalized, respectable—and violent." Influential Americans began to debate the true nature of the Russian regime. *Harper's Weekly,* which previously had run issue after issue with festive illustrations of

Russian life, editorialized that there is "no question as to the existence of the most cruel, arbitrary and oppressive despotism in Russia."

Just as he had defended Russia's role in the Great Game in Central Asia several years earlier, Kennan again came to Russia's defense. He publicly addressed only the emerging criticism of the Siberian exile system, and not the pogroms, but privately he expressed the belief that the Russian government had been "grossly misrepresented" in the reports of the mistreatment of Jews even though he did not then have "the facts" to prove it. In a widely publicized lecture in 1882 at the American Geographical Society, Kennan argued that while the exile system was hardly without flaws, "whatever exile may have been in the past, it is not now, in any just sense of the words, a cruel or unusual punishment," but on the contrary should be regarded as a "more humane punishment than that inflicted upon criminals generally in other European states."

He especially stressed that, unlike penal practices elsewhere, exile did not break up families because wives and children could accompany their exiled husbands and fathers to Siberia. The lecture drew extra attention because at the end Kennan departed from his topic to suggest that no hope existed for the missing captain and several crew members from the highly-publicized Arctic Ocean expedition of the USS *Jeanette,* which had been trapped and crushed by ice. The *New York Herald,* the sponsor of the *Jeanette's* expedition, challenged Kennan's pessimistic assessment while acknowledging his authority as an Arctic expert. The bodies were found a few months later on the Siberian coast.[88]

Kennan's defense of the exile system was vigorously challenged by William Jackson Armstrong, a student of Russian affairs who had served as an inspector of US consulates during the Grant presidency. The two men engaged in a fiery debate that, as one historian observed, "stirred up public interest in the exact 'nature' of the Russian Empire, as could be clearly displayed in the Siberian exile system." The heightened interest in the exile system set the stage for an encounter in the summer of 1884 between Kennan and Richard Watson Gilder, the editor in chief of *The Century Illustrated Monthly Magazine,* formerly *Scribner's Monthly.*

Kennan described to Gilder his idea for an investigation of the Siberian exile system to resolve the controversy. Since returning from the Caucasus in 1870, Kennan had presented proposals for journalistic ventures and explorations to newspapers and exploration societies, including to the Dead Sea in Palestine, Central Asia, and Siberia. Lack of money thwarted him but now he had found a magazine with ample funds and a large readership that was shortly to become even larger.[89]

Gilder, a spare, elegant man with brilliant eyes, edited the *Century* in the belief that exposing the American middle class to the highest standards of art and literature would create a "just, ordered, and gracious society," albeit one largely on white Protestant terms. Together with publisher Roswell Smith, an astute businessman who looked like a grizzled New England sea captain, Gilder turned the *Century* into a formidable challenger to *Harper's Magazine* and *The Atlantic Monthly*. Typewriters clicked and clacked incessantly in the *Century's* opulent New York City office and some of the era's most famous personalities walked its halls of polished floors, Turkish rugs, and stained-glass doors. Only an iconoclast like *Century* contributor Mark Twain, though, had the audacity to smoke a cigar and wear a hat in the magazine's office when he came to meet with Gilder. In late 1884, the *Century* burst into the national consciousness with a series, "Battles and Leaders of the Civil War," which consisted of essays from the top generals to the foot soldiers on both sides about their experiences in the war. A *Century* editorial assured readers that "motives will be weighed without malice, and valor praised without distinction of uniform."

The *Century* intended that "Battles and Leaders" would end the persisting bitterness between the northern and southern states and in effect complete the reunification of the United States. The series timely coincided with a "national mania for all things having to do with the Civil War," and a growing national desire for sectional reconciliation. Letters poured into the *Century's* offices, some accompanied by documents and pictures from veterans and their families, and the series more than doubled the magazine's circulation to a quarter of a million readers. On some days the *Century*'s offices had the feel of a military reunion as famous Union and Confederate generals came to confer with their editors over forthcoming articles. "Grant one day and Beauregard the next!" Gilder wrote his wife. By the time the series ended in 1887, the *Century* had published two hundred and thirty essays by Civil War veterans.

The series illustrates both the *Century*'s influence and the limits of Gilder's idealistic vision for America. The series helped to create a consensus narrative that celebrated the survival of the Union and the gallant courage of the Confederate armies, but any reconciliation was between whites only because Blacks were left out. Indeed, the essays scarcely acknowledged that the war was fought over slavery. It would take nearly a century to change the Civil War narrative to include slavery, Reconstruction's failure, and the rise of Jim Crow.

But the success of "Battles and Leaders" allowed Gilder the economic freedom to introduce a captivated readership to serious literature. The *Century* ran three installments from Mark Twain's forthcoming *The Adventures of Huckleberry Finn,* itself a scathing depiction of slavery and racism. Gilder, with Twain's approval, edited the excerpts by removing, as one Twain scholar points out, "references to nakedness, offensive smells, and the blowing of noses . . . He thus left nothing in the text that might make Mrs. Watson blush." Gilder evidently did not think his readers would be offended by the word "nigger," which remained in the excerpts. In a triple literary triumph, the final installment of *Huckleberry Finn* ran in the same issue of the *Century* as excerpts from *The Bostonians* by Henry James and the *Rise of Silas Lapham* by William Dean Howells.[90]

Kennan's suggestion to Gilder for an investigation of the Siberian exile system was well-timed because American newspapers and magazines had begun to develop a sense of "social responsibility" to their readers. Until the latter part of the nineteenth century, the press had largely depended on political parties for printing contracts and patronage and newspapers were accordingly partisan. The explosive growth in American literacy and a revolution in mass printing technology meant that publishers could make more money boosting their circulation with compelling stories about the dark side of human life than by giving favorable political coverage to one party or another. Well before the famous early twentieth-century muckrakers, investigative reporters—and they were not just men—began taking unusual risks. In 1887, a twenty-three-year-old reporter in New York City, who wrote under the pen name Nellie Bly, feigned madness to have herself committed to an asylum to write stories about the mistreatment of the insane (she found that it was easier to get in than get out). A few years later, Ida B. Wells, a young Black journalist in Memphis, Tennessee, at considerable risk began an investigation of lynching in the South.[91]

Gilder asked Kennan for a formal proposal for an investigation of the Siberian exile system and, apparently at his own expense, Kennan went to Russia in August of 1884 to research it. He stayed at the Hotel D'Angleterre in St. Petersburg, where he met with members of the American legation, gathered information about Siberia and the exile system, partly by browsing in bookstores (where he found copies of the Russian translation of *Tent Life in Siberia*) and, most important, ascertained that the Russian government would not stand in the way of an investigation of the exile system. He wrote detailed accounts of St. Petersburg to Emiline, whom he missed. "I am very, very lonesome," he wrote her while on a side trip to Moscow. Her letters awaited him at the Hotel D'Angleterre on his return. "Your letters yesterday were a great treat to me, Sweetheart, & I am hoping to get one more today. I love you dearly & tenderly & shall almost certainly have you in my arms within a very few days after you get this letter. I kiss your heart."

Kennan saw and heard nothing in St. Petersburg and Moscow that changed his belief that uninformed critics had unfairly maligned the Siberian exile system and the Russian government. "Neither the country nor the people look as if they were oppressed by an iron handed despotism," he wrote a colleague in the Associated Press office in Washington, "and many of my acquaintances in St. Petersburg simply laughed at the stories which I told them about the alleged reign of terror here, the severity of the police &c." Kennan did note that "at the same time it is unquestionably true that the Russian press is practically muzzled and that very little public discussion of political affairs is permitted."[92]

After returning to the United States, Kennan mailed a proposal to Gilder. "My object in going to Siberia, as I have already said to you in conversation, is to obtain, by careful and thorough personal investigation, the materials for a graphic and picturesque account of exile life . . ." He proposed to investigate the workings of the Bureau of Exile Administration in Western Siberia, visit the forwarding prisons, and inspect the convict mines in Eastern Siberia. Kennan hoped to "actually participate in the life of a marching exile party, so far as I can persuade or bribe the officer of the convoy to allow me to do so . . ." He believed that an impartial, thorough investigation, rather than expose cruelty and mistreatment, would rebut the critics who claimed that the Siberian exile system was inhumane. It also offered an opportunity, as he later wrote Emiline, to make his "reputation and a fortune."

After the success of the "Battles and Leaders" series the *Century* had contracted with Lincoln's former secretaries, John M. Hay and John G. Nicolay, for the serial rights to their biography of the late president. Kennan's investigation of the exile system could be the magazine's third great nonfiction series. The name Siberia conjured up a vast, cold, lawless, and woeful land, which was the reason why mothers, as one English traveler in Siberia put it, "have for ages quieted their noisy children with, 'Hush, or I will send you to Siberia!'" But Siberia was also alluring in the manner of the American western frontier as a source of endless fascination and myth. Gilder commissioned Kennan to write twelve articles for a total compensation of six thousand dollars (he ended up writing more than twice as many articles for more than twice that amount).[93]

The *Century* had a well-deserved reputation for the quality of its graphics. "Battles and Leaders" had been accompanied by seventeen hundred illustrations and photographs, including some by painter Winslow Homer and Civil War photographer Mathew B. Brady. Gilder wanted an established artist to accompany Kennan to Siberia to create drawings and take photographs, which a *Century* artist would later render as illustrations for the series. But every artist approached by the magazine had declined to go and finally Gilder asked Kennan to find one. He had difficulty thinking of a suitable artist. "Why don't you ask Mr. Frost to go?" Emiline suggested.

"Why, he is married."

"Well, so are you married. If I can stand it to let you go, why can't Mrs. Frost stand it to let her husband go? It won't be any harder for her than it is for me."

Kennan immediately got on his bicycle and pedaled to a telegraph office, sent a telegram to Frost, came home, and wrote a follow-up letter to "My dear Frost" (it's unclear whether Kennan ever called Frost by his first name). The next morning Kennan wrote him a much longer letter with a detailed itinerary for the Siberian trip. George Albert Frost, then forty-two years old, lived in North Cambridge, Massachusetts, where he was a landscape painter of what is now called the White Mountain School, with a successful sideline in portraiture. He was a well-built, hearty man, six feet tall with black curly hair, long, bushy sideburns, and a thick mustache. He had begun his artistic career drawing sketches of landscapes and war scenes while serving in the Union Army and might be better known today if a fire had not destroyed his studio and many of his works. Frost appeared to be an ideal companion: he was a Civil War veteran, spoke some Russian, and was a former member of the Russian-American Telegraph Expedition, where he and Kennan had shared a cabin in Gizhiga. Unknown to Kennan, however, the artist had suffered a nervous breakdown while on a recent trip to Europe.[94]

Kennan's letters to Frost had a sense of urgency because it was

mid-April 1885 and he intended to sail in early May from New York
City. His plan, he wrote Frost, was to follow the historic route of exile parties from St. Petersburg through the Russian cities of Nizhny
Novgorod and Perm; cross the Ural Mountains to Ekaterinburg; visit
the Siberian exile forwarding prisons at Tiumen and Tomsk; and, skirting the borders of Mongolia and China, travel east as far as the Lake
Baikal region, where they would investigate the convict mines. "I hope
also to have opportunities of talking with nihilist exiles and of getting
their stories." Traveling by train, river steamer, horseback, and horse-
drawn carriage, they needed to reach the convict mines of the Trans-
Baikal in Eastern Siberia before winter set in. Even a one-week delay
could interfere with his plan, as he wrote Frost, "to see as much of Siberia as I possibly can and get into as many out of the way and unvisited
places as I can." They would be gone for eight months, he advised Frost
(it would prove to be much longer).

Kennan assured Frost that there was no one he would rather have
as a companion. "I hope that you will see your way clear to go with
me, because it will really be a magnificent trip; we know one another
so thoroughly that we can work well together, and we are sufficiently
in sympathy to enjoy such an experience together." They would be
traveling through southern Siberia which, he explained to Frost, would
be very different from the Siberia they experienced on the Russian-
American Telegraph Expedition. They would be in "the most civilized
parts of Siberia and [we] shall sleep in houses nearly all the time." Kennan underestimated the rigors and hardships ahead of them. The exile
investigation would be more demanding and exhausting than anything
he had experienced on the telegraph expedition, not to mention that
at age forty he was no longer the young daredevil who had thrived in
northeastern Siberia and the Caucasus.

Frost was interested and the *Century,* after reviewing some of his
sketches, engaged him. Kennan wrote Frost that he should take mosquito netting, a warm overcoat, both a rugged traveling suit and formal
attire, field glasses, a strong leather shoulder bag, and, although not

Kennan during his Siberian exile
investigation, 1885 (courtesy New York
Public Library)

essential, "a small pocket revolver & a few cartridges if you have them."
He also asked Frost to bring a "songbook" of American songs, which
probably baffled the artist. Kennan brought similar attire and gear but
also packed a banjo and a Winchester repeating rifle, plus two hundred
and fifty cartridges, "for hunting large game" in Siberia and "as a means
of defense." Other items, such as photographic equipment, would be
purchased during their stopover in London or else in St. Petersburg.[95]

The Siberian expedition of *The Century Illustrated Monthly Magazine*,
as Kennan and Frost thought of themselves, sailed from New York
City on May 2, 1885. "Although fully aware of the serious nature of
the work in hand, we were hopeful, if not sanguine, of success." Their
journey went smoothly until they reached the Russian border, where
customs officials, without any apparent justification other than to supplement their own salaries, confiscated Kennan's rifle and ammunition
over his angry objections and a later letter of protest from the American

legation in St. Petersburg. In mid-May, Kennan and Frost arrived in St. Petersburg and began meeting with officials in the Ministries of the Interior and Foreign Affairs to procure official letters of introduction to Siberian authorities. Kennan explained why he and Frost had come to Russia, along the following lines.

> *I have been commissioned by* The Century Illustrated Monthly Magazine, *a respected journal read by hundreds of thousands of Americans, to conduct a thorough investigation of the Siberian exile system. My companion, Mr. George Frost, a well-known Boston artist, will create the accompanying illustrations. I have argued publicly in the United States that Russia's historical development and unique circumstances justify the exile system and I have no motive to undercut my own arguments. A truthful account of the Siberian prisons and mines could well be to Russia's advantage.*[96]

Kennan did not expressly promise to defend the Russian government but neither did he hide his sympathies. The St. Petersburg officials provided Kennan with letters of introduction to, among others, governors of Siberian provinces, explaining that with these letters the Americans could go where they liked, but they would have to make their own arrangements with local officials to gain access to prisons. The officials pointedly expressed concern, however, that Kennan and Frost could be misled by any nihilists they happened to encounter in Siberia, which perhaps was their way of discouraging Kennan from seeking them out. The label "nihilist," which the regime indiscriminately applied to its opponents, whether nonviolent or otherwise, was inflammatory not least because of the assassination of Alexander II.

Their apprehension created a dilemma for Kennan. He could not conduct a comprehensive investigation without interviewing nihilists, but by far the best place to find them was in Siberia because the ones in European Russia were likely all in hiding. Kennan regarded the nihilists as a group of often violent men and women, possessed of some education and courage perhaps, but in the grip of utterly impractical visions for Russia. He did not reveal his intention to interview nihilists in Siberia lest the officials change their minds and block his investigation. He later reassured himself that, since no deliberate falsehood was involved, he had not deceived the Russian authorities.[97]

Counting both the official letters of introduction and unofficial ones from private contacts in St. Petersburg, Kennan and Frost procured more than fifty letters to present to Siberian government officials, educators, and businessmen. The Russian government held Kennan in such high regard that reportedly from behind the scenes Tsar Alexander III "help[ed] to smooth Kennan's travels." In a letter to Roswell Smith, the *Century*'s publisher, Kennan characterized the Russian officials, despite the help they had given him, as wary of his Siberian investigation. "They have been so much misrepresented that they naturally feel a little afraid of foreign writers and they are furthermore conscious perhaps that their administrative methods <u>have</u> shortcomings which it is not necessary that the world should know." He assured Smith, whom he wrote frequently during his investigation, that nonetheless "I shall find out what I wish to know all the same. The official string is by no means the only string to my Siberian bow."

Kennan did not limit himself to contacts with government officials and, true to his commitment to a "careful and thorough personal investigation," he sought out opposing views, including that of Nicholas Mikhailovich Iadrintsev, a native Siberian who published an influential journal in St. Petersburg about Siberia that was under constant pressure from government censors. Iadrintsev was especially knowledgeable about Siberian prisons since he had spent three years in them. He provided Kennan with "the anti-government side of the exile question" and hosted a dinner for him to meet explorers from Siberia who lived or happened to be in St. Petersburg. "I felt almost like a [Thomas] Cook tourist," he wrote Roswell Smith, "in the presence of men whose daring explorations had extended to the remotest corners of Siberia, Mongolia, Manchuria, Central Asia and Eastern Turkestan."

Kennan asked Smith to arrange for Iadrintsev to receive a subscription to the *Century*. He and Frost boarded a train for the Volga River city of Nizhny Novgorod (known for part of the Soviet era as Gorky).[98]

For the next week or so, Kennan and Frost resembled ordinary American tourists. Emerging from the train station, they walked to the grounds of the great trading fair of Nizhny Novgorod which, like a flower that blossoms only in one season, comes to life between mid-July and mid-September. During that fleeting period millions of Europeans and Asians, from merchants to peasants, some traveling by huge camel caravans from the Tatar desert, flock to the seven-hundred-acre fairgrounds on a sandy plain flanked by the Volga and Oka Rivers.

Kennan had seen the bustling fair on his way to the Caucasus in 1870 when he wandered among the six thousand shops, organized by markets with names like "Fur Row," "Linen Row," "Clock Row," and even a church bell market, and explored the wharves along the left bank of the Oka River piled high with bales of cotton from Khiva, casks of dried fruit from the Caucasus, and tea from China. The Oka River was almost hidden from his view by a wilderness of vessels. He crossed the half-mile-long temporary floating bridge, traversed by tens of thousands each day, which connected the fair to the kremlin, or old walled city, of Nizhny Novgorod.[99]

But now in the off-season, as a traveler observed, the fairground is left to "solitude and the high waters" of the Volga and Oka Rivers. Kennan and Frost walked along empty streets, past padlocked stores and shops, and below gilded belfries with silent bells. They crossed the Oka River on a barge towed by a small steamboat and visited the kremlin with its domed cathedrals and churches. After two days of exploring Nizhny Novgorod they boarded a steamer for a thousand-mile journey down the Volga, one of the world's great rivers, and up the Kama River to the city of Perm. Kennan and Frost sat on the hurricane deck, sipping tea from a samovar, taking in the scenery as the steamer swerved from one side of the river to another to avoid sandbars, listening to the chimes of church bells from the villages, and making notes and sketches. The left bank of the Volga was low and monotonous, but along the high, grassy banks of the opposite shore village girls ran down to the river to wave at the steamer. Kennan and Frost even talked briefly with peasants in red shirts and black velvet trousers lazily reclining on a bluff. At night they spread out blankets and pillows on the leather couches in the steamer's main cabin.

The commercial activity on the river astonished Kennan. He watched a tugboat towing a caravan of ten giant black barges and a solo barge slowly winching itself upriver along a cable that the crew carried ahead and anchored on the shore. A Russian hamlet of fully built houses with ornately carved gables floated by on a huge, towed timber raft. The crew sat around a campfire at one end of the raft, drinking tea. "I could not help fancying that I was looking at a fragment of a peasant village which had in some way gotten adrift." One night, Kennan heard in the distance a boatman on the river singing.

Their steamer stopped at Kazan, an ancient Tatar city of colorful houses. One house was painted entirely metallic green. A brown house had yellow window shutters and a bright green roof. A blue house had a red roof and one dwelling "displayed the whole chromatic scale." The steamer turned onto the Kama River where "everything seemed stranger, more primitive, and in a certain sense, wilder." On a riverbank, six women wearing bright red, blue, and pink dresses, and one man, hauled a large wooden barge with a rope that ran from their harnesses to the barge's mast. Peasant children swarmed the steamer at landing places, offering to sell bunches of lilies of the valley to the passengers. Kennan and Frost left the steamer at Perm, a city of about thirty thousand.[100]

On the afternoon of their arrival, they set out for a hilltop east of the city to give Frost a commanding view for a sketch of Perm. On the way, they passed the city prison, but the hilltop proved farther than they had expected, and it was already late in the afternoon. Kennan and Frost turned around and went to their hotel, passing the prison again. The next morning, they took the same route to the hilltop, where Frost made a sketch, and then returned to the city. On their fourth stroll past the prison, they were stopped by two carriages of gendarmes wearing full-dress uniforms and armed with revolvers and swords. In Russia gendarmes were independent of the regular police and concerned themselves only with state security, which included surveillance of foreigners. As historian Richard Pipes observed, "Before the First World War no other country in the world had two kinds of police, one to protect the state, and another to protect its citizens."

The senior gendarme, a man of about thirty, got out of his carriage and bowed to Kennan and Frost. "Will you permit me to inquire who you are?"

Kennan explained that they were American travelers on their way to Siberia.

"But tourists," said the gendarme, "are not in the habit of going to Siberia. You must have some particular object in view. Tell me, if you please, exactly what that object is."

Kennan replied that Americans are always interested in learning about the people and their locales in the countries they happen to travel in.

"You devoted all your attention to the prison. Now, what were you looking at the prison in that way for?"

Kennan's insistence that they had only innocently glanced at the prison on their way to obtain a view of Perm did not allay the suspicions of the gendarmes, who asked to see their passports. Kennan and Frost could not produce them, having left their passports in their hotel room. The gendarmes placed them under arrest, put each in a separate carriage, and took them to their hotel. A large crowd gathered outside the hotel to watch "what they thought must be the arrest of two important political criminals." In their hotel room the senior gendarme examined Kennan's and Frost's passports and then looked at Kennan "as if I were some new species of dangerous wild animal not classified in the books, and consequently of unknown power for evil."

Kennan brought the "comedy of errors" to an end by producing a letter of introduction signed by the Minister of Foreign Affairs, which caused the senior gendarme's face to redden. He held a whispered consultation with his colleagues and then apologized profusely for having mistaken Kennan and Frost for wanted German criminals. Would the two shake their hands to show that they had not taken any offense? The Russians and the Americans stiffly shook hands and the Russians left, bowing as they went. Kennan felt some anxiety because "if we were arrested in this way before we even reached the Siberian frontier, and for merely looking at the outside of a prison, what probably would happen to us when we should seriously begin the work of our investigation?"

From Perm they went by train across the Ural Mountains, which are comparable in size to the Appalachian Mountains, to the city of Ekaterinburg, a prosperous mining center just outside the Siberian frontier (even today, the residents vehemently explain to visitors that the city is *not* actually *in* Siberia). Kennan and Frost hired a *tarantas,* a four-wheeled carriage, and a driver and horses to take them down the Great Siberian Post Road, which was a seventy-foot-wide dirt way with wheel tracks in the middle, to Tiumen and its forwarding prison. The passenger compartment of their carriage resembled a truncated boat partly covered by a leather hood. The compartment sat on long wooden poles suspended between the axle frames because metal springs would have shattered on the Post Road. Three or four horses typically pulled a carriage, whose driver sat on a coach-box in the front, but the passengers had no seats. Experienced Russian travelers brought thick pillows or mattresses for any lengthy carriage journey, but unprepared passengers had to sit on their luggage.[101]

Kennan had traveled west on the Post Road on horse-drawn, partly covered sleighs during his return trip from northeastern Siberia in

1867 after the abandonment of the telegraph expedition. The carriage
system operated in the same manner in warm weather with thousands of horses, drivers, and carriages available for a modest rate at
hundreds of post stations. The destination-obsessed drivers maintained
speeds of around five to ten miles per hour, depending on road conditions, by constantly exchanging tired horses for fresh ones. Passengers
often tried to sleep at night in their moving carriages, usually without
success, rather than stop and sleep on the benches or floors of the overcrowded, noisy, vermin-infested, foul-smelling traveler rooms at the
post stations. After a few days on the road, Kennan and Frost decided
to purchase their own carriage rather than carry their luggage from one
rented carriage to another at the post stations.

Traveling in a horse-drawn carriage on a rutted, rock-strewn, mud-
ridden, "foul smallpox of a road," as Anton Chekhov called it after his
own ordeal on the Post Road, proved to be a different experience for
Kennan than gliding along on a sleigh on a carpet of snow. The drivers,
recalled one traveler who had also purchased his carriage, "care nothing
about your bones, and what is worse, nothing about the carriage."
The head-snapping, body-slamming, spine-crunching, bone-shaking,
sleep-depriving jolts during thousands of miles of carriage travel would
debilitate Kennan and Frost.

On the road to Tiumen, their first destination, Kennan and Frost
passed by west-bound caravans of small, single-horse-drawn transport
wagons called *obozes*. Each horse was tied by a rope on its collar to the
wagon ahead. Drivers wearing long kaftans and scarlet or blue shirts,
and carrying whips, walked alongside the wagons, which were laden
with produce and goods from Siberia and tea from China. Some of the
caravans were so long and the road so curved that for days the wagons
in the rear never caught sight of the ones in the front. On his first day
after leaving Ekaterinburg, Kennan counted more than fourteen hundred *obozes* traveling to European Russia. But the *obozes* going east into
Siberia seemed to carry just one commodity. As one Siberian traveler

Bivouac of freight wagon drivers, 1885 (from *Siberia and the Exile System* 1:51)

noticed, "almost every caravan we met going eastward was a caravan of big-wheeled barrels carrying vodka."[102]

At night the drivers, whose families sometimes accompanied them, halted the caravans, set up camp, and built cooking fires. Frost sketched a group of drivers, rough-faced men with thick, uncut hair and beards, around a blazing fire next to an *oboze*. One eats his dinner, another lies on the ground peacefully gazing at the night sky, and a third fills his cup with tea from a samovar. A woman sits by the fire with a warm smile on her face as her child reaches for the food in her hands. Beyond the campfire, against the backdrop of a dark pine forest, a driver tends to a horse. Kennan called the scene "a strange, striking, and peculiarly Russian picture."

On the second day after leaving Ekaterinburg, Kennan and Frost's driver stopped the carriage in a forest clearing and called out, "Here is the boundary." The two men got out to contemplate the grieving convicts in chains who had once paused there. "After picking a few flowers from the grass at the base of the boundary pillar, we climbed into our carriage, said 'Goodby' to Europe, as hundreds of thousands had said good-by before us, and rode away into Siberia."[103]

7

Every Respiration Seemed to Pollute Me to the Very Soul

For a time Kennan had the impression that he was traveling through an elegant park. Double and even triple rows of tall silver birch trees lined this stretch of the Great Siberian Post Road. Bright sunshine warmed the air and forget-me-nots grew in such density that in places they resembled a deep blue lake. Then Kennan and Frost rode through fields where peasants toiled on land that belonged to the throne and passed villages of shabby, weather-worn log houses where bristly, razor-backed pigs roamed or lay on muddy streets. The villages reflected a lack of pride and initiative that Kennan attributed to the "paralyzing influence of a paternal and all-regulating government." The inhabitants of these impoverished villages, he decided, could only "obey orders, await the pleasure of the higher authorities and thank God that things are no worse."[104]

They left behind the open farm country and entered a marshy forest. It took four hours to travel eighteen miles because the wheels of their carriage kept sinking into black mud, sometimes up to the hubs.

At the last village before Tiumen, the gatekeeper came out of his house in a long black gown and hailed the carriage to a stop by ringing a hand bell. He bowed, crossed himself, and blessed the travelers. Kennan and Frost handed him a few coins and continued their journey. They crossed a marshy plain and, late in the afternoon of June 18, 1885, the driver gestured with his whip. "There is Tiumen." The two Americans, their faces covered with mosquito bites and their clothes splattered with mud, saw green-domed belfries in the distance. They passed a group of soldiers at target practice to the accompaniment of bugles, glimpsed the forwarding prison, and entered Tiumen, which had a population of nineteen thousand. Since leaving the boundary pillar two days and nights earlier, Kennan and Frost had traveled more than two hundred miles while sitting in painfully awkward positions on their luggage. They found lodging in a furnished apartment, but Kennan was so stiff that he could barely climb the flight of stairs to their room. "I could not have made a bow to the Tsar of all the Russias."[105]

Wearing their formal attire—waistcoat, trousers, and morning coat—as a sign of respect, the next day Kennan and Frost presented themselves and their letters of introduction to Boris Krasin, Tiumen's chief police officer. They asked Krasin for permission to inspect the forwarding prison, where exiles stayed for an average of two weeks before leaving for Siberian prisons, farms, factories, and mines. Somewhat to their surprise, especially after their encounter with the gendarmes in Perm, Krasin readily granted their request. He warned Kennan and Frost that the prison was overcrowded and unsanitary but with the guidance of the *smatritel,* the prison warden, they were welcome to see it for themselves. Krasin, mentioning that he already knew about their Siberian investigation, invited his visitors to lunch, and later wrote out a note for Kennan and Frost to show the prison warden.

The Tiumen prison began as a single, three-story, tin-roofed brick building but it soon overflowed with exiles. The prison authorities ordered the construction of adjacent log-walled *kameras,* barracks-like cells, but they too overflowed. By the time of Kennan's inspection, the prison had become a compound of penal and administrative buildings surrounded by a fifteen-foot-high, whitewashed brick wall topped by sentry posts, which were manned by soldiers with Berdan rifles and fixed bayonets. Seventeen hundred exiles, including women and children accompanying their husbands and fathers, now occupied a prison with space only for a third that number.

Kennan showed Krasin's note to the guards at the gate, and after a few minutes, he and Frost were admitted to a large courtyard where dozens of prisoners wearing gray shirts, gray trousers, and gray overcoats with diamond patches of black or yellow cloth sewn on the backs wandered aimlessly about or lay sprawled on the ground. Most were in chains, which filled the courtyard with what sounded like "the continuous jingling of innumerable bunches of keys." The warden met them and escorted Kennan around the prison, while Frost stayed behind to sketch the scene in the courtyard.

The warden first led Kennan to one of the log-walled overflow cells where one hundred and sixty prisoners inhabited a space built for forty. A sleeping platform, built like a low-slope roof, stretched nearly the length of the cell. Its peak, which rested on wooden supports, was two feet above the floor. With their heads nearly touching at the peak, prisoners slept in tightly packed rows on the opposite, inclined sides of the platform. Since the platform was too small to accommodate one hundred and sixty men, scores had to sleep on the filthy floor. All prisoners slept in their chains and used their overcoats for bedding. The cell's only other furniture was a large open *parasha,* or excrement tub. "How do you do, boys?" asked the warden as he entered. Their chains clinking, the prisoners who had been lying down got to their feet and all prisoners removed their caps.

"We wish you health, your high nobility," answered a hoarse chorus.

"You see how it is," said the warden to Kennan. He spoke as though the overcrowded conditions were so obviously bad that there was no point in pretending otherwise. He took Kennan, now joined by Frost, to more similarly crammed cells. As Kennan and the warden entered one cell, several sick-looking prisoners, wriggling like worms, emerged from the cramped space under the sleeping platform. In each cell, where there were only a few small, grated windows for air, the smell of its excrement tub merged with the odors of unwashed and mostly unhealthy men. A former inmate of Siberian exile prisons described the air in the cells as "saturated with a stench as if from a disinterred grave." Another recalled that on hot summer days the foul air "reduced the occupants to a condition of semiconscious madness."

The warden led Kennan and Frost into the main prison building. As they passed a ground-floor cell whose inmates appeared to be so-phisticated men, the warden removed his hat. Kennan guessed that these were nobles who had been convicted of political offenses. The three men climbed a stairway to the second floor where the air, this close to the hospital wards on the floor above, was even more foul-smelling than in the cells. Kennan felt as though he was trapped in a hospital sewage pipe. Nauseous and close to fainting, he tried to breathe as little as possible, but "every respiration seemed to pollute me to the very soul."

The warden, noticing Kennan's pale face, held out a cigarette case. "You are not accustomed to prison air. Light a cigarette: it will afford some relief, and we will get some wine or vodka presently in the dispen-sary." Smoking a cigarette somewhat helped Kennan. The warden led Kennan and Frost through the prison workshops on the second floor and took them to the basement, where Kennan inspected the kitchens. Half-naked prisoners were baking bread and boiling soup in large iron kettles. Kennan tasted the soup and found it surprisingly good. "Do you wish to go through the hospital wards?" the warden asked him. "Certainly, we wish to see everything that there is to be seen in the prison."

With a shrug the warden led them back up the stone stairs to the third floor. Kennan had never smelled anything like the hospital wards, where prisoners lay on beds with thin mattresses and the air was "poi-soned with the breaths of syphilitic and fever-stricken patients, loaded and saturated with the odor of excrement, disease germs, exhalations from unclean human bodies, and foulness inconceivable." Each year several hundred prisoners died in the hospital wards. "Never before in my life had I seen faces so white, haggard, and ghastly." The warden mentioned to Kennan and Frost that the prison was plagued by typhus and that even his own assistant had contracted the disease. He hastily reassured them that they would not be in the prison long enough to be infected.

Kennan visited the lying-in ward for the pregnant women, but he could take no more and told the warden that he had to go outside. The warden took the Americans to the dispensary, where they drank vodka. At his suggestion, they were sprayed from head to foot with diluted carbolic acid, a disinfectant that, "after the foulness of the prison atmosphere, seemed to us almost as refreshing as spirits of cologne." In the prison courtyard Kennan and Frost gulped the fresh air like men who had come close to asphyxiating. Before finishing the inspection, Kennan tried on the heavy chains worn by convicts and observed the arrangements for disposal of the contents of the excrement tubs. The prison odors lingered in their clothing for hours after their inspection.[106]

The next morning Kennan and Frost returned to the prison so that Frost could make more sketches and take pictures with their photographic equipment. As they neared the gate Kennan heard chains clinking, crying children, and low, indistinct murmuring, and came upon hundreds of prisoners outside the main prison wall. A third were women and children voluntarily going into exile with their husbands and fathers. The men wore gray convict clothing and chains, but the women, who were allowed to wear their own clothing, were dressed gaily in colorful calico gowns with bright scarves around their heads. The exile convoy would first march fifty miles to the town of Yalutorfsk, where some of the men would stay to work as forced colonists. The rest would continue to other towns and villages in southern Tobolsk Province where they would be put to work. Kennan could not understand how anyone, after confinement in the forwarding prison, could walk at all, but compared with the exile parties he later encountered in Eastern Siberia suffering in far worse conditions, this party had an easy march. The convoy did not carry food for the exiles, who instead received a few coins each day to buy food from roadside vendors.

Lined up across the street from the prison were some twenty crude horse-drawn carts filled with the aged, the sick, and children under twelve. "Please put my little girl in a wagon," a woman pleaded with the commanding officer of the exile convoy. "She isn't ten years old, and she has a lame ankle." The officer, a heavyset man with blond whiskers and an expression devoid of pity, briefly glanced at the child's bony legs. "She can't ride, I tell you—there's no room. I don't believe there's anything the matter with her ankle, and anybody can see that she's more than twelve years old. Move on!" He coldly told the child, "You can pick flowers better if you walk." The mother and child faded into the crowd. The commanding officer shouted, "Form ranks!" Cossacks, in dark green uniforms, mounted their horses and soldiers shouldered their rifles. The exiles made the sign of the cross and bowed in the direction of the prison chapel. "March!"

The column set out on a muddy road, Cossacks in the lead, followed by the main body of men, women, and children over the age of twelve, the carts with small children and the infirm, a rear guard of soldiers and Cossacks, and finally more carts piled with small sacks containing the prisoners' belongings. As the column disappeared out of sight, Kennan heard the Cossacks shouting at the youngsters in the marching party to stay in the procession. One of Frost's sketches shows a cart carrying worn-out women in coats and headscarves, feeble-looking men in loose-fitting overcoats, and a soldier cradling his rifle. The driver's whip is poised to strike a horse, a woman leans against the side of the cart with her eyes closed, and a man with long, disheveled hair is half-turned in his seat, staring in the direction he had come from, like a sailor hoping for a last glimpse of land. Ahead, more carts carrying the weak travel in single file on a dirt road under dark clouds pierced in spots by an occasional shaft of sunlight.[107]

Before leaving Tiumen, Kennan and Frost watched the loading of a convict barge. It was one of three black-hulled, two-hundred-foot-long convict barges that in warm weather made the seven-to-ten-day voyage between Tiumen and Tomsk, seven hundred miles to the east. The barges could each accommodate hundreds of convicts and their wives and families, in seventy-five-foot-long cages bolted to their decks between two yellow-painted deck houses, and in below deck cells. They would disembark in Tomsk, where many, including women and children, would begin marches of thousands of miles to Eastern Siberia.

The convicts and their wives and families waited on the riverbank while the barge was cleaned and disinfected. An officer shouted, "Let them go on board." For an hour, carrying gray sacks with their belongings, men in clinking chains and women, some holding the hands of small children, made their way down a zigzag wooden bridge from the landing onto the barge. Kennan recognized mountaineers from Dagestan, Tatars from the lower Volga, Turks from Crimea, Jews from Podolia, and peasants from all over European Russia. Some of the men had good-natured expressions, others appeared intelligent, many looked loutish and dull, but Kennan thought that most did not have the cruel features of American criminals. The women and children filed into a separate cage from the men.

Fresh-faced Russian soldiers closed the cage doors. Dozens of peddlers came to the landing to sell hard-boiled eggs, black rye bread, pretzels, and salted cucumbers to the men and women in the cages, who had also been given coins. Food and coins were passed back and forth through the openings in the latticed cage wire; the soldiers sometimes opened the cage doors to allow larger items, such as the loaves of bread, to be given to the convicts. The peddlers frequently handed over food without first demanding payment. A Russian priest in a black gown, carrying a smoking incense burner by its chains in one hand and an open prayer book in the other, walked onto the barge. He first held services for the women, who kneeled in their cage and pressed their heads to the floor, and then moved on to the men's cage. A peasant woman came on board, went to the women's cage, and pushed small, sweet cakes through the cage wire for the children.

Frost began sketching the male convicts in their cage, which attracted their attention. The prisoners combed each other's hair, affected dramatic attitudes, and tried on a borrowed red fez or an embroidered Tatar cap for effect, all the while shouting instructions to Frost of

Inside the women's cage on a convict barge, moored at Tiumen, 1885 (from *Siberia and the Exile System* 1:118)

whom to sketch. "This arranging of figures in groups for Mr. Frost to draw, seemed to afford them great amusement, and was accompanied with as much joking and laughter as if they were schoolboys off for a picnic, instead of criminals bound for the mines." A steamer pulled up, its crew tied a line to the barge, both men and women tried to get a final glimpse of Tiumen from their cages, and "the great black-and-yellow floating prison slowly moved out into the stream." Two months later Kennan and Frost arrived in Tomsk and inspected what they believed was the same barge that they had observed in Tiumen. Its most recent cargo had just disembarked. "Then [in Tiumen] it was scrupulously clean . . . but now it suggested a recently vacated wild-beast cage in a menagerie."[108]

The Siberian postal system was well organized. Carriages plied the Siberian roads between cities, villages, and towns carrying leather pouches filled with mail. Each day Irkutsk, the largest city in Siberia, received mail from Moscow, which was twenty-six hundred miles away, and delivered it back three times a week. The system allowed Kennan's and Frost's wives and friends to send them letters care of the post offices in larger Siberian cities, based on their expected itinerary, and for them to send letters back to the United States. Kennan mailed a letter to *Century* publisher Roswell Smith reporting that their success in gaining access to the Tiumen prison was "beyond my expectations" and that Frost had made numerous sketches and taken many photographs despite the balky equipment. Kennan had seen the prison in its "every-day aspect" and was confident that "nothing was fixed for my inspection" because "such a prison as that cannot be temporarily fixed."

Overall, it was a positive report but for a note of self-doubt. Kennan described the forwarding prison as "the worst" he had ever encountered and, if it turned out to be representative, "I shall have to take back some things that I have said and written about the exile system."[109]

The Siberian exile system was not planned to be loathsome and vile. For much of its existence, little planning went into it. The system was the product of imperial ambitions, bureaucratic incompetence, corruption, and inadequate funding; Siberia's vast size and harsh terrain and climate; and the extraordinary Russian capacity to inflict and endure suffering. Centuries of grotesque penal evolution had spawned disease-ridden prisons, exile parties driven like cattle, virtual enslavement, and lunacies like the punishment of the Bell of Uglich. Other countries have exiled their criminals, but none on the scale of the Russian exile system. Between the 1780s and 1860s, the British transported about one hundred and sixty thousand convicts to Australia. In the last half of the nineteenth century, the French overseas penal population was between five and six thousand. Russia stands out because between 1801 and the Russian Revolution of 1917, the tsarist regime exiled more than a million of its subjects to far-flung destinations within its own vast borders, creating what has been called "an enormous prison without a roof."

As Siberia's vast natural resources became apparent, the regime began employing the penal code as a tool for supplying Siberia with a labor force because too few Russians would go voluntarily. The offenses punishable by Siberian exile grew to include not just common-law crimes but political offenses, religious dissent, army desertion, and vagrancy. In 1753, the death penalty was formally abolished, and instead of being hanged, capital offenders underwent a public mutilation followed by "eternal penal labour" in Siberia. The death penalty would reclaim a place in the Russian judicial system in the nineteenth century, most notably in cases involving assassination plots against tsars.

Abolition of the death penalty did more than free up laborers for Siberia. As historian Andrew A. Gentes points out, abolition emphasized the divine-like power of the ruling Romanovs to either execute their subjects or show them mercy:

I could kill you, but I choose instead to spare you out of Christian mercy (*milost*). Therefore, although you have been flogged nearly to death and have had your face branded and your nose cut off, you should be grateful that you have been allowed to commence a two-year, three thousand mile journey in chains for the purpose of sowing grain in His Majesty's fields near the Arctic Circle.[110]

For centuries convicts began marching to Siberia from Moscow, St. Petersburg, and other cities in European Russia, often starting their march on the Vladimirka road. At the first post station, which was called *Gorenki*, from the word *gore*, meaning grief, family members who were not accompanying a convict to Siberia could get a last glimpse of their loved one. In his iconic *Vladimirka*, the Russian artist Isaac Levitan painted the view ahead of a marching exile: a dirt road stretching to the horizon under a vast sky. By the time of Kennan's investigation, trains and then barges transported convicts into Siberia but many of them still had to march more than halfway across a continent to their final destinations in parties of three hundred or more guarded by Russian soldiers on foot and by mounted Cossacks.

The sight of an exile party stunned travelers in Siberia. In January 1828, a young woman making her way through Siberia in subzero temperatures to join her exiled fiancé heard a strange noise from her carriage. "It was the noise of the fetters . . . an entire party of people was in chains—some were even chained to a metal pole. These unfortunates were a terrible sight. To protect their faces from the cold they had covered them with some dirty rags into which they had cut holes for their eyes." On an overcast morning in 1856, an English traveler observed, beneath a double row of birch trees on the Great Siberian Post Road, "a long line of drab-clad figures marching in the same direction as ourselves. We instinctively know what it is but can still hardly believe that a story so sad, so strange, so distant, is being realised before our eyes." Kennan never carried out his plan to march with an exile party, possibly because he was denied permission but equally likely because he had observed the experience of the exile parties to be so dreadful.

No one seemed to question or care whether, after a forced march of thousands of miles, cold-blooded killers and an assortment of thieves, incorrigibles, misfits, malcontents, and regime enemies could become productive workers in the Siberian mines and factories. In fact many of the convicts who reached Eastern Siberia, according to one report from local authorities, "arrived exhausted, prematurely enfeebled, having contracted incurable diseases, having forgotten their trades, and having grown quite unaccustomed to labour." Local Siberian officials regularly commandeered the healthiest convicts from the marching parties to meet their own needs, which further aggravated the shortage of able workers.[111]

So many exiled convicts died on Siberian roads that the peasants, who had to dispose of the bodies, protested to the government in St. Petersburg, which only sent back orders to the local authorities to pay for the burials. Some convicts took years to reach their destinations but their time on the journey did not count as part of their sentence. One convict was on the road for eight years, but his eight-year sentence did not start until he finally entered a prison factory in Irkutsk. The authorities did not want the convicts to run out their sentences by feigning illness or otherwise finding ways to delay their arrivals at the prisons, factories, and mines.

Notwithstanding the human wastage, enough productive convicts reached their destinations to justify the exile system to the St. Petersburg and Siberian bureaucracies. As Kennan wrote, "One is surprised not that so many die but that so many get through alive." Factories, salt works, distilleries, farms, and mines in Siberia continued to demand more workers and the regime continued to send them by, for example, allowing landowners and monasteries to turn over their troublesome serfs to the state for exile. Siberia became the jewel in the Romanov crown and played a role in the rise of the Russian Empire comparable to that of India in the ascension of the British Empire.

The regime, never a model of efficiency to begin with, could not control a penal system the size of a continent that even the most modern and efficient state would have struggled to administer. Finding ways to free themselves of chains, or evidently even while wearing them, prisoners dug tunnels and cut holes in the prison roofs. Prison guards often looked the other way so that they could keep the subsistence allowance of the escaped prisoners. Tens of thousands of desperate fugitives moved west through Siberia, sleeping in the forests, begging for food in the villages, and hoping to cross the Ural Mountains to their homes. On their way east in Siberia, Kennan and Frost passed a solitary "hard looking" man walking in the opposite direction. He wore a weathered cap and dirty tunic, a gray bag was strapped to his back, and a small kettle hung from his belt. Traveling at night they sometimes glimpsed the glow of a campfire in the forest.

Some escaped convicts formed marauding bands who murdered entire families and raped Siberian women. They were hunted down and killed by local farmers, who took their clothes to sell or wear, like animal pelts. In the spring the melting snow in the forests exposed the corpses of escapees who had died in the winter. As one Siberian exile official said to a convict who had been caught trying to escape, "The tsar's cow-pasture is large, but you can't get out of it; we will find you at last if you are not dead." If they managed to cross Siberia and get over the Ural Mountains, the escaped convicts, as well as the relative few who were able to return after finishing their sentences, found that their villages or towns in European Russia would not readmit them.

Captured escapees typically were punished with the lash, a length of rawhide ending in two long, braided tails, or a rod made of slender birch switches. With these tools, an experienced torturer could render a man unconscious with just a few blows or slowly shred his flesh. Some convicts were so frequently lashed that the skin never fully regenerated over their shoulder blades, whose pinkish-white bones were left permanently visible. Kennan did not witness a lashing but a few years after his investigation of the exile system, Anton Chekhov watched a captured escapee named Prokhorov receive ninety lashes in the prison colony on Sakhalin Island off Siberia's Pacific coast. As crimson welts formed on his back, which was already covered with scars from previous lashings,

Prokhorov pleaded for mercy, squealed, bellowed, wheezed, and vomited. "Ninety at last . . . His teeth are chattering, his face is yellow and wet, his eyes are wandering. When he is given medicinal drops, he bites the glass convulsively." Since the exile system ran on the fuel of inflicted pain and fear, those convicts who kept escaping only to be recaptured and stoically tolerate repeated lashings were lionized by their fellow convicts.[112]

Exiled convicts formed brutal, Mafia-like organizations called *artels*. Kennan noted that if a convict "disobeys [the *artel*] or betrays its secrets to the prison authorities, even under the compulsion of the lash—he may count himself dead already." In the exile convoys, the *artels* tracked down, punished, and returned convicts who escaped in defiance of the *artel's* orders. In return, the convoy commanders permitted convicts to beg for food in Siberian villages and sometimes even to remove leg fetters. As an exile party passed through a town or village, once the *artel* had secured permission, the exiles sang the *miloserdnaya,* or the "Begging Song," which brought Siberian women and children out of their homes carrying food.[113]

Lack of recordkeeping and administrative controls produced chaos. A peasant in European Russia innocently bought a stolen horse and found himself transported as a murderer to the Siberian mines, where he worked underground for decades. A Siberian governor banished a local official from the province of Irkutsk with the stipulation that the official could not live in any one location in Siberia for more than ten days. The official spent the rest of his life wandering from place to place. The Siberian authorities did not even know how many exiles were in their midst. In 1822, the Russian reformer Mikhail Speransky was tasked with bringing a semblance of organization to the exile system. It was an ironic choice because Speransky had previously spent time in exile within European Russia for advocating reforms that evidently offended too many nobles.

One Speransky reform was to establish a centralized exile administrative agency, the Bureau of Exile Administration, whose records Kennan used to compile statistics for his later articles and book. Another was the creation of subordinate bureaus throughout Siberia to better manage the exile system. Speransky accelerated the construction of yellow-painted *etapes* and *poluetaps,* which were way stations along the routes of the exile parties, who marched about fifteen to twenty miles a day. The *etapes,* which could house exile parties for two nights and a rest day, were two days' march apart. The *poluetaps* were positioned halfway between the *etapes,* or about a day's march from or to an *etape,* and could accommodate an exile party for a single night.

Speransky mistakenly assumed, however, that no more than two thousand exiles would enter Siberia each year. It proved to be many times that number because the tsarist regime, which was reluctant to tax nobles to pay for growing military expenditures, instead "squeeze[d] as much as it could out of the rest of society," including through greater exploitation of Siberian resources. By the time of Kennan's visit, eighteen thousand exiles a year, including women and children who went voluntarily, entered Siberia. The surge of exiles overwhelmed the prisons and the way stations, which deteriorated into crumbling, vermin-infested, overcrowded buildings that more resembled animal barns than overnight jails. Even after the Speransky reforms, according to Andrew A. Gentes in *Exile, Murder and Madness,* which was published in 2010, "the death rate among Siberia's exiles was considerably higher than even the worst adult death rates found in the world today."[114]

Exiles to Siberia fell into two broad categories: those who were given at least some semblance of a judicial process and those who got none. In the first category were the *katorzhniki,* the convicts sentenced to *katorga,* or hard labor, in the Siberian prisons, mines, and factories, and the *poselentsi,* the convicts forced to work in existing Siberian settlements. The word *katorga* was derived from the Greek word for a galley. Both the *katorzhniki* and the *poselentsi* went to their Siberian destinations in chains; their heads had been half-shaved to the scalp to mark their status as convicted criminals (in an earlier era, they were identified by slit noses or brand marks made by hot irons); they could not return to European Russia after their terms of exile ended; and they lost all civil rights, including the right to marry or remain married (unless their wives accompanied them). The judicial system that sent them to Siberia was corrupt and dysfunctional. One appellate court's backlog was cleared up by a gendarme who stood behind a judge until he had decided the court's pending appeals by alternately stamping "upheld," "reversed," "upheld," "reversed" on the case files until the mountain of legal papers was gone.

In the second category were those exiles sent to Siberia without any judicial process at all. From the 1830s on, according to Daniel Beer in *The House of the Dead*, "more than half the exiles who set off for Siberia had never seen the inside of a courtroom or heard the rulings of a judge." They had been subject to "administrative exile," which sometimes meant exile on someone's whim. To keep up with the demand from Siberia for more laborers, the regime empowered local authorities in European Russia to use administrative exile to permanently banish villagers to Siberia on almost any pretext, such as being "obnoxious to fellow citizens" or for "immoral behavior." These exiles were called *silni*, or the banished ones. Many of the exiles in the party that Kennan and Frost observed outside the Tiumen forwarding prison had been sent to Siberia by their village communes.[115]

The wives of exiles, especially those with children, had an impossible choice in deciding whether to accompany their husbands. If they remained behind, they faced social isolation and an impoverished life in communities that had no desire to support fatherless families. If they went with their husbands, they faced a grueling march in an exile convoy whose guards considered them a perquisite of their jobs and where convicts were known to sell their wives to other convicts for money, vodka, or protection. One exile recalled that, for their own protection, every woman in his convoy had to take a lover who was chosen for her in an auction run by the convicts. The authorities tried to separate single males from women and children in exile parties, but as Kennan wrote, "even 'family parties' contain large numbers of depraved men and boys." Nonetheless, many wives, taking their children, went with their husbands. Some set out in the mistaken belief, often because their husbands had lied to them, that the Siberian authorities would support them at their destinations and that they were free to return to European Russia. But once in Siberia, the wives had to fend for themselves, which for many meant begging, prostitution, or starvation. Examples of husbands accompanying into exile the relatively few wives convicted of crimes are few, possibly because men had more economic options than women if they declined to follow a spouse to Siberia.

Some women were already pregnant at the start of the march while others became pregnant on the road after being raped. Pregnant women, who rode in the wooden carts that also carried the aged, the sick, and small children, often died on the road, sometimes during childbirth. By one estimate half of the children who accompanied their mothers perished on their Siberian journeys. In February 1858, an exile wrote in his diary that "two of our party died today, an old man and a little baby. Both froze to death on the carts." By 1885, when Kennan began his investigation, nearly one third of the exiles in Siberia were the *dobrovolni*, innocent women and children who had gone with their husbands and fathers into exile.[116]

One of the most famous examples of a wife following her husband into Siberian exile was Princess Maria Volkonsky, the beautiful twenty-year-old daughter of a military hero of the Napoleonic Wars. She was married to Prince Sergei Volkonsky, a serving Russian army officer whose mother jealously guarded her friendship with the empress. In March 1826, Maria learned that Sergei had been arrested for plotting with other young, reform-minded army officers, many from noble families, to depose Tsar Nicholas I and end autocratic rule in Russia. Maria, who was unaware of her husband's activities, was stunned by Sergei's arrest but also relieved because she had thought that his moodiness and frequent absences meant that he was having an affair.

The coup had spectacularly failed in a bloody battle in December 1825 on Senate Square in St. Petersburg. Russian soldiers loyal to the throne defeated rebellious army units led by the plotters, who became known as "the Decembrists." On the frozen Neva River, which runs next to Senate Square, blood splashes around holes in the ice marked where men had been shot and fallen through. Five ringleaders were sentenced to die by hanging but the night before the execution a downpour swelled the ropes, which weakened them. In the morning, three of the ropes snapped and three condemned men went sprawling into a ditch, still alive. The priest, who had just heard the men's confessions, fainted. The half-strangled men were assisted back onto the scaffold and successfully hung on the second try, but not before one expressed his satisfaction that he could die for his country, not just once, but twice. A similar scene took place more than half a century later at the hanging of the assassins of Alexander II.

Sergei Volkonsky was sentenced to fifteen years hard labor in Siberia, followed by exile for life. He and seven of the other exiled Decembrists left St. Petersburg at night in a procession of troikas escorted by Cossack guards on horses. The troikas passed by the home of the minister of the interior where three thousand candles illuminated a fashionable ball on the second floor, which was attended by St. Petersburg society, including Sergei's mother. Some revelers, hearing the jingle of the horses' bells, looked down and saw the troikas. Sergei's mother apparently did not notice her son, bound in chains, on his way to Siberia because she was just then dancing with Tsar Nicholas I, who had assured her that Sergei's treason had not damaged her standing at court.

Maria begged Nicholas to be allowed to follow her husband into Siberian exile. The tsar gave her permission but warned Maria of the "danger" that awaited her if she traveled beyond Irkutsk. She left her infant son Nikolenka in the care of her family and set out in winter in a horse-drawn sleigh with a passenger compartment. She wrapped herself against the cold in a bearskin given to her by a friend and, to occupy her mind during the journey, recited poetry and dreamed of seeing Sergei. Sixty years later, Kennan and Frost would visit several of the Siberian towns and cities where the exiled Sergei and the self-exiled Maria had once been.[117]

The exiled political opponents of the regime, many from the aristocracy and intelligentsia, included both those convicted of criminal offenses that were political in nature and those administratively exiled without judicial process. The latter's ranks were enlarged by the emergency decree, previously mentioned, that had been enacted in the aftermath of the assassination of Alexander II in 1881 and gave the regime the power to administratively exile to Siberia anyone whose presence was "incompatible with public tranquility" for three to five years (later extended to eight years). All over Russia men and women disappeared, often without their families finding out what had happened to them. The absence of procedural safeguards turned some regime opponents into the central figures in their own surreal tragedies. A well-known journalist was administratively exiled to Siberia because he possessed a "dangerous" and "pernicious" manuscript, which was only a copy of an article on a mundane economic issue that the journalist had submitted to one of Russia's most widely circulated magazines. After arriving in Siberia, the journalist learned that the magazine had since published his article with the express approval of the censors.[118]

In some respects, the administratively exiled regime opponents were treated leniently compared with the exiled convicts; for example, they were typically allowed to ride in the carts to their Siberian destinations. But these educated men and women underwent a form of torture devised by the exile system. Once in Siberia, unless the local provincial administration took pity on them, among other restrictions, they were forbidden to teach or give public lectures, participate in scientific studies or meetings, take part in theatrical performances, practice law or medicine, or have any involvement in bookstores, libraries, and art or printing establishments. They had to survive on a tiny government payment, which allowed only for the barest necessities, and local authorities kept them under close surveillance, including by opening, or even withholding, their letters and through unannounced searches of their rooms.

In effect they had been sentenced to "compulsory inaction." The governor of the province of Archangel warned the minister of the interior that this policy was producing "ruinous consequences" for intellectually cultivated and gifted men and women exiles, who were "going insane, attempting to commit suicide, and even committing suicide." The governor presciently cautioned that administrative exile for political reasons was turning these mainly nonviolent men and women into "extremely dangerous" revolutionaries.

In the early 1880s in the province of Tobolsk, the mother of a local mayor lay dying from an accidental gunshot wound to her leg. Since the local doctor had no surgical skills, the mayor pleaded with Nifont Dolgopolof, an administratively exiled medical student in the village, to operate on his mother. Dolgopolof first cited regulations forbidding him from practicing medicine but eventually gave in to the mayor's pleas, operated on his mother, and saved her life. The authorities jailed Dolgopolof for violating the terms of his exile in a proceeding with a fittingly absurd legal caption, "The Affair of the Unauthorized Extraction of a Bullet, by the Administrative Exile Nifont Dolgopolof." When the angry townspeople protested his arrest and imprisonment, the police transported Dolgopolof, now suffering from typhus contracted in jail, to a prison more than one hundred miles away.

At the time of Kennan's investigation, the overall exile population in Siberia was approximately three hundred thousand, of whom several thousand were political exiles. They were a small percentage of the exile population, but these journalists, writers, students, merchants, state officials, and sons and daughters of the nobility, represented Russia's best and brightest. They were about to have an impact on George Kennan.[119]

The Exile System Is Worse Than
I Believed It to Be

It rained on the third day after Kennan and Frost left Tiumen, but the weather improved overnight and the next morning the sun rose against a sky of nearly unbroken blue. Their carriage traveled on a pot-holed and muddy road that ran through vast, unfenced fields of waving wheat. As Kennan looked around for the village whose inhabitants tilled these fields, the driver suddenly shouted "Heekh-ya-a-a" and furiously lashed the horses, who broke into a frantic gallop. It meant they were approaching a post station because whenever this driver had neared one before, he drove the horses at a lunatic speed as though prize money was at stake.

Kennan knew from painful experience to brace himself, but he still was not prepared for the tremendous jolt when the carriage hit a large hole in the road, briefly became airborne, landed with a crash, and lurched and bumped its way down the road. Both men, clinging to ropes and struts, were slammed about the passenger compartment. Kennan could have leaned out to yell at the driver to slow down, but it would only gain him a face full of the mud flying up from the hoofs of the horses, and the driver would ignore him anyway.

At the gatekeeper's hut, which was a hole in the ground covered by a peaked sod roof, an old man with a white beard climbed out, bowed, and tipped his tattered cap to Kennan and Frost as they flew by. They would have liked to stop to photograph the quaint scene—the gatekeeper reminded Kennan of "Rip Van Winkle after his twenty years' sleep"—but the driver was unstoppable. The carriage raced by a signpost. VILLAGE OF KRUTAYA. HOUSES 42. MALE SOULS 97. With a triumphant cry, the driver pulled the horses to a stop in front of a log house with a corral, which was the post station. "Bring out the horses!" A boy appeared and went to fetch horses.[120]

Time passes slowly in a small village on the southern steppe. Old men with scraggly beards wearing ragged sheepskin coats came walking along the muddy road to see who had arrived and to watch the changing of the horses. "Permit us to ask," one inquired, "where is God taking you to?" Kennan replied that they were going to Omsk and Semipalatinsk, which were their first stops on the way to Tomsk.

"A-ah-ah!" The onlookers reacted as though the strangers had announced that they were going to the end of the earth.

"Where do you condescend to come from?" asked the same old man.

"From America."

"A-ah-ah!"

An argument broke out among the villagers over whether America was a Russian town. The driver cracked his whip over the new team of horses, shouted "Noo-oo!" and they rode off, leaving the arguing men behind. Past Krutaya, orange asters, spotted tiger lilies, white clover, and daisies carpeted the steppe. Kennan asked the driver to stop. He climbed out of the carriage, walked away from the road to the top of a gentle hill, and lay down amidst the flowers. The serenity was broken only by the faint buzzing of bees, the pulsing chirps of katydids, and the hoarse cry of a circling hawk. The warm air and the sweet scent of the flowers made Kennan think of wild honey. On the road again they passed a carriage with a single passenger going in the opposite direction and later they overtook an exile party plodding along under guard. Their driver kept going at night, but the jolts of the carriage prevented Kennan and Frost from getting much sleep.

After traveling more than four hundred and twenty miles in less than ninety hours since leaving Tiumen, they reached Omsk, a city of about thirty thousand. Both men were so exhausted, bruised, and aching that they could barely climb out of the mud-splattered carriage. After checking into a hotel, since it was July 4th in the United States, they sang patriotic songs, such as "Hail Columbia!" and "My Country 'Tis of Thee," with Kennan playing his banjo. Once, in a long stretch without letters from Emiline, he wrote her that "since I stopped getting letters from you the banjo and my luggage seem to be the only connecting links between me and home." While in Omsk, Kennan looked for the *ostrog,* or prison fort, where Fyodor Dostoevsky had served a four-year hard labor sentence in the early 1850s, but he was told that it had been torn down.[121]

Already a well-known author by his late twenties, Dostoevsky had been arrested, convicted, and sentenced to death on several political charges, including the accusation that he had read out loud a letter written by one intellectual to another that the regime regarded as subversive. Tsar Nicholas I, who liked to display an all-powerful but merciful image to his subjects, commuted Dostoevsky's death sentence to hard labor in Siberia. The law required that in such cases of imperial mercy the accused undergo a ritual, mock execution but no one told Dostoyevsky about the commutation until he was terrifying moments away from what he thought was an actual firing squad.

Traveling in the winter in an exile party transported by horse-drawn sleighs, Dostoevsky passed through the town of Tobolsk, where he would have seen the Bell of Uglich, another prominent Siberian exile.

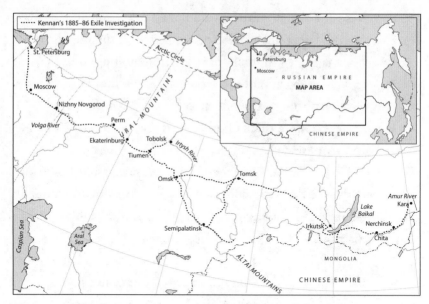

Kennan and Frost's journey during their investigation of the Siberian exile system, 1885–1886 (from *Siberia and the Exile System*)

The wooden floor of his prison in Omsk was covered by a slippery, inch-thick layer of filth. He wore chains day and night and shared an excrement tub with hundreds of convicts, many of whom hated the elite inmates. "They would have eaten us alive, given the chance." Convicts in Siberia had murdered old people and children without the slightest remorse or fear of divine retribution. "In the furthest flung places," a convicted murderer once explained to a prisoner sentenced for political offenses, "where crows don't even carry bones and where animals don't go, we've seen neither God nor the Devil."

But there were worse things in the Siberian prisons than bloodthirsty convicts. After his release, Dostoevsky wrote an account of his time in Omsk in *Notes from the House of the Dead*. To get the book by the censors, he invented a semibiographical central character named Goryanchikov, who describes the torture of never having a single moment to himself. "I could never have conceived how terrible and agonizing it would be not once, not even for one minute of all the . . . years of my imprisonment, to be alone. At work to be constantly under guard, in the barracks to be with two hundred other convicts and not once, never once to be alone!" Dostoevsky's time in the Omsk prison "was crucial for the development of his writing and philosophy," according to historian Daniel Beer. "The men with whom he shared his captivity offered compelling psychological studies for the thieves and murderers who filled the pages of his great post-Siberia novels."

Kennan had insisted to American audiences before his Siberian investigation that the cruelest features of the exile system had been "greatly modified or entirely done away with." He evidently thought that Dostoevsky's experience was the relic of a bygone era in Siberia.[122]

Their carriage was a tiny moving speck on a steppe under an overarching sky. Chekhov wrote of a steppe crossing that "on and on you travel but where it all begins or where it ends you just cannot make out." Kennan had chosen to take the roundabout steppe route to Tomsk as part of a ruse. The ministries in St. Petersburg understood from their meetings with Kennan and Frost that the Americans planned to take the Great Siberian Post Road east to Tomsk. The ministries had almost certainly telegraphed local officials in towns along that route to monitor their activities, especially for any contacts with banished regime opponents. No one in St. Petersburg would have thought to notify officials on the sparsely traveled steppe road, which veered south, away from the Post Road, to the Mongolian border. If the ruse succeeded, Kennan and Frost could visit several political exile colonies on the steppe route without interference; as well, they could also make a side trip to the scenic Altai Mountains before resuming their trip to Tomsk.[123]

The flowers thinned out and vanished, the landscape became sandy with short, withered grass and scraggly bushes, and the temperature rose steadily. The road was dry and smooth, which lessened the jolting, and the two men fell asleep on their luggage. Kennan woke up at two-thirty in the morning to find the carriage softly gliding, like a sleigh on snow, over the sand-covered streets of Semipalatinsk. Their driver brought them to the Hotel Sibir, where they pounded on the front door until it opened. St. Petersburg was now more than twenty-five hundred miles of travel behind them.

Semipalatinsk lay on the Irtysh River, one of the longest rivers in Asia (the town is now within the borders of Kazakhstan and called Semey). It was the governmental seat for the province of Semipalatinsk, with a population of about fifteen thousand Russians, Kirghiz, and Turkic-speaking Tatars. The town, which was nicknamed "the Devil's Sandbox," dashed the popular notion of Siberia as a frigid, snow-covered wilderness. The temperature was nearly ninety degrees Fahrenheit and five-foot sand drifts lay against the houses. Semipalatinsk, with its heat and sand, arriving and departing camel caravans, white turbaned mullahs, and mosques and minarets, most resembled an outpost on a desert trade route somewhere in the Middle East.[124]

The next day Kennan and Frost donned their formal dress and made a courtesy call on the provincial governor. Kennan, explaining that he was an American journalist with an interest in Siberia and its inhabitants, presented their letters of introduction from the Ministries of the Interior and Foreign Affairs in St. Petersburg. The governor, who was quite cordial, gave them permission to go anywhere in the town and suggested that they pay calls on town officials. He did not appear to have been alerted by St. Petersburg to expect their arrival, which Kennan found reassuring. The governor, who may have suspected that his guests were more than travelers, expressed the view that the exile system was an evil even though Kennan had not mentioned his interest in exiles. Kennan did not comment and they left. Frost went to sketch the Tatar end of town, while Kennan began exploring Semipalatinsk and making the rounds of local officials. One, whom Kennan later identified with the fictitious name of Mr. Pavlovsky, asked an unexpected question.

"Mr. Kennan, have you ever paid any attention to the movement of young people into Siberia?"

"I have not," Kennan cautiously replied. "Perhaps I do not fully understand the meaning of your question?"

"I mean that large numbers of educated young men and women are now coming into Siberia from European Russia. I thought perhaps the movement might have attracted your attention."[125]

Kennan wondered whether St. Petersburg had alerted local officials to expect him, after all, and whether Mr. Pavlovsky was setting a trap to obtain an admission that he planned to contact the political exiles in Semipalatinsk, who likely were nihilists of the kind that the St. Petersburg officials had warned him against contacting. If he revealed his interest in such exiles to Mr. Pavlovsky, he might be escorted out of town, or worse. After hesitating he decided to take the risk.

"Mr. Pavlovsky, are you talking about the political exiles? Are they the young people to whom you refer?"

"Yes. I thought you understood."

"Of course I am interested. I don't know where to look for political exiles, nor how to get acquainted with them; and I am told that the government does not regard with favor intercourse between foreign travelers and politicals."

Mr. Pavlovsky assured Kennan that the political exiles were easy to find, in fact, dozens of them lived in Semipalatinsk. "I find them to be quiet, orderly, reasonable human beings. We certainly have no trouble with them here." He suggested that Kennan visit Paul Lobonofsky, a young exile and an artist whose sketches he might find interesting. They climbed into Mr. Pavlovsky's *droshky*, a single-horse-drawn carriage, and rode on sandy streets to the log house that Lobonofsky used as a workshop. Mr. Pavlovsky didn't bother to knock. As they entered, Kennan probably would not have been surprised to find the domineering, scornful Bazarov, the fictional nihilist from Turgenev's *Fathers and Sons*, declaiming "Liberalism, progress, principles! Why have you ever considered the vanity of those terms? The Russian of today does not need them."[126]

Paul Lobonofsky was a blue-eyed, well-built young man with poorly cut blond hair who, like the other exiles in Semipalatinsk, had been exiled to Siberia without a trial. He was fortunate to have ended up in Semipalatinsk, where the provincial governor treated political exiles humanely, even allowing them to engage in forbidden work, and some officials, such as Mr. Pavlovsky, evidently sympathized with them. Lobonofsky wore a brown linen suit and stood in front of a half-painted white sheet that was the local theatre's drop cloth. In one hand he held an artist's brush and in the other a palette with dabs of paint in varied colors. His face was flushed and wet with perspiration. Mr. Pavlovsky introduced Kennan as an American traveler who had heard of Lobonofsky and his sketches. Might he look at some? Lobonofsky brought out some sketches. He apologized for their drawbacks, explaining that he had only crude paper on which to draw. The sketches were limited to portraits of exiles or the stretches of the towns that Lobonofsky had glimpsed from the forwarding prisons and the way stations on his exile party's march.

Kennan devoted less than his full attention to the sketches because he was struggling to reconcile his preconception of political exiles with Lobonofsky, a polite and evidently cultured individual who could easily have been an artist member in good standing at the Lotos Club in Manhattan. Kennan realized that he was staring at Lobonofsky, who was surely aware that the American was more curious about him than his sketches. Lobonofsky invited Kennan to his home that evening. Later that day Kennan met another political exile who from outward appearances could have been a young scientist at the Smithsonian Institution. He returned to his hotel wondering whether he would have to modify his opinion of political exiles. That evening he and Frost arrived at Lobonofsky's tiny apartment. Kennan noticed several books by Herbert Spencer, including *The Principles of Psychology,* lying on a crude handmade table.[127]

Lobonofsky was explaining to his guests that he sought a constitutional form of government for Russia when several exiles, including a woman, entered the apartment. Kennan was especially intrigued with Madame Dicheskula, which is how Lobonofsky introduced her, because she did not have the hard look that he expected to find in women political exiles in Siberia. She was about thirty years old and wore a plaid dress of soft material, with white lace ruffles at neck and wrists, which nicely set off her spare, stately figure. Madame Dicheskula had an intelligent, animated face and thick, brown hair, which, as she explained ruefully, was unwomanly short because her head had been shaved while she was in a Moscow prison.

She did not talk about her political activities or whatever charges had led to her imprisonment, but she did recount, sometimes with amusement, some of her experiences in prison, matter-of-factly mentioning that she had spent a year in solitary confinement. Madame Dicheskula was an attractive woman, but her imprisonment and subsequent march, as a state criminal in an exile convoy, to Semipalatinsk had roughened her complexion and thinned her face. Her composure faltered only when she recalled her exile party's arrival on Trinity Sunday at a way station in Kamishlova during the hard march to Tiumen. Before the arrival of her exile party, the peasants of Kamishlova had cleaned their way station and decorated it with wildflowers. Kennan thought he saw tears in Madame Dicheskula's eyes as she recalled the kindness of the peasants. Lobonofsky brought out a samovar and the Americans and the Russians spent the evening drinking tea around a small pine table. They talked comfortably, as though they had known each other for years.

Kennan and Frost met more political exiles in Semipalatinsk with whom they discussed the Russian government and the exile system. Kennan was introduced to two exiled teenage girls who blushed when he shook their hands. He could not conceive what anyone so young could have done to deserve exile. In his letter to Roswell Smith at the *Century* about the encounter, Kennan asked, "Is it possible that the Russian government cannot protect itself against young girls like these, without banishing them to Siberia? Or on the other hand, is it possible that such young girls have energy, courage, and force of character enough to be really dangerous to a powerful military despotism like Russia? . . . I hope to be able to answer [these questions] before I return to America."

The Tiumen forwarding prison had disturbed Kennan. Semipalatinsk confounded his preconception of the political exiles. But his
investigation was still at an early stage, and he had many unanswered
questions, not just about the two girls but whether in Semipalatinsk he
might have happened on the most intelligent and polite political exiles
in Siberia and whether the fanatical nihilists, as he imagined them,
had been exiled to regions farther east. After a week in Semipalatinsk,
Kennan and Frost resumed their journey.[128]

A Russian army officer in Omsk had warned Kennan that he should
avoid traveling on the steppe on hot afternoons under cloudless skies.
Several soldiers under his command, explained the officer, had become
nauseated and fainted after foolishly traveling in those conditions. Kennan could not suppress a smile at the idea of having sunstroke in Siberia. Now, traveling through a barren landscape where the leaves and
grass had been scorched brown by the sun and the temperature reached
103 degrees Fahrenheit in the shade, Kennan wished he had taken the
officer's advice because he was nauseated, extremely thirsty, and close to
fainting. A sandstorm overtook them during a stop at the Voroninskaya
post station but their driver set out anyway and, with the one-hundred-
foot-high sandstorm as a tailwind, raced the carriage down the road
while Kennan and Frost struggled to breathe. At the Cheremshanka
post station they drank copious quantities of milk to soothe their raw
throats and quench their thirst. "If anybody thinks that it doesn't get
hot in Siberia," rasped Frost, "just refer them to me!"

They ascended the foothills of the Altai Mountains near the Mongolian border. Almost magically, as though a curtain had parted to let
them into a Siberian Shangri-la and then closed behind them to block
out the steppe, they came upon a vista of meadows, cool breezes scented
with the smell of flowers, turquoise lakes fed by glacial runoff, thickly
wooded valleys, and a beckoning range of snow-laden mountains. The
sudden transition from a sunburnt, bone-bleached landscape to some-

thing resembling the Swiss Alps stunned both men. Kennan and Frost decided that they deserved a vacation from their exile investigation.

They procured horses and the guiding services of a young blond peasant who wore a bloodred shirt overlaid with a pattern of yellow harps, buckskin trousers embroidered with bouquets of roses and sunflowers, and a hat reshaped into a piratical appearance. Their prismatic guide led them on trails that zigzagged up and down valleys, across slopes covered with purple flowers, and through huge moraine fields below glaciers whose ice cracked and split with the sound of an artillery barrage. Water gushing from the bottom of one glacier became a roaring waterfall that cascaded thousands of feet to the valley floor. On the descents, some as steep as the ones Kennan had experienced in the Caucasus, both he and an unnerved Frost more than once came close to sliding off their saddles. They spent ten days exploring the mountains, gazing at snowcapped peaks nearly fifteen thousand

View of mountain peaks in the Altai, 1885 (from *Siberia and the Exile System* 1:219)

feet high, and soaking in hot springs comparable to Europe's fabled Carlsbad hot springs. Much refreshed, they resumed their journey to Tomsk, now seven hundred and fifty miles to the northeast.[129]

Heavy downpours had left the normally bad roads to Tomsk nearly impassable. They traveled at night through mountainous terrain until their carriage capsized in a rain-worn gully. They were rescued by several mail carriages from Bukhtarma whose drivers helped pull their carriage out of the gully. They again proceeded in the dark, but this time Kennan walked ahead, waving a white handkerchief in the air to guide the driver around gullies and dislodged boulders whose location he ascertained by stumbling into them. Exhausted after an hour, Kennan climbed back into the carriage, which shortly capsized again. He and Frost spent the rest of the night shivering under the upended carriage while their driver, taking one of the horses, went for help. He returned the next morning with a Cossack from Alexandrofskaya who had ropes, crowbars, and fresh horses, and their carriage was on its way.

They made such slow progress on the mountainous road to the small village of Ulbinsk that Kennan and Frost got out, walked alongside the carriage, and collected goldenrod and hollyhocks to decorate their passenger compartment. In Ulbinsk, the political exiles bore their banishment with such quiet dignity that Kennan began to doubt whether, no matter how far east he went, he would find the nihilists of his imagination. Kennan and Frost decided to leave Ulbinsk after staying only a day and a night because their sojourn in the Altai Mountains had left them behind their demanding schedule to reach the convict mines in Eastern Siberia before winter. Two of the Ulbinsk political exiles rode with them on horseback as far as the Ulba River. After crossing the river on a ferry, Kennan and Frost turned to look back. On the other side of the river the two exiles took off their hats and bowed low.

By day they journeyed through dried-out steppes, where Kirghiz horsemen tended flocks of fat-tailed sheep, and passed by fields of cultivated sunflowers and half-ripe watermelons. Rather than endure the perilous road in the dark, they spent the nights in post stations, which were so infested with bedbugs that Kennan abandoned any hope of sleep and instead wrote until dawn. Letters awaited both men at the post office in the mining town of Barnaul. Kennan had eight from Emiline and letters from his father, mother, and sister Jennie. Frost's letters included one from his wife enclosing, to his delight, a recent photograph of their young son. Kennan's hotel room in Barnaul afforded no relief from bedbugs. Desperate for sleep, he stretched out on a small table but it constantly capsized. "Before we left Barnaul, I was reduced to a state bordering on frenzy."

After Barnaul they rode through a landscape of gently rolling hills and birch groves that led Frost to say that he could imagine he was "up Berkshireway." They crossed the Ob River on a paddle-wheeled ferry and on August 20 rode into Tomsk, a provincial capital with a population of about thirty-one thousand. Since departing Tiumen and its forwarding prison, they had traveled a distance equal to that between New York City and Austin, Texas. Kennan and Frost checked into the European Hotel, which mercifully had clean beds without bedbugs.

A senior provincial administrator in Tomsk, who had read the Russian translation of *Tent Life in Siberia,* readily gave Kennan and Frost permission to visit the forwarding prison. "I think you will find it the worst prison in Siberia," said the official, who advised them to stay away from the hospital wards. Another official took Kennan aside. "The prison here is unfit for human habitation—it isn't fit for a dog." The sky was an ominous shade of ash gray when they arrived at the Tomsk forwarding prison, which was a stockade on the open prairie outside the city. Although it was August, the air was so damp and chill that Kennan was glad that he wore his heavy overcoat. The inspection party consisted of Kennan, Frost, the prison warden, the chief of the local exile bureau, and an officer from a convict barge. Kennan heard the familiar jingling and clinking of chains as he entered the prison.[130]

Hundreds of convicts, who wore chains and frayed, military-like overcoats, sat or wandered aimlessly in the three-acre open area in the stockade. Armed sentries stood watch on the walls. The scene evoked for Kennan the illustrations of the dreadful Andersonville Prison in the Civil War, where the Confederacy had crammed thousands of captured Union soldiers into an open-air enclosure. The warden, a young, round-faced official named Ivanenko, tried to rush the Americans along, which did not escape the notice of the convict barge officer. "Are you going to show them the family *kameras* and *balagans*?" he asked Ivanenko, referring to the one-story log barracks in a corner of the prison that housed, among others, the families accompanying exiled convicts.

"Certainly. I will show them anything that they wish to see," replied Ivanenko, who led the party to the family barracks. The *kameras* were fully enclosed but the *balagans,* which were surrounded by ditches filled with filthy water, had no walls. Instead, thin cotton sheets hung from each *balagan's* roof around its perimeter. Kennan inspected a *balagan* crammed with women, children, and their husbands and fathers, who could not move without bumping into or shoving one another. Mothers with handkerchiefs tied around their heads sat in awkward positions holding or nursing infants. Men and women sat or lay on the sleeping platforms, others had squeezed into the tight space beneath the platforms or lay on the squalid floor, and many just stood with vacant looks in their eyes. Damp underclothing hung from the crossbeams below the roof and the entranceways were partly obstructed by bags, bundles, clothes, and utensils. The smell of urine and excrement rose from holes and gaps in the floorboards. Throughout the inspection the warden was besieged with appeals for relief.

One man pleaded that sleep was impossible because of the cold, the overcrowding, and the crying babies.

"You will go on the road pretty soon, and then it will be easier," Ivanenko told him.

"*Batiushka!* [My little father! My benefactor!]," called out a young woman nursing an infant, "Won't you, for God's sake, let me sleep in the bathhouse with my baby? It's so cold here nights; I can't keep him warm."

A family prison cell in the Tomsk forwarding prison, 1885 (from *Siberia and the Exile System* 1:313)

"No, *matushka,* (My little mother)," replied Ivanenko, "I can't let you sleep in the bathhouse. It is better for you here."

But when one man repeatedly demanded a clean shirt, Ivanenko rounded on him. "Silence! How dare you talk to me in that way? I'll take the skin off from you! You'll get another shirt when you go on the road, and not before. Away!" More young mothers with infants vainly pleaded with Ivanenko for permission to sleep in the bathhouse. Kennan asked why he refused the mothers' requests. "It is cold here now and it must be much worse at night. These thin walls of cotton-sheeting don't keep out at all the raw night air."

"It is impossible," Ivanenko replied. "The atmosphere of the bathhouse is too hot, close and damp. I tried letting some of the nursing women sleep there, but one or two of their babies died every night and I had to stop it." Ivanenko seemed sympathetic to the plight of the mothers and their children, but they were beyond the help of even a humane warden. Kennan did not press the issue, and they moved on to the prison hospital, which was filled with patients suffering from typhus, scurvy, dysentery, rheumatism, anemia, and bronchitis. Dozens of patients lay on benches or on the floor because there were not enough cots. One physician told Kennan that he had tried without success to persuade the authorities to burn down the hospital because it was so saturated with disease. He mentioned that he sometimes fainted from the smell while working in the wards.

Kennan, who had defended the exile system as humane because, unlike other penal systems that broke up families, wives and children were allowed to accompany husbands and fathers to Siberia, had trouble falling asleep that night. He was experiencing the quandary of Prince Nekhlyudov in Leo Tolstoy's later novel *Resurrection*. Nekhlyudov's seduction of the servant-girl Maslova sets in motion events that lead to her exile to Siberia for a crime of which she is innocent. The guilt-ridden Nekhlyudov follows her and learns what happens to the exiles. "Am I mad because I see what others do not," Nekhlyudov asks himself, "or are they mad that do these things that I see?" After falling asleep, Kennan dreamed of the families in the *balagan*, dead babies in bathhouses, and the dying hospital ward patients whose faces were as cold and pale as moonlight. "It was enough to make one sick at heart," he later wrote, "to see, subjected to such treatment and undergoing such suffering, hundreds of women and children who had committed no crime, but had merely shown their love and devotion by going into Siberian exile with the husbands, fathers, or the brothers who were dear to them."[131]

Kennan and Frost met with several of the political exiles living in Tomsk. Kennan found one, Felix Volkhovsky, a former law student in St. Petersburg who was fluent in English, to be especially "attractive and sympathetic." He noticed that when Volkhovsky's face was "in repose there seemed to be an expression of profound melancholy in his dark-brown eyes." He had first been jailed in 1868 at the age of twenty-two on charges that the regime never proved. By the time he was released nearly three years later, his hair was white, his voice cracked when he spoke, and he suffered from splitting headaches. He was rearrested in 1874 as part of the crackdown on the Going to the People movement and held in pretrial detention for three years. Once a guard whispered something to him out of pity, but by then Volkhovsky was losing his hearing. The tribunal in the Trial of the 193 found him guilty of belonging to a society "that intends, at a more or less remote time in the future, to overthrow the existing form of government" and exiled him to Siberia for life.

For some exiles like Volkhovsky, who thought of themselves as prisoners of war, the unexpected appearance of a journalist, especially one from a country whose democratic governance and individual freedoms they admired, meant a great deal even though Kennan did not appear sympathetic to Volkhovsky's revolutionary views. Years later, after escaping from Siberia, Volkhovsky recalled Kennan's visit and how he "was always prepared to listen silently and without any preconceived animosity to what we had to say. And that was, in fact, all we were longing for. . . . Until then we had been talking either to acknowledged friends or to prejudiced enemies, never to an impartial outsider." After Tomsk, however, Kennan had to struggle to maintain journalistic impartiality.[132]

Tomsk was a turning point. "It was not until we reached Tomsk that we were brought face-to-face with the tragedies of exile life. From that time, however, until we recrossed the Siberian frontier on our way back to St. Petersburg, we were subjected to a nervous and emotional strain that was sometimes harder to bear than cold, hunger, or fatigue." He wrote to publisher Roswell Smith at the *Century* to confess that his preconceptions of the political exiles as fanatics had been badly mistaken. "On the contrary they are simple, natural, perfectly comprehensible, and often singularly interesting and attractive. One sees at once that they are educated, reasonable, self-controlled gentlemen, not different in any essential respect from one's self."

He ended the letter by acknowledging that "the exile system is worse than I believed it to be, and worse than I have described it. It isn't pleasant, of course, to have to admit that one has written upon a subject without fully understanding it; but even that is better than trying, for the sake of consistency, to maintain a position after one sees that it is utterly untenable."[133]

A *Telega* Will Simply Jolt
a Man's Soul Out
in Twenty-Four Hours

The Tomsk prison authorities gave Kennan and Frost permission to accompany a convoy of hard labor exiles for a few days on its march to the Trans-Baikal mines. They arrived early in the morning at the prison in their carriage. Several hundred male convicts in chains stood in parallel rows outside the prison gate. Each had a gray bag with personal belongings, small kettles hung from the waist chains of many convicts, and one man held a dog in his arms, which he apparently intended to take with him to the mines. A blacksmith went up and down the rows of convicts, stopping here and there to make repairs or replace a fetter. During a roll call convoy officers handed each convict a few coins to buy food. Capt. Gudim, the commander of the exile convoy guard, came out of the prison. "Boys!" he called to the convicts and asked, perhaps for the benefit of the American visitors, "how many of you are now going to the mines for the sixth time?"

"There are lots of them," shouted several convicts in unison. Capt. Gudim permitted Kennan to speak to the convicts. One asked him whether a convict in the United States could earn money by doing extra work so as not to leave the prison destitute. Kennan told the convict that most prison inmates in America could earn money in prison. "It is not so with us. Naked we go to the mines, and naked we come out of them; and we are flogged, while there."

"Oh no!" said Capt. Gudim, who had been listening to the conversation. "They don't flog at the mines now."

"Yes, they do, Your Nobility," the convict responded with polite insistence. "If you are sick or weak and can't finish your [work] you are given twenty blows with the cat."

Kennan wanted to speak further with the convict about his prison experiences but Capt. Gudim interrupted to ask if he would like to observe the loading of sick prisoners. "All prisoners who have certificates from the doctor, step out!" Capt. Gudim shouted. The sick or disabled with doctors' certificates climbed into the waiting carts. Convicts jeered and booed as one man, a malingerer known to be skilled in faking illness, seated himself in a cart. Capt. Gudim took off his cap, made the sign of the cross, and bowed to the prison church. He turned to the convicts. "Well, boys! Go ahead! A safe journey to you!" The column of convicts, carts, and the flanking guards set off. Kennan and Frost followed in their carriage. No women and children accompanied this convoy.

The convoy traveled in a dust cloud tossed up by the shuffling feet of the convicts on a dry road on a hot, windless day. Their carriage stayed close enough to the convicts for Kennan to hear the experienced ones, those who had escaped and been caught multiple times, point out the features of the road and the personalities of the convoy officers to the newcomers. After five or six miles, the convoy passed a roadside shrine with a Christ effigy. Two-thirds of the convicts removed their caps, crossed themselves, and said short prayers. "A Russian peasant may be a highway robber or a murderer, but he continues, nevertheless, to cross himself and say his prayers."

After ten miles the party was allowed a midday rest stop. Nearly every convict, weak from lack of exercise in the forwarding prison and weary from the burden of their chains, sprawled out on the ground. A dozen women and girls from a nearby village, who had been waiting by the roadside, came forward with baskets of food, bottles of milk, and small jugs of beer to sell to the convicts. After ten more miles, the party reached a way station, where they would spend the night. Convoy officers assembled the convicts, held a roll call, and then threw open the gates to the decaying building.

A political exile who had spent sixteen years in Siberia recalled that at one way station on his journey to the mines convoy officers and convicts lost all sense of why they were there and sat down together to a meal purchased from the peddlers, eating, drinking and talking like close friends. No such scene took place at this way station where, with a noisy clanging of their chains, several hundred convicts stampeded inside, pushing and elbowing to claim a space on the sleeping platforms. Behind them the convoy guards slammed shut and locked the doors. The guards slept in separate quarters in the way station, while Kennan and Frost spent the night in their carriage. Kennan planned to ask a convoy officer to let him sleep overnight with the convicts at the next stop but he abandoned the idea in the morning "after breathing the air of one of those cells when the doors were reopened."[134]

After two days on the road with the exile convoy, Kennan and Frost returned to Tomsk. They said farewell to the town's political exiles and began a thousand-mile journey to Irkutsk. They traveled through fields where, under a bright sun, men and women peasants in scarlet-and-blue shirts slashed and hacked at the ripe wheat with sickles. The weather was cool and the rolling countryside teemed with flowers. "Many of them were blooming out of their proper season and were represented by only a few scattered specimens; but of the others we might have picked millions." They passed through empty villages whose residents, other than small children and post station masters, appeared to have left for the harvest. *Kabaks,* drinking taverns that vastly outnumbered schools in Siberia and "bring revenue to the government and demoralization to the peasants," could be identified in these villages by the tree branches nailed to their doors. In the village cemeteries many graves were surrounded by cheerful red, white, and blue picket fences. To Kennan the graves proved that the "Russian love of crude color triumphs even over death."

In one otherwise empty village they saw a blond, five-year-old child, ambling along, sometimes sinking knee deep in mud, while taking bites from a large, raw turnip. Someone had hung a cowbell on a string around his neck, but Kennan and Frost could not tell whether it was to distract him or a means for the parents to find the child at the end of the day's work, or both. At another village they came upon a handcuffed horse grazing on grass, which left Kennan wondering whether the horse had engaged in conduct "incompatible with public tranquility." He inquired about the horse at the next post station, whose station master explained that the horse tended to wander away, so the owner had handcuffed the horse but then lost the key.[135]

They crossed the border between the provinces of Tomsk and Yeniseisk and entered Eastern Siberia. Past the town of Achinsk five horses had to pull the carriage because the road climbed high ridges and descended into gullies filled with thick, wet clay. On flat, hard stretches, where the passage of countless *obozes* had carved deep furrows in the road, the Americans were constantly thrown against the sides or roof of the carriage compartment until Kennan felt "as if I had been beaten from head to foot with a club and left for dead." Frost was ill and suffering from bad chills. They later learned that the road's contractor had been jailed because of the state of the road, which was the one autocratic measure in Russia that Kennan and Frost found to their liking. At the town of Krasnoyarsk, they had a decent meal and slept soundly in a small hotel. Armed with a letter of introduction from a St. Petersburg contact, they called on a wealthy Krasnoyarsk gold-mining entrepreneur who invited Kennan and Frost to his home for dinner.

That evening a servant opened the door to the entrepreneur's home and showed the two into "one of the most beautiful and tastefully furnished drawing-rooms that we had seen in Russia." The fifty-foot-long room had a polished oak floor, Oriental rugs, a grand piano, potted ferns, and cherrywood cabinets filled with bronze Buddhist idols and fine china. A fire of birchwood blazed in a fireplace. The entrepreneur and his brothers and sisters spoke fluent English and some had traveled extensively in the United States. It was a relief for Kennan and Frost to spend time with cultured and sophisticated men and women "who did not tell us harrowing stories of imprisonment and exile."[136]

They climbed back into their carriage, "which we were beginning to dread as a once-tortured criminal dreads the rack," and resumed their journey. They crossed the Yenisei River on a ferryboat and rode through the bright red and yellow fall colors of poplars and birch trees and alongside fields where peasants were stacking sheaves of wheat in long rows. Heavy rains slowed their progress. They overtook an exile party as it slogged through the downpour on its way to the convict mines. Neither man got any meaningful sleep, the food at the post stations on this route was abysmal, and the temperature dropped sharply at night.

A plague of vermin, which they had acquired while inspecting the filthy exile way stations, accompanied the physical beating administered by their carriage. "Cold, hunger, sleeplessness, and fatigue I could bear with reasonable patience and fortitude; but to be forced to live for weeks at a time in clothing infested with fleas, lice or bedbugs from the unclean bodies of common criminal convicts . . . gave me a humiliating sense of physical defilement that was almost as bad as a consciousness of moral degradation." Kennan discarded several changes of underwear until finally "I abandoned all hope of relief and reconciled myself to the inevitable as best I could." At a post station near Irkutsk, Kennan noticed a sign in the waiting-room:

POST STATION OF BOKOFSKAYA

DISTANT

FROM ST. PETERSBURG 5601 VERSTS [3712 MILES]

FROM IRKUTSK 13 VERSTS [8.6 MILES]

"You may subtract 13 from 5601, or divide 5601 by 13, or put the two numbers through any other mathematical process that you choose, but you will never fully appreciate the difference between them until you have travelled 5601 *versts* in the Russian Empire and have only thirteen *versts* to go." In mid-September 1885 they crossed the Angara River on a ferry and, entered Irkutsk, which had a population of thirty-six thousand. They came upon countless taverns, and passed by peasants, peddlers, tramps, and soldiers on foot and in carts. "Nearly half of them were more or less intoxicated." They found a hotel room where Kennan changed his clothes for the first time since leaving Tomsk. His underwear was bloodstained, and his body so covered with rashes that he thought he had acquired an infectious disease.

Kennan had passed through Irkutsk on his return trip from northeast Siberia after the Russian-American Telegraph Expedition came to an end. The city charmed him, after more than two years in the wilderness, as "very striking and beautiful."[137]

Decembrist wife Maria Volkonsky also found Irkutsk, with its wide streets and brick merchant houses, charming. Trying to catch up with her exiled husband, she arrived after a sleigh journey through a Siberian winter so cold that she could not lean out of the passenger compartment's window for fear of frostbite. In the city she learned what Nicholas I had meant when he warned her to go no farther than Irkutsk. The governor of Irkutsk handed Maria a decree from Nicholas that any wife of a Decembrist who followed an exiled husband into Siberia would be stripped of all titles and rights of nobility, forfeit all valuables and sums of money, and would never be allowed to return to European Russia, not even on the death of her husband. The governor told Maria that she had to sign the decree if she wanted to go farther but pleaded with her to return to her son. Even though proceeding past Irkutsk meant that Maria would never see her child again, she unhesitatingly signed the decree and immediately left for Nerchinsk where her husband, Sergei, had been put to work in the silver mines.[138]

Irkutsk charmed neither Kennan nor Frost when they arrived in 1885. Several years earlier a fire had destroyed nearly four thousand buildings and the city was still disfigured by blackened buildings and vacant lots. After a needed night's sleep, the two men left their passports at the police station and went to the post office to collect their mail, which included five letters for Kennan from Emiline, the most recent dated two months earlier. For the rest of the day, Frost sketched scenes at the riverfront and Kennan explored an open-air bazaar teeming with Buryats, Mongols, Cossacks, and Russian peasants.

After they returned to the hotel, a uniformed official, whose boots had jingling spurs, entered their room. "I am Makofski, chief of police." Kennan rose from his chair, expecting the worst. Sooner or later, he feared, the police in a town where they had stopped would send a telegraph to the minister of the interior: "Kennan and Frost are establishing intimate relations everywhere with administrative exiles and state criminals. Was it the intention of the government that this be permitted?" Telegraphed orders would come back from the ministry to detain the Americans at their next stop. The telegraph lines on Siberian roads "hung over our heads like an electric sword of Damocles, threatening every moment to fall and cut short our career of investigation."

But Capt. Makofski astonished Kennan by saying, "I have the pleasure of knowing you by reputation—I have read your book—and when an eminent foreign traveler comes to Siberia to study the country, I regard it as only my duty to call upon him and offer my services. I understand that you are interested, among other things, in prisons and the exile system." Capt. Makofski said that he had learned of Kennan's and Frost's presence from their passports, but he could have known about their interest in the exile system only from St. Petersburg officials. Evidently the authorities, whatever their suspicions, still regarded Kennan as sympathetic to the regime because Capt. Makofski did not arrest them. Instead, he arranged for Kennan and Frost to visit the Irkutsk prisons and confided his view that the exile system was a burden to Russia. Kennan was skeptical of Capt. Makofski's friendliness, especially when he visited an Irkutsk prison where the local prison authorities had spread white sand on the floors to improve its appearance. "I felt, however, that I had no right on this ground to throw stones at anybody, since I myself was living in a very large and very fragile glass house."[139]

Before starting the twelve-hundred-mile journey from Irkutsk to the convict mines, Kennan and Frost sold their carriage. Instead, they planned to travel "on transfer" by carriages called *telegas,* which they could hire at the post stations. They thought the smaller *telegas* better suited to winter travel, although it meant carrying their luggage from one hired *telega* to the next at the post stations. They anticipated a difficult trip. The Trans-Baikal was the most isolated region of Siberia on their journey and the convict mines, which could not be found on maps, were dispersed over thousands of square miles of rough terrain. They could not even be sure that they would receive permission to inspect the mines.

On September 24 Kennan and Frost left Irkutsk in a hired *telega* for Lake Baikal, forty miles away. They came upon a wagon, pulled by four horses, going in the opposite direction and carrying a large crate. Their driver suggested that the crate might contain a tiger from the Amur River region on its way to an exhibition in Irkutsk. Curious, Kennan and Frost hailed the wagon's driver, who stopped and obligingly removed the crate's covering boards to indeed reveal a giant Siberian tiger in an iron cage. The orange-and-brown-striped animal, enraged at its captivity, roared and battered itself against the cage bars, rocking the wagon violently. "We thought for a single breathless instant that he was coming through [the bars] like a three-hundred-pound missile from a catapult." The driver poked and jabbed at the tiger through the bars with an iron rod until the animal retreated to a corner of the cage with resentful growls.

Shaken, Kennan, and Frost continued to Lake Baikal, whose scale can be grasped by imagining a fifty-mile-wide gash in south-central Siberia as long as England, as deep as the Grand Canyon, and containing one-fifth of the world's supply of fresh water. The lake has a mercurial temperament: storms abruptly arise, churning out six- or seven-foot waves, and then just as suddenly vanish. The two Americans boarded a lake steamer where Kennan spent most of the crossing below decks writing a wedding anniversary letter to Emiline and reflecting on their married years. As the steamer approached Boyarskaya on the eastern shore, sudden heavy winds and waves forced the captain to anchor out in the lake instead of docking. Kennan and Frost spent a seasick night in a tiny cabin on the tossing steamer. The winds subsided overnight and the next morning the steamer tied up to the wharf. The two men went ashore cold, hungry, and sleep-deprived.

At the closest post station Kennan and Frost hired a *telega,* which they reluctantly got into because they had learned by now that the smaller carriage was even more brutal to travelers than the larger *tarantas* they had ridden through Western Siberia. An English traveler wrote after traveling in a *telega* that "I don't think there is much to choose between the top of a *telega* and the back of a buck-jumping horse." The springless *telega's* smaller size and weight magnified the jolts and its shallow passenger compartment forced Kennan and Frost to perch high on their trunks and cling to any available rope to avoid being hurled onto the road. A *telega* "will simply jolt a man's soul out in less than twenty-four hours."

At the post station in Ilinskaya, they drank tea and ate crusts of bread for dinner and immediately went to bed. But Kennan, lying on a narrow bench, barely slept because noisy drivers and passengers kept entering the post station all night along with blasts of cold air. A government official arrived and complained loudly to the station master about the condition of the road, awakening Kennan. A family came in but instead of going to sleep the parents talked and drank tea and their baby coughed incessantly. By four in the morning they had quieted down but then two portly merchants arrived and loudly discussed gold-mining techniques. Just as their conversation was subsiding, and Kennan was dozing off, a white-bearded elderly man carrying a double-barreled shotgun entered and began talking about gristmills with the merchants. Kennan gave up, rose, drank tea, and conversed with the newest arrival about the recently discovered gold deposits in Mongolia.[140]

He now had a violent headache, a backache, and an acute pain in his lungs that made it hard to breathe. Even though winter would not wait for them to get to the convict mines, he and Frost decided that they needed another vacation. "We were tired of prisons and the exile system; we had had misery enough for a while; and it seemed to me we should be in better condition to bear the strain of the mines if we could turn our thoughts temporarily into other channels and travel a little, as boys say, 'for fun.'" They detoured south toward Mongolia to visit the famous Buddhist lamasery of Goose Lake near the town of Selenginsk in Buryat country. The Buryats, skilled horsemen, had fought off Genghis Khan, but the Romanov rule over Siberia forced them to adapt to Russian civilization, which for many meant giving up their nomadic ways. Some became Cossacks while others took to cattle breeding. The tribal shamans gave way to Lamaist (a Tibetan form of Buddhism) priests.

Kennan and Frost stayed overnight in Selenginsk's post station, where Kennan did not so much fall asleep as pass out. He awoke in the morning to find his face so disfigured by bedbug bites that he could not open one eye until he had reduced the inflammation with cold compresses. After Kennan made himself more presentable, he and Frost called on the local police chief, Khainuief Munku, a bullet-shaped

Buryat about sixty years old who wore a gray gown belted at the waist. Munku, who was drunk when Kennan and Frost entered his office, demanded a sum to guide them up a stony road to the lamasery and act as their interpreter that Kennan regarded as robbery, but afterward considered well spent given the Buryat's showmanship.

An hour later, Munku arrived at Kennan's and Frost's post station in a carriage pulled by three shaggy horses. He had changed into a flamboyant, ultramarine silk gown with a scarlet sash around the waist and wore a dishpan-shaped red felt hat. On the way to the lamasery Munku berated the driver for not going faster, sipped what he called "insanity drops" from a flask of vodka, and once stopped the carriage and got out to coax an attractive young Buryat woman in a blue kaftan, who was riding into Selenginsk, to get off her horse and kiss him. She did it with a mix of mortification and fun. Munku climbed back into the carriage with a grin that Kennan interpreted to mean, "There. What do you think of that? That's the kind of man I am! *You* can't make a pretty woman get off her horse just to kiss you." As they neared the lamasery, Munku asked Kennan and Frost, "How are you magnified?" Seeing their puzzled looks, Munku rephrased the question. "What is your rank?" Frost explained that they were only private American citizens without rank or titles, which left Munku crestfallen because his stature would suffer from introducing two inconsequential travelers to the Grand Lama.

At the lamasery the acolytes and servants who answered the door spoke to Munku in whispers, "as if there were a dead body in the house or as if the Grand Lama were asleep and it would be a terrible thing if he were awakened." Munku, who now showed not the slightest sign of drunkenness, finally persuaded them to announce the visitors. The Grand Lama, who had a pleasant, sympathetic face, made a theatrical entrance wearing a gown of orange silk embroidered with golden thread, a red silk scarf, and a pointed orange felt hat. Munku introduced Kennan and Frost as two "Lord High Commissioners from the great American republic," which satisfied both the lamasery's protocol needs and preserved Munku's prestige, even though the Grand Lama had never heard of America. Over dinner, which included copious amounts of vodka for Munku, it emerged that the Grand Lama thought that the world was flat. Kennan explained that he had personally circumnavigated the globe and "returned to my home from the direction exactly opposite to that which I had taken in leaving it. If the world was flat, do you think I could have done this?" The Grand Lama seemed saddened. "It is not in accordance with the teachings of our books; but the Russians must be right."

Kennan and Frost spent more time exploring the area, including a Russian town and a Mongolian town that faced each other across the border. In a short walk the Americans left behind log houses, churches with golden domes, and Russian merchants in loose waistcoats to mingle with Chinese traders in skullcaps and stare as "wild-looking sunburned horsemen in deep orange gowns and dishpan-shaped hats ride in now and then from some remote encampment in the great desert of Gobi." But overall, the "fun" detour to the Goose Lake lamasery and Buryat country did not have the refreshing effect of their earlier excursion to the Altai Mountains.

In one ancient Mongolian town Kennan fell ill with chills, fevers, dizziness, and severe headaches. "It is one thing to be sick at home in a good bed, in clean linen, and with somebody to take care of you, but it is quite another thing to lie down sick like a dog . . . with all your clothes on, and in the paroxysms of fever be tormented to the verge of frenzy by bedbugs." The illness did not subside for almost two weeks. "Up to that time I had had at least strength to bear the inevitable hardships of life and travel in such a country; but after that time, I was sustained chiefly by willpower, quinine and excitement."[141]

On October 15, Kennan, although still weak and dizzy, managed to climb into a hired carriage alongside Frost to begin the two-day journey back to Selenginsk. He found that it was no worse to be ill in the lurching carriage, where he could at least breathe fresh air, than to collapse feverish and vermin-ridden, as happened on one occasion, in a room adjoining a bakery in the frontier town of Troitskosavsk. They were returning to Selenginsk because a political exile in Irkutsk had told Kennan that, before leaving for the convict mines, he must meet Catherine Breshkovsky, who was in exile there. During his ten months in Siberia, Kennan met more than a hundred political exiles but perhaps none more colorful, tougher, and better versed in the hellish circles of the exile system than the diminutive woman exile in Selenginsk who later became known as the "Little Grandmother of the Russian Revolution."

Catherine Breshkovsky was then forty-one years old. She had been born to wealthy, loving parents but grew up ashamed that they owned hundreds of serfs, whom she dreamed of helping in some way. She gave up material comforts, the advantages of a first-class education, which included studies at a Swiss boarding school, and both her husband and her baby (handing her baby to her brother and sister-in-law broke her heart, but "I knew that I could not be a mother and still be a revolutionist") and went into small villages with the other narodniki in the Going to the People movement. To better pass for a worn peasant, she put on a black jacket and coarse sack skirt and used acid to age her face and hands but was found out anyway. The local police threw her into a jail called the Black Hole, where she slipped because the floor was covered with excrement. She fainted onto a pile of straw, but was stung awake by the vermin swarming over her body.

"And this was the beginning of Siberia," she later wrote. She was held for three years with the other narodniki in pretrial detention, where she conceived the idea of assassinating the governor of St. Petersburg, which Vera Zasulich later attempted to do. She was found guilty by the tribunal in the Trial of the 193, and sent to the mines of Kara. After finishing her sentence at Kara, Breshkovsky was sent in an exile convoy to a settlement near the Arctic Circle. Her party halted at an exile way station where a party of dozens of women of childbearing age, all of them dressed in white and wearing makeup, had also stopped for the night. The women were on their way to the penal colony on Sakhalin Island, where they would be used to increase the island's population. That night Breshkovsky heard "cries, sobs, shouts, the coarse voices of drunken men." She rushed to a window, looked out, and nearly went mad.

She escaped from the Arctic settlement and began walking to the Pacific coast, but was caught and sent back to Kara to serve another sentence, which included forty lashes. She demanded that prison officials carry out the lashing, but they backed down and put her in a windowless room the size of a horse stall. For three years she breathed foul air, fought vermin, and subsisted on a diet of soup, black bread, water, and, occasionally, rotting meat. Twenty young women political exiles, many from noble families, had also been confined in her dilapidated building. Most fell ill, their bodies turning blue from scurvy. Breshkovsky nursed them as best she could, but half of the women died. She was then sent into permanent exile in Selenginsk, which she found the hardest to bear because she was the only educated woman within a hundred miles. To maintain her sanity, she sometimes ran into the countryside and sang grand opera arias. "I languished like a hawk in a cage."[142]

At their meeting in Selenginsk, Breshkovsky and Kennan discussed the Russian revolutionary movement and its progress over the past fifteen years. Kennan told Breshkovsky of his plans to visit the convict mines. She rummaged through her meager possessions and gave him a few teacups, a hand mirror, and a small red feather duster to bring to her friends at the mines of Kara. She asked him to give the feather duster, with her best love, to her dear friend Natalia Armfeld.

Kennan thought that this cultured and intelligent woman, who spoke several foreign languages and was an accomplished musician, would spend the rest of her life in lonely exile under police surveillance, cut off from family and friends in a town that was the dreariest he had yet seen in Siberia. "The town looked empty, deserted, and dead as if it had been stricken by a plague." At the end she would be buried in a graveyard by the Selenga River "where no sympathetic eye might ever rest upon the unpainted wooden cross that would briefly chronicle her life and death." Because so much of Breshkovsky's past had been dreadful and her future seemed so bleak, he was stirred by the "unshaken courage" of her parting words to him. "Mr. Kennan, we may die in exile, and our children may die in exile, and our children's children may die in exile, but something will come of it at last." He wrote in his journal that "she is evidently a woman of much character, education and warm affections."

Much of Kennan's youth and early adulthood had been spent reassuring himself that he possessed courage. He had precariously walked around the bell tower of a church in Norwalk, roamed the rough waterfront streets of Cincinnati at night, and spent two and a half years in northeastern Siberia. Until he met Catherine Breshkovsky, perhaps apart from his mother's pioneer experience, Kennan appears not have associated women with daring or valor and, if anything, thought of them as less courageous than men. On the telegraph expedition he once willed himself not to faint from a sudden, extreme temperature change because he did not want to show "womanish weakness" to a group of American men.

The long-suffering but still defiant Breshkovsky changed Kennan's appreciation of both courage and women. "I cannot recall her last words to me without feeling conscious that all my standards of courage, of fortitude, and of heroic self-sacrifice have been raised for all time, and raised by the hand of a woman." After he returned to the United States Kennan wrote about their meeting, concluding, "I have never seen nor heard of [Catherine Breshkovsky] since that day. She has passed as completely out of my life as if she had died when I bade her goodbye." Eventually much of the world would hear of her and the two would meet again.[143]

Six days after leaving Selenginsk, Kennan and Frost descended a mountainous ridge. They had traveled so far east that the United

States felt closer than St. Petersburg. In village shops Kennan saw American goods, including tinware, lanterns, and "Yankee notions," and half expected to "catch sight of San Francisco and the Golden Gate" from a hilltop. They stopped in Chita, the capital of the Trans-Baikal, and then began the three-hundred-mile journey to the Kara mines. For much of that distance Kennan and Frost had the unaccustomed luxury of traveling on a reasonably good road, which first ran through the valley of the Ingoda River and then along the left bank of the Shilka River.

The late-October weather turned against them, the temperature dropped to zero degrees Fahrenheit and several inches of snow fell. At Stretinsk the colliding chunks of ice on the Shilka River forced them to abandon their plan to take a skiff downriver to the Kara mines. Leaving their carriage in Stretinsk, they hired a guide and horses even though Kennan, still weak from his illness at the Mongolian border, doubted that he had the strength for an eighty-mile ride through a mountain wilderness. In places the switchback trail, high above the Shilka River, was covered with ice and snow, which forced them to dismount and lead their unshod horses because a slip or stumble while mounted "would unquestionably put an end to our Siberian investigations." After several days on the trail they reached the peasant village of Shilkina. Kennan's pulse, "running at the rate of 120, warned me that I was near the extreme limit of my endurance." They spent the night on the floor of a peasant's hut, but the worst of the trip was over. They were only a short ride to Ust Kara, the nearest of the Kara penal settlements.[144]

10

The Mines of Kara

Greek mining engineers advised Peter the Great in the late seventeenth century that mineral wealth lay underground in the regions east of Lake Baikal. Hard labor convicts were soon digging down to the silver veins in the vicinity of Nerchinsk. Gold mining began later near the Kara River, a name derived from a Tatar word meaning "black." The Nerchinsk Mining Region, as it became known, eventually stretched over thousands of square miles from the eastern shore of Lake Baikal to the Chinese border.

In late October 1885 Kennan and Frost rode their horses through the valley of the Kara River to the prison complex at Ust Kara, or Kara mouth, the first of the prisons, convict settlements, and open placer gold mines stretching twenty miles up the valley. In addition to Ust Kara, there were the Lower Prison, the Political Prison, the Lower Diggings, Middle Kara and Upper Kara convict settlements, and the Upper Prison. Their total exile population was around twenty-five hundred, of whom two-thirds were hard-labor convicts and the rest women and children who had accompanied their husbands and fathers to the mines. Many of the political convicts in Eastern Siberia were held at Kara.[145]

Kennan and Frost left their horses and guide at Ust Kara and found a carriage to take them to the administrative center at the Lower Diggings settlement, where they had their first glimpse of convict life at the mines. The settlement was a village of whitewashed cabins, tin-roofed officers' residences, and a dark, forbidding log prison. A thin layer of snow did not disguise the ugliness of the placer craters that surrounded the Lower Diggings. Several dozen convicts in long gray overcoats worked on a new log building guarded by armed Cossacks in fur caps, sheepskin coats, and felt boots. "In the waning light of the cold, gloomy autumnal afternoon, the dreary snowy square, the gray group of convicts working listlessly as if hopeless or exhausted, and the cordon of Cossacks leaning upon their bayoneted rifles, made up a picture that for some reason exerted upon me a chilling and depressing influence."

Kennan and Frost went directly to the prison commandant's residence where they were greeted by Maj. Potuloff, who was in charge of Kara's common-law convict prisons. Potuloff, a tall, cordial man in his fifties with a bushy beard and soldierly bearing, explained that he had been alerted by telegram to expect Kennan and Frost, but he never thought that the two would make it through from Stretinsk at this time of the year. He laughed when Kennan inquired where they could find a place to stay for the night. Other than the accommodations for criminals, he explained, the only place to stay was in his home, which they were welcome to do. Kennan and Frost had no alternative than to accept his offer "and in minutes [we] were comfortably quartered in a large, well-furnished house, where our eyes were gladdened by the sight of such unfamiliar luxuries as long mirrors, big soft rugs, easy-chairs, and a piano."[146]

They found themselves effectively under twenty-four-hour surveillance in Maj. Potuloff's home. He never left them alone, in fact, he seemed to have relinquished his official duties during Kennan and

Frost's stay in order to keep an eye on them. Once, when Kennan moved in the direction of his overcoat, Maj. Potuloff asked, "Where are you going?"

"Out for exercise."

"Wait a minute and I will go with you." Kennan's bedroom, which was on the ground floor across the front hall from the sitting room, had no door but only a thin curtain. The sentries posted night and day outside the house could even look in his bedroom through its curtain-less windows.[147]

Under Maj. Potuloff's watchful eye, Kennan inspected prisons that were the now-familiar "perfect hell[s] of misery," from the impossible overcrowding to the filth and vermin to the lack of any bedding for the inmates. "Civilized human beings put straw even into the kennels of their dogs." But no matter how many Siberian prisons Kennan inspected, he always marveled at the unendurable smell. His descriptions of prison odors steadily grew more vivid and literary the farther east he went. Of the air in the Ust Kara prison, which Maj. Potuloff readily acknowledged was repulsive, Kennan later wrote, "I can ask you to imagine cellar air, every atom of which has been half a dozen times through human lungs and is heavy with carbonic acid; to imagine that air still further vitiated by foul, pungent, slightly ammoniacal exhalations from long unwashed human bodies; to imagine that it has a suggestion of damp, decaying wood and more than a suggestion of human excrement—and still you will have no adequate idea of it."[148]

During Kennan's prison inspections, convicts complained to Maj. Potuloff and even approached Kennan on the assumption that "I must be an inspector sent to Kara to investigate the prison management." Several convicts pleaded with Maj. Potuloff that they had been imprisoned for months but still did not know what they were charged with. Another insisted that he had already finished his sentence. One man explained that he had gotten drunk on the exile march and exchanged names with another convict and ended up at Kara serving a hard labor sentence when, had he kept his name, he only would have been sent to a settlement as a forced colonist.

Bartering names for food, drink, or clothing was a common practice among the exiled convicts and not easily detected since the convoy and prison guards could hardly familiarize themselves with the faces of hundreds of convicts. The exchange, which the *artels* ruthlessly enforced, invariably improved one barterer's position to the distinct disadvantage of some hapless exile who had spent his money or gambled away his clothing, and thereby gotten himself, as Kennan explained, "into such a condition that for five or ten rubles and a bottle of vodka he will sell his very soul." Maj. Potuloff ignored the convicts and their complaints.

In his Siberian travels Kennan encountered a variety of attitudes among Siberian prison officials. Some defended the conditions in their prisons, while others openly acknowledged their true nature. Kennan learned of a prison official, a drunkard and thief, who embezzled the money sent to convicts by their relatives. A rare official, such as the near-legendary Col. Vladimir Konovich, the head of the Lower Kara Prison in the early 1880s, did what he could to help the convicts. When a Siberian prison official demanded that Col. Konovich explain why prisoners praised him, he replied, "What explanation could I give? Did you expect me to excuse myself [apologize] because somebody regarded me as a human being and not a beast?" As they went through the Ust Kara prisons, Kennan noticed that Maj. Potuloff was at turns uncommunicative, irritable, and downcast. "He did not attempt to explain, defend or excuse anything, nor did he then, nor at any subsequent time, ask me what impression the Ust Kara prisons made upon me. He knew very well what impression they *must* make."[149]

After finishing one prison inspection, Maj. Potuloff, Kennan, and Frost rode together in a carriage to the stockaded Upper Kara convict settlement. From there they walked toward the Kara River and came upon dozens of convicts laboring under Cossack guard in deep gravel placer pits which had once been a creek bed. "The day was cold and dark, a light snow was falling, and a more dreary picture than that presented by the mine could hardly be imagined." Some convicts broke up the bottom of the pit with crowbars while others shoveled the loosened clay, sand, and small stones into wheelbarrows or onto pallets. Since the convicts were forbidden from talking, the only sounds in the pit were the clinking of chains, chipping and scraping of crowbars, and curt orders from the mine overseer. Convicts pushed the wheelbarrows and hand-carried the pallets about one hundred and fifty yards and dumped out the contents, which were fed into a sluicing apparatus that separated the gold particles from the sand and gravel. Several Cossacks on a rest break huddled around a fire trying to warm their hands.

At the end of their shifts, the convicts shuffled from the placer pits to the penal settlement. Frost sketched a long column of mostly bearded men in caps, gray overcoats, and chains marching three or four abreast. Cossack guards flank the column on both sides. A flag flies over a nearby building and in the distance a cross rises into the sky from a church dome. Most of the convicts' heads are bowed, but a few appear to be staring at something, likely at the well-dressed, well-fed man sketching them from the side of the road.

Passing Frost, the convicts entered the stockade, crossed a courtyard with churned-up earth, and went into the prison for the night. Some convicts, Kennan learned, entered the prison after a work shift pushing a miner's wheelbarrow to which they were chained, even at night, as a disciplinary punishment.

After Kennan had spent five days at Kara, Maj. Potuloff was called away on business. Perhaps by now more trusting of Kennan and Frost, he did not assign an officer to keep watch on them during his absence. Kennan decided to first visit Capt. Nikolin, the gendarme commander of the political convicts at Kara, hoping to obtain his permission to visit the Political Prison. After that, he planned to seek out Catherine Breshkovsky's friend Natalia Armfeld, who was now in the "free command."

As a reward for good behavior in prison, common-law and political convicts were allowed to live under close surveillance in a shantytown of shacks and huts around the Political Prison called the free command.

Political convicts typically did not work in the mines because the local Siberian authorities regarded them as unfit for hard labor and believed that forced inactivity was the cruelest punishment for these

Convicts at work in the Kara gold mines, 1885 (from *Siberia and the Exile System* 2:163)

educated men and women. "Immunity from hard labor, however, does not render the lot of state criminals an easy one," an Eastern Siberian official stressed in a secret report to Tsar Alexander III that Kennan later managed to secretly obtain. "On the contrary, complete isolation and constant confinement to their own limited circle make their life unbearable. . . . There have been a number of suicides among them and within a few days one of them, Pozen, has gone insane. A number of others are in a mental condition very near to insanity."[150]

Capt. Nikolin received Kennan courteously, ordered an aide to bring in a samovar, and offered Kennan a cigarette. He was a heavyset man in his early fifties with pursed lips, icy eyes, and an opaque expression. One former Kara prisoner described him as a "fat, spiteful old tom-cat" who was always poised to "pounce on a victim and stick his claws into it." Kennan knew that Russian army officers throughout Kara loathed Capt. Nikolin and that his relationship with Maj. Potuloff was strained. After small talk, Capt. Nikolin asked, "Suppose that you were going to search a political convict as thoroughly as possible, how would you do it?" Kennan suggested a strip search. "Is that all you would do?" replied Nikolin, who proceeded to describe, among other feats, how he had once found a small dose of poison concealed in a wax cap in a convict's hollow tooth. "Ah-h-h! They are very sly, but I know all their tricks," gloated Nikolin, rubbing his hands.

Kennan suddenly remembered the red feather duster, the gift from Catherine Breshkovsky for Natalia Armfeld. He had hidden it in the lining of his overcoat, which now hung in the hallway of Nikolin's house. A gendarme distrustful enough to search a tooth in a convict's mouth could well order a search of his overcoat. He half expected that a Cossack would enter the room with a red feather duster in his hand, for which there was no innocent explanation. "I might as well try to explain the presence of a mouse-trap and a fire-extinguisher in a diving-bell!"

No Cossack entered and Capt. Nikolin changed the topic to the comfortable lives, as he described them, that political convicts led at

Kara. Kennan found it hard to act the role of a naïve traveler who was "naturally surprised and delighted to find that political convicts . . . were really treated with humanity, consideration, and benevolent kindness by an intelligent and philanthropic commandant." At the end of their meeting, Capt. Nikolin declined Kennan's request for permission to visit the Political Prison but unexpectedly suggested that Kennan, if he wanted, could visit the political convicts in the free command. Kennan, who did not disclose that he planned to go there next, wondered whether Nikolin's casual suggestion was some kind of trick. Nonetheless, he intended to see Natalia Armfeld even if Capt. Nikolin was trying to entrap him. He left Capt. Nikolin's house and, following the directions given him by other exiles, he made his way to Armfeld's hut just after sunset and knocked on the door. The meeting with Capt. Nikolin had left him tense and anxious.[151]

A woman in her early thirties opened the door. She had a spare figure, dark, short-cropped hair, luminescent eyes, and a chalk-pale face that suggested tuberculosis.

"Does Miss Armfeld live here?"

"I am Miss Armfeld."

"My name is George Kennan. I am an American traveler, and I have come to Siberia to investigate the exile system." Kennan explained that he had a letter of introduction from a political exile who knew her and a gift from one of her friends. She stared at him in bewildered astonishment. "Pray come in." Kennan entered a tiny room with a bare wooden floor, log walls, and a ceiling made from rough planks. The homemade furniture consisted of a pine table, three pine chairs, and a narrow bed covered with a rough gray blanket. Shelves on either side of the door held a few cooking utensils, plates, cups and saucers, and a samovar. Behind a low partition was an oven with a chimney that rose through the roof. "Everything was scrupulously neat and clean, but in other respects the house looked like the home of some wretchedly poor Irish laborer."

Kennan started to hand her the letter of introduction, which he had

The Armfelds' cabin at the mines of Kara, 1885 (from *Siberia and the Exile System* 2:185)

kept in his pocket, and the red feather duster, but she blocked his arm. "Stop. Don't do that!" With shaking hands, she closed the shutters, bolted the door, and lit a candle. "You are not accustomed to the atmosphere of alarm and apprehension in which we live. You might have been seen through the window giving me a letter." She took the letter and the feather duster but instead of opening the letter, stared at Kennan with no less amazement than if a long-dead relative had walked in.

"How did you ever get here?"

Kennan described how he had crossed the mountains on horseback from Stretinsk. "But how were you ever *allowed* to come here?"

Kennan briefly summarized his investigation of the exile system, including his visits to prisons and encounters with political exiles, but did not mention his meeting with Capt. Nikolin. Natalia, who spoke three languages, switched from Russian to English. "You are the first foreigner that I have seen since my exile. Excuse me for staring at you so, and pardon me if I have not seemed to welcome you cordially; but I can hardly believe that I am awake. I feel as Livingstone must have felt when Stanley found him in Central Africa."[152]

Natalia Armfeld had grown up in a prominent family in European Russia. Her father had been a Russian army general and her sister was a writer on scientific subjects. She became a revolutionary but that part of her life ended in 1879 when gendarmes raided her secret cell in Kyiv. Gunfire broke out and both sides had casualties. The authorities hung two of the cell members and the rest, including Armfeld, were sentenced to Siberian prisons followed by exile for life. Less is known about Natalia Armfeld than other women revolutionaries, but she might be understood through the fictional Maria Pavlovna in Tolstoy's *Resurrection*.

Tolstoy, who was a friend of the Armfeld family, apparently drew on Natalia in creating Pavlovna, who speaks three languages and whose father is a general. Pavlovna becomes a revolutionary because, like many young Russian women from well-to-do backgrounds, she loathes her upper-class life and loves, as Tolstoy wrote, "the life of the common people. And she was always being scolded for spending her time in the servants' hall, in the kitchen or the stables instead of the drawing-room." Sexual love repels Pavlovna, who regards it as mystifying and distasteful, and she dedicates her life to helping others "so naturally that those who knew her no longer [were grateful] but simply expected it of her." After Pavlovna and her fellow revolutionaries fight a gun battle with the gendarmes, she is sent to Siberia.[153]

"How did the remarkable idea of coming to Siberia and investigating the life of political exiles ever enter your head?" Natalia asked Kennan.

Kennan was answering her question when he was interrupted by a frail voice.

"Who is there, Natalia? With whom are you talking?"

"It is an American traveler, Mother, who has found us even here at the mines."

Natalia's mother, Anna Vasil'evna, emerged from behind the partition where she had been sleeping. Russian mothers often supported their revolutionary daughters even when they did not approve of their activities. They let their daughters use their homes for secret meetings, helped them to smuggle funds, and even visited them in their hiding places. Sophia Perovskaya, who led the People's Will assassins of Tsar Alexander II, wrote her mother that "in every moment of doubt and hesitation your image has sustained me." Anna Vasil'evna sympathized with and even took pride in her daughter's revolutionary deeds. Following Natalia's imprisonment, but before she was sent to Siberia, her mother obtained the plans for her prison and recruited persons to dig an escape tunnel, which was half-completed when Natalia was transferred to another prison. After hearing frightening reports of beatings and suicides at the Kara mines, Anna Vasil'evna, gray-haired and in her sixties, traveled across Siberia to be with her daughter. She would soon be leaving because her other children in European Russia also needed her.

When Anna Vasil'evna came into full view from behind the oven, and Kennan saw the dark circles around her eyes, he almost had to look away. He explained that he had to return to Maj. Potuloff's home for dinner but would come back later that night. At seven o'clock he returned to the hut, where political convicts from the free command had begun gathering to meet the American journalist. A lit samovar stood on the pine table. Every few minutes, someone tapped softly on a window shutter and Natalia went to the door. She cautiously asked who was there and, once satisfied that it was a political convict, unbolted and opened the door. Kennan recognized by name one political convict who entered the cabin, Maria Kolenkina, who had set out in 1878 to kill a prosecutor in the Trial of the 193 but could not gain access to his residence and was caught months later after a gun battle with gendarmes.

The soft knocks, the gloomy interior of the cabin, and the intensity of the captured young men and women sitting around the pine table, had a dreamlike quality, as though Kennan had entered a revolutionary netherworld where the overthrow of the regime was as certain as the rotation of the earth. He listened to their harrowing stories of life at Kara and answered as best he could their many questions about the latest revolutionary developments. Kennan was no longer surprised by the strength and commitment of the revolutionary women like Armfeld and Kolenkina. In fact, they impressed him with their "power of endurance and a stern inflexibility of character rarely found in men." But he was always struck by how often the exiled revolutionary women he met in Siberia, some of whom had taken part in horrific events, were delicate girls. Had he not known of their activities "I should have taken [them] for teachers in a Sunday-school or rather timid pupils in a female seminary."[154]

As Kennan made notes, he heard a loud, angry-sounding knock on a window shutter. Maria Kolenkina whispered that "it's the gendarmes! Don't let them come in. Tell them who of us are here, and perhaps they'll be satisfied." Natalia went to the door and calmly said to the men outside, "We are all here: my mother, I, Kurteief, Madame Kolenkina—" Kennan could not hear the other names but he was not nearly as calm as Natalia appeared to be since Capt. Nikolin could easily claim that he had never given him permission to visit the free command. After a few minutes' discussion, Natalia closed and rebolted the door. "They were satisfied; they didn't insist on coming in," she told the gathering. For Kennan's benefit, she explained that "the gendarmes visit us three times a day to see what we are doing, and to make sure that we have not escaped. Their visits, however, have grown to be formal, and they do not always come in."

As the conversation resumed, Kennan's attention was attracted to a man in his early thirties with vacant eyes. Unexpectedly he spoke to Kennan. "We—have—a—graveyard—of—our—own—here. Would—you—like—to—see—it?" Taken aback, Kennan struggled for a reply, but then realized that the man may have gone mad. "This strange, unprompted question, with its suggestions of insanity and death, seemed to render more vivid and terrible the stories of human suffering that I just heard." Kennan stayed until midnight and then walked back to Maj. Potuloff's home where everyone had gone to sleep, except for Frost who had been anxiously waiting up. Kennan tried to fall asleep, but "all that I had just seen and heard kept surging through my mind."

The next morning Kennan returned with Frost to the Armfeld hut which, in the daytime, appeared even more threadbare than it had at night. Natalia had placed in the middle of the tiny room a crudely made easel holding an unframed oil painting of Anna Vasil'evna. "I have been trying to make a portrait of my mother," she explained. "Of course I shall never see her again—she is too old and feeble to make another journey to Eastern Siberia—and I want something to recall her face to me when she has gone out of my life." Natalia did not lack for artistic skills, but the rough canvas and the limited paint colors, especially with which to capture skin tones, had defeated her. At best, it was a grotesque likeness of her mother. "I know that it is a bad portrait, and I am almost ashamed to show it to you; but I wish to ask your help. I have only a few colors, I cannot get any more, and perhaps Mr. Frost may be able to suggest some way of using my scanty materials to better advantage."

Frost examined the painting and Natalia's few brushes and paints and glanced at Kennan with a guarded, hopeless expression. Kennan could have suggested that Frost make a sketch of Natalia's mother, but he could not bring himself to in any way "criticize a work of love executed under such circumstances in the face of such disheartening difficulties." Several political convicts, including Maria Kolenkina, entered the hut, which distracted Natalia's attention from the painting.

That evening Kennan made his fourth visit in twenty-four hours to the Armfelds, who clung to him "with an eagerness that was almost pathetic." He agreed to deliver letters from Natalia and her mother to their family members in European Russia even though carrying letters from a political convict was a crime under Russian law. "If they were willing to run the risk of writing such letters, I was willing to run the risk of carrying them." Before leaving Kennan promised to visit Count Tolstoy after his return to European Russia and give him a report on the Armfelds' circumstances.[155]

Maj. Potuloff returned late that night. Kennan devoted the next morning to working on his notes in a secluded part of the house. Capt. Nikolin came to the house and went with Maj. Potuloff into a room that opened on to the drawing room, where Frost was making a crayon portrait of the major's children. After discreetly listening to their conversation, Frost went to Kennan and whispered that he had overheard Nikolin and Potuloff discuss Kennan's meetings with the political convicts in the free command and then argue whether to search the Americans' luggage. Capt. Nikolin had insisted on a search, Frost explained, but Maj. Potuloff defended Kennan and Frost and pointed out that searching the luggage of foreigners might create a diplomatic incident. Nikolin responded that, whether in Kara or not, at some point the luggage would be searched.

Kennan spent the rest of the day in a state of anxious indecisiveness. Discovery by Capt. Nikolin of the Armfeld letters in his luggage could send Natalia back into the prison and even result in his own arrest but destroying the letters would betray his promise to deliver them. Kennan avoided being alone with Maj. Potuloff for fear that he would ask whether he was carrying letters from political convicts and he did not want to lie to a man he had come to like. Pleading a headache, Kennan went to his room early in the evening. He lay awake all night and by morning decided that the letters had to be destroyed. As happened each morning, a soldier came into his room, lit the coals in a brick oven, and left. Kennan waited for the sentry at the front door to move to a position where he could not see through the bedroom window. He quickly opened the iron door to the oven and shoved in the Armfeld letters, which crisply burned to ashes. He erased the names of political exiles in his journals and wrote codes in their place.

On November 12, 1885, Maj. Potuloff took Kennan and Frost in his carriage from the Lower Diggings to Ust Kara. They passed two free command political convicts in long gray overcoats, who removed their caps and bowed. Kennan and Frost slept that night in the house of the overseer of the Ust Kara prison and the next morning they prepared to begin the return trip over the mountains to Stretinsk. Maj. Potuloff had brought a bottle of white Crimean wine and three cups. He offered a toast before they mounted their horses. "Here's to the beginning of a journey to America." Kennan and Frost planned to visit the silver mines while on the way to St. Petersburg, but it was the start of their return journey.

Within a year, Natalia was dead, and her mother soon after. Kennan regretted burning the letters because his luggage was never searched. He also came to question whether his companion had actually heard Capt. Nikolin and Maj. Potuloff discuss searching their luggage or had only imagined it.[156]

11

There Are People Who
Intend to Murder Us

The return horseback ride across the mountains to Stretinsk so depleted Kennan that he struggled afterward to walk even a short distance. He and Frost rested for several days in a peasant's log house on the bank of the Shilka River and then set out in a carriage for the silver mines despite reports that smallpox had broken out along their route. After twenty miles they were so cold and hungry that they stopped in the village of Kopun and knocked on a door, hoping it would be safe to buy food.

"Will you be kind enough to tell me whether you have smallpox in the house?" Kennan asked the woman who opened the door.

"Yes, we have."

Kennan and Frost had tied a bag of bread to the back of the carriage before leaving Stretinsk. They opened it, brushed off the dirt thrown up by the carriage's wheels, broke off pieces, and gnawed at the frozen chunks. "O Kennan!" said Frost, "if I only had some warm milk-toast!" Under cloudy skies they traveled between mountains with stunted, leafless bushes. In Shelapugina, where the driver stopped to change horses, the station master assured them that the post station was free of smallpox. Kennan and Frost, too worn out to go any farther, took their chances and slept that night on the station floor. The next morning, restored by a decent night's sleep and a hot breakfast, they continued to the mines. The temperature fell to minus fifteen degrees Fahrenheit and frost coated the horses.[157]

Since they were first dug in the 1700s, the silver mines, and later the placer gold mines, had been worked by Siberian peasants, exiled Decembrists, Polish insurgents captured after their failed 1863 rebellion against Russian domination of Poland, and convicts sentenced to hard labor. Exiles feared being sent anywhere in the Nerchinsk Mining Region, but the deep underground silver mineshafts may have been the most dreaded destination of all. The mineshafts were primitive, cramped tunnels dug into the hillsides where hard-labor convicts worked shifts of twelve hours each; the day shift existed in near-perpetual darkness. The convicts thought of the shafts as monsters intent on devouring them, which reflected a Russian superstition that the "earth was a dark underworld populated by a host of evil demons."

The superstition had some truth. Convicts died in cave-ins, from dynamite explosions, or by suffocating from lack of oxygen. The mining authorities treated the convicts, who had little modern mining equipment, like beasts of burden. A hard-labor sentence to the mines, wrote historian Daniel Beer, was "so arduous and soul-destroying . . . that many convicts resorted to drastic measures to avoid it." Some claimed to have committed gruesome murders, hoping that an investigation would at least temporarily keep them out of the mines. Others exposed their bare hands to subzero temperatures in the winter to induce frostbite and, perhaps the best outcome, the amputation of their fingers. They even simulated the symptoms of syphilis by inserting tiny filaments of horsehair into minute cuts on their penises.[158]

Kennan and Frost stopped for tea in Kavwikuchigazamurskaya, whose name struck Kennan as having more letters than the village had people.

They inspected a prison in Alexandrofski Zavod, where they found lunatics and sane inmates crowded together in the same cells. Their carriage followed a road that ascended one side of a low range of mountains that were not much more than towering mounds of dirt, and then plunged down the other side to the village of Algachi, where they found a lodging house. The peasant hostess brought out a steaming samovar and served them buttermilk. Kennan and Frost thawed their bread by toasting chunks of it over a crackling fire. "We went to bed on the floor about nine o'clock—warm, comfortable, and happy."

The next morning the warden of the Algachi prison and the resident mining engineer readily agreed to show them the prison and the silver mine but insisted on first serving breakfast to their American guests, which included vodka, Crimean wine, and to Kennan's amazement, Boston canned lemonade. The warden told Kennan and Frost that "I am afraid that you will find our prison the worst you have ever seen." The prison was a dilapidated one-story log building that tilted noticeably to one side. Kennan and Frost entered a cell whose walls were covered with dried blood and dotted with crushed bedbugs. "I had suffered enough in Siberia myself from vermin fully to understand and appreciate the significance of that dull-red band." They inspected hospital wards where several convicts, who had been torn apart in dynamite accidents in the mines, lay on cots under bloody sheets.

Kennan observed that half of the convicts in the prison stayed in their cells while the other half were at the mines. The idle convicts, he pointed out to the warden, might be put to work cutting trees and building a larger and better prison. "In a few months you would have here a prison fit for a human being to live in."

"My dear sir. I cannot send convicts into the woods without orders to do so. Suppose some of them should escape—as they probably would—I should be held responsible." The warden added that he had continually reported the condition of the prison to St. Petersburg. If prison officials baffled Kennan, so did the inmates who, instead of revolting, submitted to an existence that, he wrote in his journal, was "as hard as human life can be made . . . Our convicts would pull down the [Algachi] prison and all make their escape in less than a week, but patient endurance + submission to authority are a part of the Russian character."

Kennan and Frost finished their inspection of the prison and rode in the mining engineer's carriage to the Algachi silver mine, passing double-humped Bactrian camels grazing on frozen grass poking above the snow. The mining engineer declined to accompany Kennan and Frost into the mine and turned them over to a convict who had six sticks of dynamite casually jammed into a pocket of his sheepskin coat with their long fuses dangling out. The convict handed Kennan and Frost each a candle and led them through a doorway into the mountain. Frost thought of the inscription at the entrance to Hell in Dante's *Divine Comedy:* "Abandon All Hope, Ye Who Enter Here." They lit their candles and followed the convict, who dexterously led them down a series of ladders, some with missing rungs, while holding his lit candle in one hand. Sometimes a ladder unexpectedly ended in midair. With a black void below them, Kennan and Frost had to hold on with one hand to both ladder and candle and grope with the other hand for the adjacent ladder. In places there were no ladders but only thick logs with notched, slippery steps.

After they descended several hundred feet on dozens of ladders and logs, the convict led them through a maze of horizontal passages with loose floor planks. Their candle flames frequently turned blue and flickered out and they had to continue in the dark, their heads scraping the passage roof, until they reached a space with enough oxygen to relight the candles. Frost crystals, formed in the subterranean cold, clung to the walls and ceilings like snow. Silver in the newly dynamited ore glittered in the candlelight.

Kennan's and Frost's minds, however, were not on the beauty of the frost crystals and the silver but on the dynamite sticks in the convict's sheepskin coat. As frightening as they had found the descents on the ladders and logs, they were even more terrified that their guide would trip on the floor planks and cause his candle to ignite the fuses of the dynamite sticks. The explosion, Kennan imagined, would blow them out of the mine "like wads from a Fourth-of-July cannon" and at best they would end up under bloody sheets in the prison hospital.[159]

The primitive level of the mining operation astonished Kennan. The convict-miners used crowbars and pickaxes to hack out the silver ore, which was brought to the surface by baskets hoisted by hand-operated windlasses. The ventilation system consisted of a hand-cranked fan that generated more noise than air flow. Kennan and Frost returned to the surface by the same perilous route and emerged aboveground into a sharp, cold wind. In a tool house men and women convicts sat cross-legged, breaking up silver ore with short hammers. "The way in which the work was being carried on would have brought a contemptuous smile to the face of a Nevada miner."

They continued to the Pokrofski, Kadainski and Savenski silver mines. Frost, who was tired, did not accompany Kennan into these mines. The temperature in the Pokrofski mine was comparatively warm but "why it should thaw in this mine and freeze in the mine of Alga-chi, only four miles away, I could not understand," and the resident mining engineer could not explain it either. Water dripped from the walls and often formed pools on the floors several inches deep, which Kennan had to splash through behind his convict-guide. They half crawled, half crouched as they made their way through passages filled with acrid smoke from recent dynamite explosions. He went into some caverns that had been mined since the time of Catherine the Great. One passage in the Kadainski mine was braced by crossed logs which, blackened by time, no longer bore any resemblance to wood. Kennan pulled rotten fibers from the log supports and decided that this was the most dangerous place he had ever seen. His guide suggested that they leave immediately.

With an American sensibility Kennan pointed out to a mining official that the additional costs of much-needed modern mining and ventilation equipment would be more than offset by improved

productivity. "What is the use of pottering along in the way you do? . . .
I don't see how the present state of affairs can be profitable to anyone."
The official shrugged his shoulders as if to say he did not know or did
not care. Before leaving the Nerchinsk Mining District, Kennan looked
for the graves of the Polish exiles and a Decembrist conspirator who
had died at the mines but was unable to find them.[160]

In 1827, Princess Maria Volkonsky reached the Blagodatsk silver mine
in the Nerchinsk Mining Region. She thought that it would have been
a beautiful place if the trees and vegetation had not been cut down
for thirty miles around so that guards could more easily spot escaping
convicts. Another Decembrist wife had arrived a few days before Maria and obtained permission to see her husband. "Prepare yourself for
the worst," she warned Maria. After signing a document limiting her
right to see Sergei to twice a week and only in the presence of guards,
Maria was taken to his cell, where he was confined when he was not
in the mines. The guards opened the cell door and she stepped into
darkness. She heard metal clanging on stone and then her husband, his
legs encased in heavy chains, stood before her. Maria for the first time
fully understood the sacrifice he had made for his ideals. "A feeling of
exaltation and great pride swept over me. To the bewilderment of the
guards, I knelt on the filthy floor and kissed the chains."[161]

On November 23, 1885, Kennan and Frost started out for the town
of Nerchinsk, two hundred miles away. The road ran through more
featureless mountains, the temperature dropped to well below zero, and
their hired carriages were the most uncomfortable they had yet experienced. "We suffered from cold, hunger, jolting, and sleeplessness until
we were reduced to a state of silent, moody, half-savage exasperation,
in which life or at least *such* a life—seemed no longer worth living, and
we were ready to barter all our earthly rights and possessions for a hot

bath, a good dinner and twelve hours of unbroken sleep in a warm, clean bed." The only available hotel in Nerchinsk, a town of a few thousand, instead proved to be the worst Kennan and Frost had yet experienced in Siberia.

Their dirty room had no beds, the floor was pocked with rat holes, and the air smelled of charcoal. The only servant, a boy in a red flannel shirt, brought them a brass wash pan that had been used, not just for rinsing hands and faces, but for other human functions, and looked as though it had never been adequately cleaned. Resigning themselves to the appalling hotel, Kennan and Frost spent a few days exploring the town. They met with several political convicts who had endured the mines of Kara and were now serving sentences of exile in Nerchinsk. A courteous bankruptcy receiver guided Kennan and Frost through the town landmark, which was the palatial, but deserted, residence of the Butin brothers, once prosperous mine owners who had fallen on hard times. The silken curtains, stained-glass windows, old Flemish paintings, and spacious library with a large collection of Siberian minerals, overwhelmed both men.

They resumed their westward journey but, since the road was now buried under snow, their vehicle was a horse-drawn, partly covered sleigh. Icicles hung from the nostrils of the horses, the dry snow squeaked under the runners, and the mountains had a frigid blue tinge. Just before dark they stopped fifty miles from Chita to change horses at the post station in Turinopovorotnaya, where the temperature hovered around minus twenty degrees Fahrenheit and the town was drunk. Merry, intoxicated young people rode back and forth in sleighs. Lines of inebriated peasant girls in colorful dresses, despite the cold, paraded through the town with their arms around one another, singing. Kennan and Frost went into the crowded post station to request fresh horses and a driver but everyone there was drunk, other than a baby.

In succession, Kennan asked a village official, a priest, and the station master what was being celebrated, but they were all too drunk to explain, let alone help him find a driver and horses. "In fact, we could

Kennan next to his horse-drawn sleigh during his Siberian exile investigation, 1885–1886 (courtesy Library of Congress, Prints and Photographs Division)

not find anyone who seemed sober enough to know the difference between a horse and his harness." He and Frost took their luggage into the post station and sat down on the floor in a corner "to study intoxicated humanity and await further developments." They watched a drunken young Russian army officer kiss every woman in the room and then devoutly cross himself. The celebration began to subside as some revelers left, but the requested horses had yet to appear.

Kennan told the station master that there would be trouble unless horses were brought out and harnessed to their sleigh. The station master, whose drunkenness had taken the form of "severe official dignity," expressed shock that drinking was taking place in his station. He went outside and began shouting for help finding horses and a driver, but he was met with drunken hoots from the carousers still in the streets. Finally, a driver appeared to report that he had harnessed fresh horses to Kennan and Frost's sleigh and they were ready to leave. The station master fined the driver, as far as Kennan could tell, either "for being sober or for having the horses ready." They left the drunken town for

Chita. When the shouting and laughter had faded, Kennan asked the driver, "What's the matter with everybody in this village? The whole population seems to be drunk."

"They've been consecrating a new church," replied the driver.

"Consecrating a church!" Kennan was dumbfounded. "You're the only sober man I've seen in the place. How does it happen that you're not drunk?"

"I'm not a Christian. I'm a Buryat." It struck Kennan that the only sober person in the Christian village was a non-Christian.

Kennan and Frost had stopped for two days in Chita on their way to the mines but this time they stayed for two weeks. In the daytime, Kennan called on officials and prominent citizens to allay any suspicions about their presence in the town and at night he and Frost met with the town's political exiles. While in Chita, Kennan found a discarded small portrait of one of the Decembrists, which he kept in his luggage. During his investigation, Kennan met long-serving Siberian officials who recalled the Decembrists as "men of character and education." He thought of the Decembrists as "gallant young noblemen who vainly endeavored to overthrow the Russian autocracy and to establish a constitutional form of government."[162]

After eleven months at the Blagodatsk mines, the exiled Decembrists, accompanied by their wives, including Princess Maria Volkonsky, were sent to Chita. The men lived together in a prison barracks and the wives found houses. "We see our husbands twice a week for three hours and we are allowed to send them dinner," wrote Maria from Chita. "Often the clanking of their chains summons us to the window, from which we watch with a bitter-sweet joy as they go to work." Maria's spirits had been remarkably high, but in Chita she learned that her son Nikolenka had died at age two. The poet Pushkin, a friend from her aristocratic days, sent Maria a poem that was later engraved on the boy's tomb. "With a smile he looks upon earthly exile, Blesses his mother and prays for his father." A Decembrist wife close to Maria recalled that "Nikolenka took Maria's laughter with him."

The Decembrists' living conditions gradually improved, although the tsar adamantly refused to consider amnesty. They were permitted to receive books and have a workshop in a two-story log building. A Decembrist was allowed to marry a lover who had followed him to Siberia. The clanking of the other Decembrists' chains as they filed into the church for the wedding drowned out the organ. They eventually received permission to remove their chains, which two of the Decembrists fashioned into bracelets in their workshop. The wives, who proudly wore the bracelets, could now spend time alone with their husbands and soon several were pregnant. In 1832 Maria gave birth to a son and, two years later, to a daughter.[163]

The Chita exiles were among the most cultured and appealing that Kennan encountered in Siberia, and their stories among the most tragic. Frost sketched one meeting of men in *kosovorotkas,* long embroidered shirts belted around their waists, and women wearing long dresses. Most are in their twenties and thirties. They stand or sit around a table with a tall samovar, talk, gesture, smoke, and drink tea. They seem to know each other well. Kennan's evenings with them, in the same building where the Decembrists had their workshop, were a mix of gloom and warmth.

They discussed the condition of Russia and the Russian revolutionary movement, and the exiles told Kennan what had happened to their friends and comrades in Siberia, which ones had committed suicide and how. Madame Kavalefskaya went mad at Kara, but the humane Col. Konovich sent her to Minusinsk where her husband lived in exile. In his company she recovered sufficiently, the authorities decided, to be returned to Kara, where she again went mad and killed herself. Kennan listened silently to these stories, his eyes moist with tears. "I am not ashamed of it," he later wrote. "It would have been a relief to me sometimes if I could have cried."

A meeting of political exiles in Chita, 1885 (from *Siberia and the Exile System* 2:337)

But there were cheerful moments, too. A Russian exile played romantic Russian ballads on a battered guitar and Kennan and Frost sang American songs. One evening ended with choruses of Russian revolutionary songs and the American "John Brown's Body."[164]

Kennan and Frost's hotel room in Chita was next to a room occupied by four policemen, including an officer, with only a thin wall between them. Kennan returned at two in the morning from a meeting with political exiles and lay down on the floor next to the thin wall. Frost slept peacefully on a wooden bench. A revolver shot suddenly rang out on the other side of the wall, almost, it seemed to Kennan, next to his head, and he heard what sounded like falling plaster. Frost woke up. The stillness that followed was as puzzling as the shot. Kennan and Frost heard whispers on the other side of the partition and the click of a revolver being cocked and uncocked, but no more shots were fired.

Kennan dismissed the incident as a prank played by drunken Russian policemen on two American travelers, but later wrote in his journal under
the heading "Frost's illusions" that his companion believed the men in
the next room were "concocting plots against us." Kennan did not realize
it then, but Frost, who, as mentioned, had suffered a nervous breakdown
not long before coming to Siberia, was on the verge of another.[165]

They spent a final evening with the Chita exiles and the next day
resumed their return journey to St. Petersburg. Their immediate goal
was Irkutsk on the far side of Lake Baikal, which they had crossed by
steamer the previous fall. They traveled west for five days and nights,
stopping only to change horses. Lake Baikal had not yet frozen over and
the steamers had stopped running for the season, so they had to skirt the
southern end of the lake. The absence of horses at a post station halted
them sixty miles from Irkutsk, but the two were so impatient to get to
Irkutsk, which meant civilization, that they hired a peasant to take them
in his freight-sleigh. At night on the mountainous road the peasant's
half-starved horses refused to pull the heavy sleigh uphill. Kennan and
Frost had to get out and in the dark stumble alongside the now-lightened
sleigh to the next post station.

The next day, December 15, they reached Irkutsk and eagerly went
to the post office, where they found letters waiting for them, including
seventeen from Emiline for Kennan. They checked into a decent hotel,
had a hot meal, and happily read their letters. They now only had to
cross the Angara River to the Great Siberian Post Road, which would
take them to Tiumen, where they could board a train to St. Petersburg.
But despite the frigid temperatures the Angara was still open at midriver.
Since the river had no bridges and the river ferries no longer ran, the
Americans had to wait in Irkutsk for the Angara to freeze over. They
celebrated New Year's Eve of 1885 in Irkutsk.[166]

In 1844, Maria Volkonsky received permission to move with her son
and daughter to Irkutsk, but her husband, Sergei, was not allowed to

accompany them. The appearance of an actual princess was cause for celebration in Irkutsk, even though Maria was still registered as "the wife of state criminal Volkonsky." She reciprocated the town's affection through philanthropic projects such as raising funds to expand the town's foundling hospital and to build a new theatre and concert hall. Sergei was eventually allowed to join Maria in the city (their house still stands). In 1854 Sergei's sister, Princess Sophia, traveled to Irkutsk to visit her brother. Sophia attended a concert with Maria that celebrated the opening of the new theatre. At the end the audience stood and gave a standing ovation to Maria, who sat in a box seat with Sophia.

"I see that you have a kingdom of your own out here in Siberia," said Sophia.

"A kingdom I bought with my tears," replied Maria.

After Nicholas I's death in 1855, his successor Alexander II issued a proclamation of amnesty for the Decembrists. By then Maria and her children had been allowed to return to European Russia, where copies of *Dekabristy* bracelets became the rage among stylish women.[167]

Kennan and Frost heard reports from peasants that an ice bridge had formed on the Angara River one hundred miles north of Irkutsk. On January 8, they set out in a sleigh on a road along the Angara's eastern riverbank. They stopped to visit the Alexandrofski central prison, which had a reputation as a model prison. After inspecting the prison, with its adequate space for the inmates, clean-smelling air, a decent hospital, and even a schoolroom for inmates to read books or listen to lectures by priests, Kennan told the warden that he had thus far inspected fifteen prisons and his was by far the best. While "I did not find much to approve in Siberian prisons generally," as he later wrote, "I am glad to have the opportunity to praise where praise is deserved."

Near the village of Olon on the way to the ice bridge, the riverbank became so steep that the driver had to veer onto the river, whose ice was dangerously thin in places. As the horses picked up speed, the ice gave way underneath them. The sleigh's extended, stabilizing outriggers held on to the unbroken ice, which kept it from fully sliding into the frigid waters, a reprise of Kennan's mishap on the Lena River in 1867. It was night by the time they had dragged the horses and the partly submerged sleigh out of the river. The incident left Frost especially agitated, insisting that the driver had deliberately plunged the sleigh through the ice. Kennan had to calm him down.

Crossing the ice bridge on the Angara River, 1886 (from *Siberia and the Exile System* 2:354)

Peasants on this route earned money in the winter by coming to the aid of stranded travelers. A peasant from Olon agreed, for an exorbitant amount, to take Kennan and Frost in his sleigh to the next post station. Local villagers advised them not to continue on either the river or the road but instead travel over the mountains. During a heavy snowstorm in the steep, roadless terrain the peasant lost his way and the sleigh bogged down in snowdrifts and frequently capsized. The strain of repeatedly pushing, pulling, or righting the sleigh exhausted Kennan, pain in his lungs returned, and he struggled to breathe. At the village of Kamenka their peasant driver finally found the ice bridge, which was a jumble of ice blocks that had piled up at a narrow bend in the Angara River. They crossed to the other side on a rough path carved by sleighs through the ice blocks and stayed that night in a comfortable post station on the Great Siberian Post Road.[168]

At the post station they hired a heavy sleigh suited for travel in the heart of the Russian winter and bought provisions, including tea, sugar, bread, condensed milk, boiled ham, and several roasted grouse. From peasants they purchased shaggy sheepskin coats, heavy felt boots, fur caps, and thick mittens. They acquired a heavy sheepskin sleeping bag, which was large enough for both of them, and placed it at the bottom of the seatless sleigh and then covered it with blankets. Even in a sheepskin sleeping bag buried under blankets and wearing their sheepskin coats, the two men were still so stiff from the cold after a night's ride on the Great Siberian Post Road that they had trouble climbing out of the sleigh at the post stations.

Heavy snow reduced visibility on the road. Peering ahead, Kennan and Frost glimpsed what they thought were oncoming sleighs, but, on hearing clinking sounds, they realized it was an exile convoy. Cossacks in fur hats, thick coats, and heavy boots, and shouldering muskets with fixed bayonets, appeared in the snowflakes, followed by the convicts in their chains. The plodding convicts, who wore short overcoats, loose leather boots, and gray caps, had tied handkerchiefs or rags around their ears and stuffed hay into their boots, trying to ward off the cold. Kennan asked his driver to pull their sleigh over to the side of the road.

As the half-frozen, exhausted men struggled by, a few convicts broke ranks and approached Kennan's sleigh, evidently with permission obtained by the convoy's *artel* from the guards. The convicts held out their caps and sang the "Begging Song," a mix of chanting, singing, and keening for the dead that Kennan thought was the most grief-stricken, despairing sound that he had ever heard. "Have pity on us, O our fathers! . . . We from all our kin have parted, We are prisoners! Pity us, O our fathers!" Kennan put a few coins into any cap that was held out to him, even though he knew that the convicts would use it to buy vodka on the road. Bringing up the rear of the party were single horse-drawn, open sleighs carrying convicts who had collapsed on the road and now clung to one another to keep warm. The exile party vanished into the falling snow and the clinking sounds faded away.

Thousands of horse-drawn freight sleighs traveled in caravans in both directions on the Great Siberian Post Road. Winter storms and the passage of so many freight caravans had reshaped the snow into giant frozen waves, known to Siberian travelers as *ukhabi,* that were sometimes ten feet high. Under the driver's lash the horses pulled Kennan and Frost's sleigh up to the crest of one wave, charged down into the trough, and climbed up the next wave. Crashing through the *ukhabi* "jarred every bone and shocked every nerve-ganglion in one's body." In Frost's sketch, a procession of rising and falling sleighs make their way single file through *ukhabi* that stretch to the horizon. The grizzled driver in the lead sleigh clenches a lit cigar between his teeth as he whips three straining horses through the *ukhabi.*[169]

Siberia seemed to expose the vulnerabilities in the two spent men on their return journey. Frost's weakness was his mental instability, but Kennan's was religion. One night after a rough passage through the *ukhabi,* Kennan lay down on a plank in a post station during a changeover of horses. He fell asleep and dreamed that he had been invited to address a Sunday school run by the Church of the "Holy Monopolists," a new sect that believed in "only one thing." Kennan, uncomfortable that he did know what the "one thing" was, decided to give a talk on the comparative merits of Mohammedanism and Buddhism. Before he could begin, the Sunday school superintendent asked him to identify "the first progressive-euchre [a card game] player that after his death was brought back from Alaska amid the mourning of a nation?"

Kennan, ashamed of himself for not even having heard of an

Exiles passing a caravan of freight sleighs, 1886 (from *Siberia and the Exile System* 2: Front Matter)

Ukhabi (snow-waves) near Krasnoyarsk, 1886 (from *Siberia and the Exile System* 2:362)

Alaskan euchre player, confessed to the Sunday school that he did not know who the progressive-euchre player was—and woke up to find two travelers standing over him. He struggled to recall why he was in the cold room. "What's the matter?" one asked. "You have been moaning as if you were in pain." Kennan only said, "I have had a bad dream." When the horses were ready, Kennan walked stiffly out to the sleigh and crawled into the sleeping bag next to Frost. Kennan later described the dream in his book about his Siberian investigation, but without explaining what it might mean, although it likely reflected his guilt over the pain he had caused his family, and especially his mother, by questioning their faith and leaving the church. Kennan later had a different, happier dream on his return journey, which he described in his journal as about "kissing Lena."[170]

The journey west from Irkutsk to Krasnoyarsk took nine days and required forty-three changes of horses; the temperature dropped as low as minus forty-five degrees Fahrenheit. At one post station white vapors jetted through cracks in the door and a half inch of frost covered the ends of bolts protruding into a room through the window casings. In Krasnoyarsk two young men followed Kennan and Frost, mimicking their gestures. "The intention to be offensive was so extraordinary and deliberate," Kennan wrote, "that I at once suspected some sort of police trap." Three days after leaving Krasnoyarsk, Kennan and Frost reached Minusinsk.

Soon after their arrival, the inspector of police appeared in their rented room and demanded to know what business they had in the town and "what kind of people" they were. Without a uniform, Kennan thought, the police inspector "would have been taken anywhere for a particularly bad type of common convict." Kennan handed the letters of introduction from the Russian ministries to the inspector, saying "perhaps you will be able to find out from these." The police inspector read the letters, which had protected them so far, bowed, and withdrew but the encounter further alarmed both Kennan and Frost.

Kennan's anxiety was less for himself than for his journals, letters, and other documents, some forty pounds of material. He decided to ship them to a trusted friend in St. Petersburg rather than risk their seizure by the Russian authorities. With the help of his Minusinsk contacts, Kennan found an exiled Polish carpenter, who constructed a box with hidden compartments. He packed his documents into the compartments and put the box on a mail sleigh to St. Petersburg. "From that time forward I was never free from my anxiety about it.

The package contained all the results of my Siberian work, and its loss would have been simply irreplaceable."[171]

On February 4, Kennan and Frost left Minusinsk. They were overtaken by a winter gale, which slowed their sleigh to a crawl. Every several hundred yards the sleigh became so mired in deep, soft snow that Kennan and Frost had to get out and push it. Finally the exhausted horses, despite the driver's furious curses and lashings, refused to pull the sleigh. "They were perfectly well aware that nothing was to be gained by floundering about aimlessly the rest of the night on that desert of drifted snow." Their driver cursed his fate, pleaded with God, and finally broke down in tears. In a sympathetic tone, Kennan suggested that the driver ride one of the horses to the nearest village and get help, which he agreed to do. Kennan and Frost spent the night huddled in the sleigh wondering whether they would ever see their driver again, but the next morning he appeared with fresh horses, ropes, and a peasant to help them get the sleigh underway again. They stopped briefly in Tomsk to give a report to Felix Volkhovsky, the exile who had lost hearing in prison, and the other Tomsk exiles about their friends at the mines of Kara. Volkhovsky embraced and kissed Kennan when they said farewell. "George Ivanovitch, please don't forget us!"

Kennan wrote Emiline a letter from Tomsk which began "I love you, you sweet rascal." The letter was about his emotional reaction to the tragic men and women he had met in Siberia. It reflected a notable transformation in a man who, before the exile investigation, had often seemed unmoved by human hardship, whether striking railroad workers in the United States or the subjugated women in the Caucasus.

> It will be a never ending source of regret to me Sweetheart that you cannot know some of these people. . . . With many of them I simply fall dead in love as if I were a girl of eighteen. . . . I have met among the exiles in six months more people whom I could love, more people who would be dear friends, more people whose souls are akin to mine, than I had met in all the previous ten years of my life. I kissed

*three men goodbye in Minusinsk with my arm around them and
if anybody had told me a year ago that I would do such a thing I
should have laughed at them. You know me well enough Sweetheart
to understand and realize that only <u>extraordinary</u> characters could
exert such an influence over me as that.*[172]

They stopped at Omsk, where Kennan had looked in vain for Dostoevsky's prison on his eastbound journey, and rested for twenty-four
hours before going back on the road. In the stretch after Omsk, they
did not encounter *ukhabi,* but their sleigh capsized twice in the deep
ruts left by giant freight sleighs piled high with goods and pulled by
teams of eight horses. Both men were badly bruised and neither got
much sleep on the way to their next stop at Tobolsk, which required a
detour northeast called the "merchant's shortcut." In Tobolsk, which
they reached at the end of February, Kennan briefly inspected two
convict prisons and visited perhaps the best-known political exile in
Siberia, the Bell of Uglich, which "has received ecclesiastical consecra-
tion, and now calls the orthodox people of Tobolsk to prayers." The
town of Uglich was trying to recover the bell, he learned, but the mayor
of Tobolsk insisted that after nearly three centuries of residence, the bell
belonged to his city.

Much of Kennan's time in Tobolsk was devoted to Frost, who had
become so fearful of arrest that the sight of a policeman threw him
into a panic. Frost's grip on reality had been increasingly tenuous since
their visit to the gold mines of Kara, when he heard, or thought he
heard, Maj. Potuloff and Capt. Nikolin discussing whether to search
Kennan's luggage. The terrifying descent into the Algachi silver mine,
the gunshot in Chita, and the incidents in Krasnoyarsk and Minusinsk
had only worsened his condition. Anxiety kept him from sleeping,
sometimes for five or six nights in a row. He stopped eating and drinking, even refusing tea, for fear that any food or drink contained drugs
to make it easier to murder him. Kennan had tried arguing with Frost,
getting angry with him, and playing his banjo to distract him, none of

which helped. Frost, Kennan realized, was "slowly breaking down under the combined nervous and physical strain of sleeplessness, jolting,
and constant fear of arrest."[173]

At midnight in their log hotel in Tobolsk, Frost crept over to Kennan, woke him up, clutched Kennan's arm, and put his lips close to his
ear. "Keep still. There are people outside our door who intend to murder us," he whispered, explaining that he had been listening to a man
and a woman speak in low voices. The man had lost his nerve but the
woman was urging him on. "'What are you afraid of?'" Frost quoted
her as saying. "'The servants are all drunk.'" Kennan initially was so
startled that he grabbed his revolver and cocked it, but then realized
that Frost had been hallucinating. Kennan, afraid that his companion
might go mad, decided "to get to Tiumen as quickly as possible." He
evidently did not appreciate that his own condition was hardly better
than Frost's. His mental and physical strength was failing from the
months of brutal travel, his myriad illnesses, and the emotional toll of
his meetings with the political exiles. Caring for Frost had drained his
remaining reserves.

They reached Tiumen in early March, which might have been an
occasion to celebrate with champagne and vodka because they only had
to board a train to St. Petersburg. But both men lacked the strength
to do anything but rest until they were fit enough for a train journey,
which turned out to be a revelation for Kennan. "How delightful it
was to move swiftly out of Tiumen in a luxurious railroad car." Frost's
condition improved after they crossed the Siberian frontier. Their train
pulled into St. Petersburg on March 19 and they checked in to a hotel. Leaving Frost in the hotel, Kennan, who was in a state of high
anxiety, immediately went to his friend's home to retrieve the box of
the precious documents he had mailed from Minusinsk. Without the
names, dates, and other essential details in the documents, his memory
alone would be an insufficient source for the articles he had contracted
to write for the *Century*. The friend opened the door. Kennan asked,
without any greeting, "Did you receive a box from me?"

"A box?"

Kennan struggled to maintain a calm demeanor.

"Oh yes," said his friend, recovering from the sight of Kennan, whose physical appearance would have alarmed anyone who knew him before he went to Siberia. "The big square box sewed up in canvas. Yes, that's here." As Kennan later put it, "At least four suns, of the largest size known to astronomy, began immediately to shine into my friend's front windows, and . . . I could hear robins and meadowlarks singing all up and down Nevski Prospect." Rather than take the box with him through the Russian customs checkpoints, and risk having it searched and confiscated, Kennan arranged to send the box to London via someone he identified only as a "special messenger." Frost could not be left alone in St. Petersburg, so Kennan took him along to London, where Emiline was waiting for him.[174]

Emiline and Kennan had planned to meet in London when his investigation was over. In July 1885 Kennan had written Emiline from the Altai Mountains that he could not be sure when he would be finished. It might be as early as January or February 1886, he suggested, but it could take longer. He could not bear the thought of her spending months alone in London waiting for him so he wrote that "I shall have to leave you to act on your own judgment." In December 1885 Emiline let Kennan know by telegram that she planned to wait for him in Dublin, where her brother lived, and sailed for Ireland.

His letters, some of which had been opened, reached Emiline in Dublin. She had little to do in Dublin, where it rained constantly, other than worry about her husband and write letters to his family updating them on his progress since leaving the Kara mines. Kennan's letters increasingly alarmed Emiline because they suggested that her husband was suffering from "great depression of mind and body." Then the letters stopped coming. She had begun preparations to "start for Siberia myself," when she received a telegram from the American legation in Russia that they had heard from Kennan. He was in Tomsk and expected to arrive in London sometime in March.

Emiline barely recognized her husband when they finally met in London in late March. As she later recalled, "Mr. Kennan you would scarcely have known, he was so much thinner than usual—his face was white, wrinkled and old, with such a sunken narrowness to the upper part that I felt almost as great a fear as when [his] letters stopped coming. He was too exhausted to even express much joy at our meeting and he was barely able to walk." A physician examined both Kennan and Frost and then told Emiline privately that her husband was in worse shape than Frost and expressed concern for Kennan's mental state. Emiline sat by her husband's bed in their hotel room as he talked for days in a state of semi-delirium about the cold, vermin, and man's cruelty to man. "It still seems like a dream to think that I have George with me once more," Emiline wrote home in one letter. As Kennan's condition improved, she wrote that "George is not sick but is not strong, he tires easily, and I feel he must rest a very great deal." She had to find clothes in London for her husband. "Poor child, he has no clothes but furs—his sleeves were just dropping off."

Even before he had fully recovered his health, Kennan began work on his *Century* articles. He made plans to return to European Russia for more research before going home because, once the articles came out, he might not be allowed to enter Russia again. He arranged passage for Frost, who was still weak, on a steamship to Boston, where he fully recovered. Years later, after Kennan's articles about the exile system had become a sensation in the United States and elsewhere, Frost was interviewed at his cottage in North Cambridge by a *Boston Globe* reporter. He showed his Siberian sketches to the reporter and explained the difficulties of drawing in subzero temperatures. As to the exile investigation, he had nothing to add to Kennan's "wonderful articles; suffice it that we accomplished our purpose, and the world knows the result."

From London Kennan wrote letters to friends assuring them that he was well despite his Siberian hardships. "I have suffered more in every way during the past twelve months," he wrote one friend, "than I suffered during all the three years that I spent in northeastern Siberia before." For a long time after his Siberian investigation Kennan was prone to bouts of nervous exhaustion, and had dreams of "grisly" Siberian prisons and that Emiline was calling him in distress.[175]

He and Emiline met with Russian émigrés in London and then traveled together to St. Petersburg to begin a study of the political conditions in European Russia. Later, after she became a speaker on the lecture circuit, Emiline described for one audience how "as soon as we had crossed the Russian frontier from Germany, the whole atmosphere seemed to be changed. Armed soldiers were everywhere, our passports were examined with great care, and the very air [seemed] to breathe distrust." In St. Petersburg Kennan was approached by Russians seeking information about family members or friends exiled to Siberia. One young girl brought a long list of exiles's names and begged Kennan to tell her what had happened to them. "Mr. Kennan went over [the list] carefully but could do little for her," recalled Emiline. "Some he knew nothing of; a few had returned and were in hiding, but many more were dead."

They went to Moscow and stayed in a hotel across from the Kremlin, which charmed Emiline. She walked through one of its gateways and went into the golden-domed Cathedral of the Assumption, which smelled of sheepskin from the crowds of pilgrims. After she and Kennan returned to St. Petersburg, they drove out to see sunsets in the Gulf of Finland, joining luxurious troikas with tinkling bells carrying men in uniform and gowned women. The ride back to their hotel took them by the Peter and Paul Fortress, a high-security prison that held regime opponents. Emiline thought of the men inside who "were dragging out a weary existence within its gloomy casements, [which] made me again realize how brilliantly gay and pathetically sad is Russian life."

Kennan interviewed more than fifty regime opponents in St. Petersburg and Moscow. Through them he obtained secret government reports to the tsar describing the terrible state of the exile system. The reports, Kennan later wrote George Frost, had the "Czar's comments on the margin upon the state of things set forth therein. The reports deal very frankly and openly with all of the subjects that we have been investigating including the political exiles, the exile system generally, the condition of the prisons and [way stations], the corruption and inefficiency of the local administration, the courts, etc. etc." Kennan evidently was not harassed by the police, but he left Emiline in their hotel rooms when he met with Russians living under police surveillance. She was nervous and anxious for Kennan's safety but also for her own because their trunks contained stolen Russian state documents. Emiline told an audience that if a gendarme had ever conducted a search of their hotel rooms, "I should be writing you from Siberia and not be telling you this in person."[176]

As he had promised the Armfelds, while he was in Moscow Kennan visited Count Leo Tolstoy at his estate, Yasnaya Polyana. Emiline did not accompany him, evidently because her husband and Tolstoy would be conversing in Russian, which she barely spoke. The author of *War and Peace* and *Anna Karenina,* then in his late fifties, had just finished spreading manure over the neighboring fields of a poor widow when Kennan arrived. He had been warned to expect eccentric behavior, but was nonetheless startled to find the great author dressed in peasant clothes, including loose, homespun linen trousers and a white cotton undershirt. Count Tolstoy's rugged features, sunburned face, and iron-gray hair called to Kennan's mind a Tuscan phrase, "molded with the fist and polished with the pickaxe."

Tolstoy invited Kennan into his two-story white stuccoed brick house where they talked in a sparsely furnished reception hall on the first floor. Engraved portraits of Dickens and Schopenhauer hung on one wall, but otherwise "more evidences of wealth and luxury might be found in many a peasant's cabin in Eastern Siberia." It was soon clear to Kennan that regime opponents were mistaken in thinking that they could enlist him in their cause. Tolstoy, who had become a committed pacifist, listened without evident sympathy to Kennan's description of the plight of the Siberian political exiles, including that of the Armfelds.

Kennan asked him if resistance to such oppression was justified. "That depends on what you mean by resistance," replied Tolstoy. "I do not believe that violent resistance to evil is ever justifiable under any circumstances. . . . The revolutionists whom you have seen in Siberia, undertook to resist evil by violence, and what has been the result? Bitterness, and misery, and hatred, and bloodshed! . . . It is not in that way that the Kingdom of God is to be realized on earth." The ideas were not new, but Kennan felt overpowered by Tolstoy's passion and conviction, which never wavered regardless of how many stories of suffering he told the author about the Siberian exiles.

They halted their conversation to go to a sunny room on the second floor for lunch, where Kennan met Tolstoy's family, including his wife, the countess; eldest son and daughter; two nieces; and several younger children. Lunch was an informal, playful affair where Tolstoy "manifested more boyishness and gayety than I had yet given him credit for." At one point Tolstoy held an auction of an embroidered towel to raise money for the poor peasant woman who had given it to him. Exercising his prerogative as the auctioneer, Tolstoy awarded the towel to his American guest, even though Kennan's bid was not the highest, which the rest of the gathering ratified with laughter. After lunch the two men resumed their discussion until late at night when Kennan said farewell "to a man whom I had known only one day but for whom I had already come to feel an almost affectionate respect." Kennan, while impressed by Tolstoy's "deep, earnest sincerity," thought his beliefs to be impractical. Tolstoy later wrote that Kennan was "an agreeable and sincere man, although one with partitions separating his soul from his head—partitions of which we Russians have no understanding, and I am always perplexed upon encountering them."

Kennan and Emiline returned to the United States in June 1886, a year after he crossed the Siberian frontier with Frost. Then, Kennan believed that his investigation would justify his defense of the

Siberian exile system and that his articles in the *Century* and lectures would make him wealthy and famous. Now, although he would still reap financial and reputational rewards from his investigation, relieving the suffering of the Siberian exiles and the cause of freedom in Russia would dominate his life. Kennan intended to mobilize American public opinion to pressure the Russian government to reform, if not end, the exile system. "If, however, I do not touch the hearts of the American people before I finish my series of Siberian articles," he wrote a friend, "I shall think that my countrymen have no hearts to be touched and no sympathies to be roused."[177]

12

Siberia and the Exile System

By the late 1880s the Literary Society had become one of the most prestigious and exclusive private institutions in Washington. It sought no publicity and its membership was limited to forty men and women who were among the most prominent government officials, literary and artistic figures, and social hostesses in the city. Rotating among the homes of its members, the society met on alternating weeks. Typically, the speaker read from an original paper or led a discussion without rising from his chair. On the evening of April 7, 1888, after the usual companionable supper, members of the Literary Society settled in to hear that evening's lecture.

The speaker entered the drawing room wearing pitiful, tattered clothing and bound in chains. The astonished members realized that it was the society's vice president, George Kennan, who proceeded to read letters from political exiles in Siberia. When he finished, a United States senator pronounced himself "completely unnerved." Mark Twain, openly weeping, stood and announced that he would be a revolutionary if he were a Russian and that the moral power of the world should be brought down on Russia to stop such cruelties. By some accounts, he added that "if dynamite is the only remedy for such conditions, then thank God for dynamite." While anti-tsarist sentiments had appeared before in Twain's writings, they were more in evidence after Kennan's appearance at the Literary Society.[178]

The daunting task Kennan had set himself after returning from Russia was to convince Americans to care about the suffering of the Siberian exiles. The subject was hardly pleasant and he had no reason to think that Americans would be sympathetic to the predicament of foreigners halfway around the world. Many seemed unmoved by the plight of their own countrymen and women, such as the former enslaved people and their descendants suffering from brutal racial oppression, or the tragedy of Native Americans whose independence, if not culture, the US Army was about to finally extinguish. Kennan essentially was doing the work of modern-day global human rights organizations like Amnesty International and Human Rights Watch, except that he was doing it alone.

To write his articles for the *Century*, Kennan first created an index to his journals on twelve thousand note cards and then began drafting. He wrote in the evenings and weekends because he had resumed full-time work at the Associated Press office in Washington. He found it painful to relive the prison inspections, meetings with the political exiles, and observations of the exile parties. "I put my soul into those papers," Kennan wrote a friend, "and many a page was written with eyes full of tears." It was a struggle for Kennan to write objectively without appearing, as he explained to another friend, "to take sides, or to plead the case of the Russian revolutionaries as I should if I were their retained advocate. It is evident . . . that my sympathies are with the imprisoned, but I have written under strong self-control and have tried not to let my emotions run away with my judgment or lead me into exaggeration." He did not entirely succeed.

After reading the proof of the first article, *Century* publisher Roswell Smith wrote Kennan that his Siberian exile series "will move the indignation of the civilized world and will produce such results as *Uncle Tom's Cabin,* produced in this country." The *Century* primed public interest with a "prospectus" for the series that inspired newspapers to report that, except for "Battles and Leaders" and "Abraham Lincoln: A History," the forthcoming "Siberia and the Exile System" series would be the "most important enterprise ever undertaken by the *Century.*"[179]

Between 1887 and 1891, the *Century Illustrated Monthly Magazine* published twenty-nine articles by Kennan about Siberia and his exile investigation, and related topics, under the overall title "Siberia and the Exile System." The first six articles examined how the tsarist regime dealt with political opponents before sending them to Siberia and included such topics as "Russian Provincial Prisons," and the "Russian State Prisoners." Kennan's narration of his 1885–86 journey, starting and ending in St. Petersburg, ran in nineteen consecutive issues through the end of 1889. Two articles appeared in 1890 and the series concluded with two more in 1891. That year the Century Company, the owner of the *Century* magazine, published the entire series in a two-volume, nearly one-thousand-page book, *Siberia and the Exile System,* which was later translated into the major European languages.

The articles and the book contained over one hundred illustrations based on George Frost's sketches, which Henry Sandham, a well-known artist, used to create the final graphics for publication. Most were based on scenes witnessed by Kennan and Frost but the illustration of the exiles crowded around the boundary pillar at the Siberian frontier, which especially attracted public attention, was a re-creation by Sandham based on an exile's rough sketch of the woeful scene on the Siberian frontier in earlier years, a photograph Frost took of an exiled convict, studio models, and some imagination. *Siberia and the Exile System* was a devastating indictment of the Russian regime and the exile system based on Kennan's firsthand observations, his interviews of exiles and officials, and the detailed statistics he obtained from the Bureau of Exile

Administration. It was also a survival saga, an exotic travelogue, and Kennan's personal testament to the suffering of the exiles.

In one passage, after describing how the "Begging Song" of one exile party grew fainter and fainter as the party moved on, Kennan wrote, "I felt a strange sense of dejection, as if the day had suddenly grown colder, darker, and more dreary, and the cares and sorrows of life more burdensome and oppressive." But there were wry accounts of travel in Siberia that balanced the grim passages, such as his and Frost's late-night arrival at a post station near the Mongolian border so crowded with sleeping travelers that they had no choice but to "lie down in an unoccupied corner near the oven, between two Chinese and a pile of medicinal deer-horns, and to get through the rest of the night as best we could."[180]

The Siberian exile series boosted the *Century*'s circulation, but reviewers especially praised the book because, as the *San Francisco Chronicle* observed, "when grouped together [the articles] have . . . a cumulative force, a power of conviction, which they lacked in their original appearance." In a lengthy review the *New York Times* wrote that "Mr. Kennan, who faced many a danger, is not ashamed to tell of the emotional strain that visits to these human hells caused him." The *New York Tribune*'s critic wrote that the "monstrous abuses" exposed by Kennan may "shame" the Russian government into reforming the exile system.

Nearly seventy years later, in 1958, Harrison E. Salisbury, a former *New York Times* Moscow correspondent, wrote in his review of a new, abridged edition of *Siberia and the Exile System* that "no more sensitive and perceptive book has ever been written on Russia . . . time runs at a different speed in Russia than in the West, and the journal has application to the Soviet Union today." In 1996 Norman E. Saul, in his history of the relationship between the United States and Russia, observed that *Siberia and the Exile System* "would color the American perception of Russia for over 100 years." Contemporary historians of the Siberian exile system, such as Andrew A. Gentes and Daniel Beer, have relied on Kennan's observations in *Siberia and the Exile System* in their own academic works.[181]

The *Century* asked Kennan to defer a lecture campaign until after the launch of the Siberian exile series. But once he began speaking regularly in 1889, Kennan's lectures may have been more impactful than his writings, in fact, there may never have been a lecture tour like it in American history. He resigned from the Associated Press, and from 1889 to 1898, he lectured eight hundred times, by one estimate, to as many as one million persons. He appeared fourteen times in Brooklyn, eighteen times in New York City, seventeen times in Chicago, and twenty-six times in Boston—and on his twenty-sixth appearance in that city his manager counted two thousand in the audience. In one eight-month period, Kennan delivered two hundred lectures without missing an engagement. He lectured, not just in the major cities, but in small towns like St. Johnsbury, Vermont, and Emporia, Kansas.

On the lecture tour Kennan was not simply engaged in what today is called advocacy journalism, a debated term that, some contend, combines fact-based reporting with a point of view. He had embarked on a moral crusade whose foundation he explained to an editor at the *Century*. "It must be somebody's business to defend and protect these victims of human cruelty and passion. If God in his divine wisdom has not seen fit to do it, is it not evidence that he has left the duty to us rather than evidence that he does not intend the weak and helpless to have any protection?" Kennan, while not rejecting God's existence, was again keeping Him at arm's length.

He brought to his crusade consummate speaking skills. His lecture manager, James Burton Pond, who managed among other prominent speakers Mark Twain, Walt Whitman, and Susan B. Anthony, thought him as good a lecturer as any. An acquaintance recalled that when Kennan lectured "both the story and the manner of its telling were so absorbing as to exclude entirely all other things." A Chattanooga journalist observed that "to listen to Mr. Kennan is to be with him on his travels for the time." In Omaha, a reporter wrote that "one could almost get a whiff of the vile stenches emanating from the [prison cells]."[182]

Unlike his earlier reading before the Literary Society, where he wanted to surprise his friends by wearing exile clothing and chains, Kennan began his lectures in evening dress looking like a well-regarded member of the local establishment. In a conversational tone he talked about the Russian men and women who had "given up all that is dear to them and have laid down their lives on what we regard as the essential and fundamental rights of a human being." The refined young woman, Natalia Armfeld, living in a hovel in Eastern Siberia. A Russian poet whose wife had died of a broken heart after his exile to Siberia. The vicious flogging of a woman political prisoner at Kara, who afterward committed suicide. The recent massacre of six political exiles in Yakutsk by Russian soldiers. "The pain of simply listening to such woes was almost unendurable," wrote a reporter at Kennan's Salt Lake City lecture.

Kennan described the challenges of traveling in Siberia, visits to prisons, meetings with the political exiles, and cat-and-mouse games with Siberian officials. He used stereopticon equipment, a forerunner of the slide projector, to project onto a screen the personal photographs that regime opponents had taken with them into Siberian exile, concealed in books or other belongings, and given to Kennan. He then announced to his audience that "I have a complete convict suit which was given to me by exiles, one furnishing one garment and another another, until the suit was made up. If you will excuse me a moment I will put it on."

He left the stage as a well-groomed gentleman and returned looking like a criminal. He wore coarse baggy trousers, a loose tunic made from a burlap bag, a dingy-looking gray overcoat, slippers made of thin leather, and a cap. A chain ran through a loop on a leather belt around his waist to heavy shackles around his ankles. The exiled convicts, he explained to the audience, marched thousands of miles in such chains. A reporter attending a Chicago lecture wrote that "the iron chains rattled around his legs and a chill crept over his listeners." At the same point in Kennan's Chattanooga lecture, the "silence [was] so deep that the speaker's words sounded like an echo."[183]

Kennan's stature as a national expert on Russia and a prominent journalist—he was the only journalist among the select group of Americans who formed the National Geographic Society in 1888—helped to draw crowds, but newspaper coverage and word of mouth gave the lectures a life of their own. One of the most famous lecture venues of the era was the Lowell Institute in Boston, where Bostonians had gone for decades to listen to prominent scientists, historians, theologians, philosophers, artists, and authors lecture on topics from "The Germ Theory of Disease" to "Early English Poetry." On the night of February 25, 1889, the Lowell Institute's lecture hall was filled for Kennan's lecture on "Eastern Siberia." All one thousand seats were taken, the aisles were packed with standees, people sat on the window ledges, and, as a reporter for the *Boston Globe* wrote, "almost literally clung to the walls with their fingers and toes." Outside hundreds more pleaded to be admitted.[184]

On a swing through California and the Pacific Northwest, Kennan's lecture at the Metropolitan Hall in San Francisco ended in a storm of applause from the audience, which had filled the seats and aisles. On a Midwest tour his audiences averaged between fifteen hundred and two thousand a night. So many people in Hartford, Connecticut wanted to attend Kennan's lecture that the hall had to put hundreds more general admission tickets on sale and bring in one hundred first-class seats. A reporter at Kennan's lecture in Chicago's Central Music Hall, attended by over twenty-five hundred, overheard a young woman standing near the doorway to the hall say to herself, "O, if I had that White Czar [Alexander III] here for ten minutes! Wouldn't I give him a piece of my mind!"[185]

Throughout the United States reporters described similar scenes. In "almost total darkness 1,000 people sat and wept" in Cincinnati, Kennan "moved his hearers to tears" at another Chicago lecture, and "there was scarcely a dry eye in the house and it was fully a minute before the thunderous applause broke forth" in Philadelphia. The latter audience remained in the hall after Kennan finished his lecture to organize a protest against the Siberian exile system, which led to the formation of the Siberian Exile Petition Association and Russian Exile Relief Committee. These and other similar organizations, such as the United States Siberian Exile Humane Society in Denver, by some accounts gathered more than one million signatures on petitions protesting the Russian regime's treatment of the Siberian exiles. The petition movement was the victim of its own success because its organizers could not find a way to deliver such a massive quantity of material to the tsar. One unusual protest was in the form of a letter on a child's stationery (it was embossed with four puppies) to the "Czar of Russia." The letter read, "We are five little children in America and must ask you to do something which would please us very much. It is that you will give up sending people to Siberia for we think it very wicked. . . . We will send our pictures to you on condition that you will answer this note. Please do."[186]

In May 1890 Kennan wrote a friend that "the campaign against the Russian Government & the exile system goes on victoriously . . . I had very large audiences almost everywhere." But he was also exhausted from the grueling pace, which reporters had noticed at his lectures. "He looks a man of steel," wrote one about Kennan's appearance in Kansas City, Missouri, "but who has been overworked for all that." J. B. Pond, the lecture agent, observed that, during the 1889–90 lecture season, Kennan was in "wretched health during the entire tour, devoting his nights to writing . . . he was loaded down, and almost broken down." Kennan wrote Pond that "it would take less out of me to ride night and day across Siberia for a hundred consecutive days and nights than it would to travel and lecture for the same length of time in America."

Since their return from Russia, Emiline had recopied the manuscripts of his articles, read the publisher's proofs, and run the business side of his writing and lectures. "She is a few years her husband's junior," one newspaper reported, "a companion and copartner as well as wife, and a lady of strong character and great personal attractiveness." But Emiline could not keep her husband from overworking and Kennan collapsed in Toledo during the 1890–91 lecture season. He wrote a friend that he was mentally and physically exhausted and needed to rest. "I have been virtually living in Siberia for the last five years—one year I was there and four years I have been there in spirit . . . every night I was living over again in my lecture the life of anxiety and emotional suffering that I lived in Siberia."

With Emiline, Kennan went to recuperate at their summer home in Baddeck, a town on Cape Breton Island, off Nova Scotia, which he had purchased with earnings from his writings and lectures. Alexander Graham Bell, the inventor of the telephone, owned a home on Baddeck Bay. The two men and their wives became devoted friends with shared interests. Kennan and Bell sailed and camped together and endlessly discussed astronomy, aeronautics, and meteorology, among many subjects. Emiline and Mabel Bell together started a kindergarten for Baddeck children "too young for field tasks" and taught lacemaking to the fishermen's wives to help them generate money to supplement their husbands' income.[187]

Kennan returned to the lecture trail before he had fully recovered. In late 1891 newspapers across the country reported that, while lecturing in San Francisco, George Kennan had become a "victim of nervous prostration from overwork, and, though he rallies to deliver lectures for which he is under contract, he collapses after each and barely maintains existence." He canceled his appearances, managed to resume lecturing in February 1892 and collapsed again but then recovered and returned to the lecture circuit. Apparently in better health, he spent part of the 1893–94 season in England lecturing and raising money for *Free Russia,* an English paper devoted to freedom in Russia. A *Guardian* reporter who covered one of Kennan's lectures wrote that "Mr. Kennan has a strong and striking face with piercing black eyes. He speaks with the cool precision and direct force of many Americans."[188]

Kennan's much younger cousin, the diplomat George Frost Kennan, later wrote that timing was one reason Kennan's writings and lectures had such an impact. The trauma of the Civil War had left the country "disinclined to any intensive introspective analysis of its own weaknesses," and the Russian exile system appealed to the American public's "curious Victorian capacity for sympathy and indignation over evils that were far away." The younger Kennan's caustic observation was undoubtedly influenced by his dislike of the American public. "I hate democracy; I hate the press . . . I hate the 'peepul'; I have become clearly un-American," he told his sister Jeanette in 1935.

But his point had merit because the older George Kennan, for all his communications skills, would likely not have attracted the same attention had his topic been Black sharecroppers in the South or Native Americans, which would have raised uncomfortable questions about American violations of the human rights of its own citizens. The woes of the Siberian exiles did not trigger American guilt, Kennan offered readers and audiences an adventure saga in an exotic land, and his audiences could identify with the educated political exiles to whom Kennan gave special emphasis in his lectures.

But even an above-average lecturer would not have drawn such large audiences to hear about the Siberian exile system. Kennan's theatricality (at one lecture he sang the exiles' "Begging Song"), narrative talent, and moral outrage over the Russian regime's cruelty—a reporter noted at one lecture that, despite his generally even tone, his voice sometimes "betrayed the presence of ill-concealed emotion"—were an enormous part of his appeal. So was the drama of his encounters with the Russian gendarmes and police, which he occasionally exaggerated. He described to at least one audience how "in secret" he visited Natalia Armfeld in Kara when his journal records that Capt. Nikolin, the gendarme commander of the political convicts at Kara, gave him permission to visit the political convicts in the free command.[189]

Kennan did more than write and lecture. He financially supported regime opponents who managed to escape or immigrate to the United States and even took one destitute former exile into his home for several months. He unsuccessfully fought against US Senate ratification of an amended version of the US-Russian extradition treaty that he feared would make it easier for Russia to extradite former Siberian exiles in the United States for political offenses. With the assistance of the American legation in St. Petersburg, he organized an operation that successfully smuggled out of Russia the young daughter of Felix Volkhofsky, who had to leave her behind when he escaped from Siberia in 1889. Kennan arranged to sneak copies of his writings into Russia by using a contact in England to send a few pages of the *Century* articles at a time to different Russians not yet under police suspicion or surveillance, who assembled, translated, and circulated them.[190]

Once in Russia the translations inspired Leo Tolstoy and Anton Chekhov, according to several historians, to write their own books about the Siberian exile system. Chekhov mentioned Kennan to acquaintances both before and after he investigated the prison colony on Sakhalin Island off Russia's Pacific coast, where he witnessed a savage lashing (described in chapter seven). Based on his investigation, Chekhov wrote *Sakhalin Island*, which exposed the brutal conditions in the colony. At their 1886 meeting, Tolstoy had shown little interest in Kennan's account of the plight of the exiles, but Kennan's subsequent *Century* articles filled him with "terrible indignation and horror." He began work on *Resurrection*, a novel denouncing the Siberian exile system which was published in 1899. According to historian Daniel Beer, *Resurrection* may have been "perhaps the most influential" condemnation of the exile system since it came from the country's greatest living author.[191]

Kennan hoped that his investigative reporting would have an

impact, not just on the Russian intelligentsia, but on the Russian government. "I was stirred to the very depths of my soul by the human misery which I saw in Siberia," he wrote Roswell Smith. "I wish to arouse similar emotions in their [Russian government officials] hearts . . . to force them through pity and shame to take some steps to right the wrongs and relieve the miseries for which they are in part at least responsible." Tsar Alexander III reportedly read Kennan's articles, but his reaction is unknown. His government did react to Kennan's investigation—with fury at Kennan.

After listening to one of Kennan's lectures, an agent in the United States of the Okhrana, the Russian secret police force that became especially active after the assassination of Alexander II, reported to his superiors that "the harm caused to the Russian government's interests by Kennan is enormous." The Ministry of the Interior concluded in a report that "agitation by this foreigner, who has lost his mind . . . has given powerful impetus to the revolutionary movement abroad." The minister, Count Dmitry Tolstoy, barred Kennan from entering Russia "as long as Dmitry Tolstoy was Minister of the Interior." It became dangerous in Russia to have copies of Kennan's work as witness the man who was imprisoned for possessing two of Kennan's *Century* articles, which his wife had translated. A Russian propagandist in England named Olga Novikov directed an anti-Kennan campaign in which she solicited Harry de Windt, a well-known English travel writer, to go to Siberia and then write a book refuting Kennan's articles. In his book, which was poorly researched, de Windt alleged that conditions in Russian prisons were reasonable and certainly nothing like Kennan's description. Novikov edited and wrote the introduction to *Siberia As It Is*.[192]

Kennan came under attack from former American ministers to Russia who had grown increasingly concerned that his writings and lectures were swaying American public opinion against Russia. One unsuccessfully lobbied the *Century* in private to discontinue the series, telling Roswell Smith that "Siberia and the Exile System" was damaging American interests, and publicly attacked Kennan as emotionally attached to the Russian nihilists. The incumbent vice-consul general of the American legation in Russia called Kennan a "sensationalist given to exaggeration." The incumbent minister to Russia did not directly attack Kennan but did stress the importance of the long-standing diplomatic friendship between the United States and Russia. The American diplomats had accurately gauged the impact that Kennan was having on the Russian-American relationship. As historian John Lewis Gaddis later wrote, Kennan "did much to change public attitudes toward Russia, and in an age when public opinion was having an increasingly important influence on [American] diplomacy, this shift eventually had its effect."

Roswell Smith urged Kennan not to respond to the critics and, for a while, he remained silent. But the criticism stung and Kennan began responding, sometimes aggressively. For the most part he outmatched his critics by marshaling the Russian government's own reports and prison statistics, for example, to expose de Windt's factual errors, which included confusing Siberian prisons. To a charge that he had failed to acknowledge the many Russians who lead peaceful lives without fear of exile, Kennan wielded eloquence like a weapon. "I did not go to Russia to observe happy homes, nor to make the acquaintance of congenial, kind-hearted people. . . . The balancing of a happy and kind-hearted family in St. Petersburg against an epidemic of typhus in the exile forwarding prison at Tomsk is not an evidence of fairness and impartiality, but rather the evidence of an illogical mind." By way of analogy, Kennan suggested that an investigation of the treatment of Native Americans would present a "dark picture; but to attempt to lighten it by showing that . . . there are thousands of happy families in New York that have not been driven from their homes by gold seekers . . . would be not only illogical, but absurd."[193]

But Kennan was not able to respond as effectively to two of his critics' charges. One was that, by writing sympathetically about Russian revolutionaries who had committed or condoned violent acts, he was defending terrorism. He insisted to the contrary that "I have not a word to say in defense of their crimes . . . It is not my purpose to justify the policy of the terrorists, nor to approve, even by implication the resort to murder as a means of tempering despotism." Rather, he was duty bound to report on and explain that statist tyranny was the reason that the Russian revolutionaries resorted to violence. To illustrate this point at his lectures, Kennan first displayed stereopticon slides of the corpses of political exiles who had been driven to suicide and then he showed a slide of Alexander II's body after his assassination by the People's Will. "The assassination of Alexander II was a great political crime," he told one audience, "but look at this picture and those that preceded it, and you cannot fail to trace the effect back to its cause." The line between explaining why a revolutionary resorts to terrorism and providing a rationale for it, however, can be a fine one and it may be that Kennan was intellectually on one side of the line but, as his critics seemed to sense, emotionally on the other.[194]

The other criticism concerned his condemnation of the Siberian prisons. Both admirers and critics of Kennan's articles pointed out that some American penal institutions, especially in the South, were as barbarous as any in Siberia. A lawyer in Missouri, J. G. Paxton, wrote Kennan about the "leased-convict" Black laborers on southern plantations whose overseers, as punishment, chained them to plows or forced them to wear spiked iron shackles on their ankles. Paxton urged Kennan to wield "your power as a writer, perseverance as an investigator, and knowledge of the subject," against this "stench in the nostrils of the American people and ultimately bring about its downfall." Kennan only passed Paxton's letter to Roswell Smith with the suggestion that Smith forward it to a *Century* contributor, George W. Cable, who "has been doing some good work in the field to which Mr. Paxton refers and the letter would perhaps interest him."

Kennan evidently was worried that any equivalence between American and Siberian prisons could weaken his campaign against the exile system. He added material about the Tiumen forwarding prison to his two-volume book, *Siberia and the Exile System,* which had not appeared in his *Century* articles. While Americans prisons, and especially "our leased convict system," he argued in the new material, are "bad enough, and I have no desire to excuse or palliate their evils," their death rates did not approach the death rate in the Tiumen forwarding prison, which in the last seven years had "ranged from 23.7 percent to 44.1 percent." To derive these rates for his book, however, Kennan used a methodology that, as he had written Roswell Smith from Tiumen in 1885, overstated annual mortality when applied to a forwarding prison. Kennan's emotional commitment to alleviating the suffering of the Siberian exiles, and perhaps his pride, had overcome his better judgment and commitment to accuracy.[195]

Kennan had resolved that he would devote his life to the cause of Russian freedom "as long as I have the strength to speak and the American people will listen." But by the mid-1890s, he sensed that the topic of the Siberian exiles was becoming too "sad and gloomy" for his audiences. Kennan also attributed their loss of interest to "the impossibility of keeping up a sustained state of feeling for any great length of time upon any subject that doesn't concern personal welfare." He did not give up lecturing on the Siberian exile system but did so at a less frenetic pace and increasingly lectured on other subjects, including the scenic aspects of his Siberian journey and, drawing on his earlier travels, the "Mountains and Mountaineers of the Caucasus."

In an interview before one lecture, a reporter asked Kennan to explain the cause of the terrible oppression of Jews in Russia. "It is race hatred alone that causes the persecution of the Jews," he replied, especially blaming Alexander III for their mistreatment. "He believes that in persecuting all dissenters from the Greek Church, and especially the Jews, he is spreading incense before the throne of God." He even compared the Russian mistreatment of its Jews with racist American attitudes toward Chinese immigrants. "The dislike of the Americans for

the Chinese is not so strong as the Russian hatred for the Jews." It was
a striking change from Kennan's attitude before his exile investigation
when he had dismissed as exaggerations the reports of pogroms against
Jews in Russia.

In 1899, under pressure from world opinion, which Kennan had
played a central role in generating, Tsar Nicholas II ordered the creation of a commission to address the "urgent question of abolishing
or limiting exile." Russians who regarded exile as a barbaric practice
unworthy of a civilized nation anticipated that the commission would
recommend abolishing the exile system. The commission's recommen-
dations a year later, and the resulting legislation, while implementing
some reforms, overall were underwhelming. Sentences to hard labor
no longer punished the defendant with mandatory exile to Siberia,
merchant guilds could no longer impose administrative exile (although
village governing bodies still could), and peasant communities could
no longer refuse to accept the return of an exile who had finished a
judicial sentence.

But the state retained the use of Siberian exile for political and
religious offenses, including the broad power to administratively exile
the regime's political opponents. As revolutionary upheaval intensified,
the regime would make ample use of this power in the years leading
up to the Russian Revolution. The modest reforms to the exile system,
though, appeared to fulfill Kennan's hope that, as he wrote in the preface to his book *Siberia and the Exile System,* his investigation would at
least "ameliorate, even [a] little, the lot of the 'unfortunates'" in Siberia.
But now his sights were on the more ambitious goal of replacing the
tsarist regime with a popular democracy.[196]

In early 1901, Kennan returned to full-time journalism as the
Washington correspondent of the *Outlook,* a widely read weekly news
magazine. His ability to write about political conditions in Russia soon
suffered a setback. In the summer of 1901 he traveled to Russia to meet
with regime opponents and gather information for more articles and

another book. He apparently assumed that Count Dmitry Tolstoy's ban on his entering Russia "as long as Dmitry Tolstoy was Minister of the Interior" had by its terms expired since Tolstoy was no longer in office. Kennan entered Russia by way of what is now Helsinki, Finland, and went to St. Petersburg. For a few weeks he met with opponents of the regime who, as he wrote a friend, greeted him with "love and devotion . . . They are in a state of wild excitement over my arrival, and I have been hugged and kissed by bearded men until I am in a state of exhaustion." They assured him that *Siberia and the Exile System* was accurate.

The minister of the interior, Dmitry Sipiagin, found out that George Kennan was in Russia. He was arrested, jailed for thirty hours, and permanently expelled as "politically untrustworthy." Many years later Nicholas Daniloff, an American correspondent in Moscow in the Cold War era, was deported by the Soviet regime on false charges of espionage. Daniloff subsequently took an interest in George Kennan and, as he wrote, learning of Kennan's expulsion "sealed the bond between him and me. To be expelled, after a long career of observing Russia, is to have your life's work repudiated; your person violated." Daniloff searched Kennan's archives in the Library of Congress for some indication of how Kennan felt about his arrest and expulsion. He found only a note that Kennan had written to Emiline mentioning his expulsion, but it gave no "hint of his feelings. Perhaps he did not realize what a blow he had been dealt." The expulsion indeed marked a turning point in Kennan's career, which had been built on an expertise acquired through his travels in Russia. As he wrote a *Century* editor, "Now I have to rely on such materials as the ordinary historian uses." He especially lacked visibility into a new generation of hardened revolutionaries who were anything but pro-democracy reformers.[197]

Kennan suffered from severe, recurring depressions in the early 1900s, which he attributed to contracting malaria in Cuba where he had gone as a war correspondent to report on the Spanish-American

War of 1898. In 1901, he came "near committing suicide" from "a fit
of malarial depression that was so extraordinary as to amount to acute
melancholia." Whether his own, permanent exile from Russia, which
had shaped his life, played a role is unknowable. But nine years later
he still struggled with "ghastly depression, restlessness, sleeplessness,
and mental semi-paralysis" to the point that he had to apologize to an
editor for missing a deadline. "It is hard, after such a life as mine," he
wrote the editor, "and after having been able always to rely on my nerve
absolutely, to go to pieces in this humiliating way, seemingly without
any adequate cause."

Nonetheless, Kennan accomplished in the final decades of his life
what for many journalists would be a lifetime's worth of achievements.
In Cuba, Kennan had interviewed Lt. Col. Theodore Roosevelt, the
leader of the Rough Riders, went to the front to observe the fighting,
and spent two days and nights in a field hospital where he carried
stretchers, distributed food and water to the wounded, and assisted
the overworked surgeons. In one hospital tent, Kennan found a badly
wounded American soldier who had been shot in the head. "Blood
had run down from under the bandage around his head, and had then
dried, completely covering his swollen face and closed eyelids with a
dull-red mask. On this had settled a swarm of flies, which he was too
weak to brush away, or in too much pain to notice." When Kennan
offered water, the soldier opened "bloodshot, fly-encircled eyes, looked
at me for a moment in a dull, agonized way, and then closed them and
faintly shook his head. Whether he lived or died, I do not know. When
I next visited the tent, he was gone."

He reported on the 1902 eruption of Mount Pelee, a volcano in
Martinique. "The whole mountain, from base to summit, was ablaze
with volcanic lightning, and the air trembled with short, heavy, thunderous explosions, like the firing of thirteen-inch guns from half a
dozen battleships in action." He wrote Emiline afterward that "I have
just seen an illustration on a stupendous scale of the old Biblical idea
of the Day of Judgment." With Emiline accompanying him, he covered

Emiline Kennan in Japan, 1904–1905 (courtesy New York Public Library)

the Russo-Japanese War of 1904–05 from Japan where he promoted democracy to Russian prisoners of war. He was invited regularly to the White House by now President Theodore Roosevelt, who considered Kennan to be one of the most influential journalists in America; he wrote a two-volume authorized biography of Edward H. Harriman, the railroad tycoon. He continued to fight for the cause of freedom and democracy in Russia, principally through articles for the *Outlook*.[198]

As they grew old, Kennan and Emiline began spending more time in Baddeck. They took their frequent visitors on overnight cruises in their sailboat, *Petrel*, camping at night on the shore. Kennan built a log cabin twenty-five miles north of Baddeck, which he named "Caribou Camp." The cabin, which took several hours by carriage and on foot to reach, was set in terrain so isolated and thickly wooded that Kennan never went for a walk without a compass. He often went to the cabin, whose walls were hung with guns and fishing equipment, to write his articles, sometimes spending weeks there at a time. Their friends, the Alexander Graham Bells, also had a rustic cabin in the same remote area.[199]

Kennan followed from afar the revolutionary developments in Russia and the regime's increasing repression, especially after the bloody, failed Revolution of 1905. In July of 1914, he predicted that "another half century may pass" before the overthrow of the Russian government. Weeks later World War I broke out between Russia, Great Britain, and France on one side, and Germany, Austria-Hungary, and later the Ottoman Empire on the other. Kennan wrote in the *Outlook* that the Russian regime's incompetence and wartime repression had put the country on a dangerous path, but that a revolution was not imminent because, among other reasons, the Russian army would not support one.

By 1917, after two and a half years of war, all the major combatants were under severe stress. But Russia, which had suffered horrendous casualties without remotely commensurate military gains, was in extremis and about to stun the world. In March, Tsar Nicholas II abdicated in the face of mounting riots, strikes, and mutinies in the Russian army and navy (the "February Revolution" in the Russian calendar). The end of the three-hundred-year-old Romanov dynasty, and the seeming advent of democracy in Russia in the form of a provisional government under Alexandr Kerensky, was the culmination of everything Kennan had worked for since his Siberian exile investigation. "The struggle for freedom in Russia, which began with the revolutionary conspiracy of the Decembrists almost a century ago," Kennan jubilantly wrote in the *Outlook,* "and which was renewed again and again, with constantly increasing violence in later years, has ended at last in the complete triumph of democracy."

Alas, as we know with the perspective of centuries, advocates of freedom in Russia are inevitably doomed to disappointment. Perhaps Kennan might have tempered his enthusiasm had he known of the conversation in St. Petersburg between two Russian soldiers just before Nicholas II's abdication. As reported by the daughter of the British ambassador, who overheard the conversation, one soldier said to the other, "What we want is a Republic." The other soldier replied, "Yes. A Republic. But we must have a good tsar at the head of it."[200]

Post-revolutionary Russia had neither a republic nor a good tsar. In early November 1917 the Bolsheviks led by Vladimir Lenin seized power (the "October Revolution" in the Russian calendar). Of the leading one hundred Bolsheviks, sixty, including Lenin and Stalin, had spent time in Siberian exile, some of them multiple times. Kennan, who was shocked and angered by the Bolshevik takeover, might have been especially distressed if he had known that, before they took control of Russia, the Bolsheviks regarded *Siberia and the Exile System* as their "Bible." Kennan wrote that, while he could not predict when, the ultimate downfall of the new communist government "was as certain as anything in Russia can be."

In 1919 Catherine Breshkovsky, now known as the "Little Grandmother of the Russian Revolution," was speaking at a social service agency, the Henry Street Settlement in New York City, when George Kennan walked in. After their meeting in Selenginsk in 1885, Breshkovsky spent more time in prison and exile until Nicholas II's abdication. Kerensky's provisional government freed her and she went to St. Petersburg where a crowd greeted her at the railway station, crying "let us see Grandmother!" By then she looked like a grandmother: her hair was white and she often wore a black dress with a thin white collar at the neck. Despite all she had been through, her face had a kind expression and her gray eyes, although half-blind, still held their fire. She battled the Bolsheviks as long as she could before fleeing into overseas exile and a life of lecture tours where she predicted the eventual collapse of the Soviet Union. "You Americans do not realize what a happy people you are," she said at one lecture in the United States,

Catherine Breshkovsky after returning
from Siberian exile, 1918 (courtesy
Library of Congress, Prints and
Photographs Division)

where her audiences applauded her to the rafters, "such a contrast to
Russia." In the Henry Street Settlement, Kennan and Breshkovsky
embraced and kissed each other in front of more than one hundred
onlookers. The far future would prove both right about the demise
of the Soviet Union but old Russia, the one they had known, was in
the past for them.[201]

Breshkovsky's powerful imagery of sacrifice and suffering at the
hands of a brutal regime that was succeeded by an even more brutal
regime created what one historian called a "sturdy narrative bridge"
between the Siberian exile system and the gulag system under Stalin.
After taking power, the communist regime began converting parts of
the Siberian exile system's infrastructure into what eventually became
known as the Gulag Archipelago, a forced labor camp system whose
scale and lethality far exceeded anything Kennan had witnessed in his
1885–86 investigation. In the mid-1930s, Stalin launched the Great
Terror whose countless victims included more than a hundred mem-

bers of the Russian Society of Former Political Penal Laborers, which had been formed by the now elderly revolutionaries who had fought to overthrow the tsar. They had survived hard labor in Siberia only to be executed by Stalin. Today, the Russian penal system and its nearly seven hundred penitentiaries have features that can be traced to the Siberian exile system. These include use of penal colonies with large inmate barracks, convict organizations that resemble the brutal *artels* that Kennan found in the tsarist-era Siberian exile parties and prisons, and the state's use of the judicial and penal system to silence and punish its political opponents.

George Kennan grasped the nature of the new regime, unlike some of his fellow journalists. Lincoln Steffens, a prominent investigative reporter, after returning from a visit to the Soviet Union in 1919, famously proclaimed that "I have seen the future, and it works." By contrast, when the communist government enacted a "constitution" for the newly formed USSR in 1923, Kennan observed that the constitution left power in a small group of self-appointed rulers without accountability to the Russian people, where it had always been since the Bolshevik takeover. With a hint of bitter realism, he warned, "But let no one be deceived. The Russian leopard has not changed its spots."[202]

Epilogue

The Changing of the Guard

Toward the end of the nineteenth century, the citizens of Uglich petitioned for the return of their exiled bell from Tobolsk on the grounds that it had been falsely accused of treason. Tobolsk argued that, over the centuries, the bell had become part of its heritage and belonged there. In 1891, after the bell had spent three hundred years in exile, Tsar Alexander III granted Uglich's petition, thus absolving the bell of its crimes. The people of Tobolsk said their farewells to the bell and in the spring of 1892, as thousands watched, a Volga River steamer carrying the bell tied up at the Uglich wharf. The bell's edges showed damage from its journey over the Ural Mountains and it wore a new clapper and ear. The bell was carried from the wharf to the cathedral where it had hung before its exile and suspended from a newly-constructed frame and crossbar. That night a citizen guard of honor stood watch over the bell and the next morning a prayer service was held to commemorate those killed, maimed, and exiled by Boris Godunov. Priests rang the bell and sprinkled holy water while townspeople prayed or sobbed. After an absence of three centuries, the Bell of Uglich had come home and its "dense and solemn tone" rang out again over the Volga River town.[203]

Relations between Russia and the United States, however, were never the same after George Kennan's investigation of the Siberian exile system. For most of the nineteenth century a friendly relationship had existed between the two countries. In 1890, as Kennan's lecture tour was in full swing, an editorial in the influential *New York Evening Post* suggested that was about to change. "The United States has a tradition of friendliness towards Russia," the *Post*'s editors wrote,

> but it is not proof against such savagery as that which Mr. George Kennan has lifted the veil from. It will not survive many floggings of delicate women or many shootings of defenseless prisoners in filthy and overcrowded [jails]. Diplomacy can probably do nothing to mitigate these horrors, but it ought to make Russia understand that the line of Christendom is drawn at her borders and no decent government wants to have anything to do with her.

Other developments influenced American public opinion against Russia, including the regime's anti-Semitism. Kennan's writings and lectures coincided with economic and diplomatic conflicts of interest between American trading ambitions in China and expanding Russian influence in Manchuria. Russian regime opponents in overseas exile, such as Sergei Kravchinsky (under the pseudonym Stepniak), and later Catherine Breshkovsky, moved American audiences with their first-hand accounts of Siberian exile. But George Kennan, more than anyone, had made human rights in Russia matter to Americans.

In 1895, in a dramatic shift from the criticism of Kennan by former American diplomats, the new United States minister to Russia, Clifton Breckinridge, advised his superiors in Washington that, despite the long and friendly relations between Russia and the United States, "as we clash upon the principles of personal liberty . . . we need to let [the

Russian government] know that, however regretful it may be to us, it is possible to cool our ardor by persistently trampling in matters concerning us, upon principles we hold most dear." Largely as a result of George Kennan's investigation of the Siberian exile system, even before the Bolshevik takeover, the era of friendship between the United States and Russia was over.[204]

When Kennan was seventy-one, he wrote about growing old to a distant cousin from a different branch of the Kennan family, Kossuth Kent Kennan, a Milwaukee attorney. "Paradoxical as it may seem, the human locomotive seems to go faster—in time, at least—as its steam pressure decreases. I haven't as much energy as I had a decade ago, and yet I seem to go through a year twice as fast." In the same letter, he took up the unfinished business of his life. He provided an account to Kossuth of his exposure to Mohammedanism in the Caucasus, how he had studied religious texts in Medina, the "great unhappiness" his studies had caused him, and the conclusions that he had reached. He did not mention the pain he had caused his mother, who had died without apparently ever coming to terms with her son's apostasy.

Kennan decided to donate his extensive collection of documents, photographs, and other materials from his Siberian journeys to the Library of Congress. But he wanted to keep personal mementos, such as the collar and crest of the Order of the Sacred Treasure given to him by the emperor of Japan, in the Kennan family. At one point he considered giving them to his namesake, Kossuth's young son George Frost. "He is still very young, and I don't know him at all," he wrote Kossuth, "but I have confidence in his parentage and in the training that you and your wife will give him."

George Kennan and George Frost Kennan met just once, in 1910, when the younger Kennan was six years old. The boy later wrote Kennan about his experience at a boys camp in northern Wisconsin. Kennan wrote back that "if you enjoy that sort of experience as much as

I used to when I was your age, you must have had a good time." He
described how, in his youth, when there were no boys' camps, he had
secretly camped out at night in the Big Woods near Norwalk. He also
wrote about the flowers he cultivated in Baddeck on Cape Breton Island: "The orange California poppy (*Eschscholtzia*) thrives even better
with us than it does in its original form." Kennan ended the letter,
"Write me when you feel like it. I shall always be interested in what
you are doing, reading, thinking, and learning. Although I am growing
old, I have not forgotten my own boyhood, nor lost my sympathy with
boys." He sent George Frost a copy of *Tent Life in Siberia*.

In a symbolic sense the 1910 meeting between the elder and younger
Kennan was the changing of the guard. George Kennan was America's
great nineteenth-century expert on the Russian Empire. George Frost
Kennan went on to become America's great twentieth-century expert
on its successor, the Soviet Union, and the conceptual architect of the
Cold War containment policy that led to the Soviet Union's downfall,
which the elder Kennan had predicted as inevitable and, in an indirect
way, contributed to. As George Frost Kennan later wrote of Kennan's
impact on his career as a diplomat, "I feel that I was in some strange
way destined to carry forward as best I could the work of my distin-
guished and respected namesake. What I have tried to do in life is, I
suspect, just the sort of thing the latter would have liked a son of his
to try to do, had he had one." George Frost helped found the Kennan
Institute, named in honor of his older cousin, for advanced research
on Russia and Eurasia at the Woodrow Wilson International Center
for Scholars.[205]

Just months before his death, Kennan wrote a friend that "I face
the end without an atom of fear. The Power that brought me here will
know what to do with me when I leave here . . . With my own life I
am content regardless of the mysteries that surround it. I don't have to
explain them, nor do I ask that they be explained to me. I have lived,
loved, suffered and enjoyed, with love and enjoyment overwhelmingly
preponderant, and that's enough." George Kennan died of a stroke in

1924 at age seventy-nine. He was mourned in the United States and Russia. Emiline passed away in 1940 at the age of eighty-six.

Kennan's unpublished autobiography begins with his early youth, before his boyhood was upended by his friend's accident, and with his dreams of adventure. "I happened to be born with . . . a thirst for adventurous experiences." At age five he sailed a fleet of ships, which he and his father had carved from wooden blocks, across the dining room carpet to "the arctic regions in the spare bedroom." From the "antipodes under the dining room table" he ventured on to the South Seas where he evaded "piratical craft whose wicked purpose it was to intercept and capture my argosies."[206]

George Kennan lived his boyhood dream of an adventurous life, and his gallant fight for freedom in Russia touched the hearts of his fellow Americans.

Acknowledgments

Peggy Ann Brown, PhD, provided essential research, especially in unearthing details about Emiline Kennan. Ivgi Oanemos was invaluable in researching Russian language sources. I am grateful to the staffs of the Library of Congress and the New York Public Library, which house the bulk of George Kennan's archives. In the midst of a pandemic, Meredith Mann and Tal Nadan of the New York Public Library's Manuscripts and Archives Division, and Chamisa Redmond and her colleagues at the Library of Congress, went out of their way to provide assistance. Historians Barbara A. Engel and Daniel Beer took time to answer my questions about women revolutionaries in Russia and the Siberian exile system, respectively. Their scholarship, along with that of Andrew A. Gentes, Frederick F. Travis, and Frith Maier, was indispensable. Bill Nelson created the maps, and my daughter, Lisanna Wallance, organized and prepared the photographs and illustrations. Peter Bernstein and Amy Bernstein, my agents at the Bernstein Literary Agency, provided their usual excellent feedback and advice. I am especially grateful to my editor, Michael Flamini, and to his colleagues at St. Martin's Press. Lies, as always, was there for me.

Selected Bibliography

Websites, blogs, and newspaper articles cited in the endnotes are not listed in the bibliography, but the URLs for any cited websites and blogs are included in the endnotes. The newspaper articles can be found in online historical databases such as Newspapers.com or major newspaper archives such as the article archive of the *New York Times*.

Books

Anderson, Frederick, Michael B. Frank, and Kenneth M. Sanderson, eds. *Mark Twain's Notebooks & Journals* I: *1855–1873*. Oakland: University of California Press, 1976.

Armstrong, William Jackson, *Siberia and the Nihilists: Why Kennan Went to Siberia*. Oakland: Pacific Press Publishing, 1890.

Baldasty, Gerald J., *The Commercialization of News in the Nineteenth Century*. Madison: University of Wisconsin Press, 1992.

Bates, David Homer, *Lincoln in the Telegraph Office: Recollections of the United States Military Telegraph Corps During the Civil War*. New York: The Century, 1907.

Beckert, Sven, *The Monied Metropolis: New York City and the Consolidation of the American Bourgeoise 1850–1896*. Cambridge: Cambridge University Press, 2001. Kindle.

Beer, Daniel, *The House of the Dead: Siberian Exile Under the Tsars*. United Kingdom: Allen Lane, 2016.

Blackwell, Alice Stone, ed., *The Little Grandmother of the Russian Revolution: Reminiscences and Letters of Catherine Breshkovsky*. Boston: Little, Brown, 1918.

Bly, Nellie, *Ten Days in a Mad-house*. New York: Norman L. Munro, 1887. Kindle.

Breshkovsky, Catherine, *A Message to the American People*. New York: Russian Information Bureau in the U.S., 1919.

Bush, Richard J., *Reindeer, Dogs, and Snow-Shoes: A Journal of Siberian Travel and Explorations*. New York: Harper & Brothers, 1871.

Camp, Walter, ed., *The Book of Sports and Games*. New York: Thomas Y. Crowell, 1923.

Chekhov, Anton. *Sakhalin Island,* Brian Reeve, trans. Surrey: Alma Classics, 2013.

———*The Steppe and Other Stories,* Ronald Hingley, trans. Oxford University Press, 1980.

Crankshaw, Edward, *The Shadow of the Winter Palace: The Drift to Revolution 1825–1917*. Middlesex, England: Penguin Books, 1978.

Cutter, William Richard, *Genealogical and Family History of Central New York,* vol. 2. New York: Lewis Historical Publishing Company, 1912.

Deutsch, Leo, and Helen Chisholm, trans., *Sixteen Years in Siberia: Some Experiences of a Russian Revolutionist*. New York: E. P. Dutton, 1904.

de Waal, Thomas, *The Caucasus: An Introduction*. New York: Oxford University Press, 2019. Kindle.

de Windt, Harry, *Siberia As It Is*. London: Chapman & Hall, 1892.

Dwyer, John B., *To Wire the World: Perry M. Collins and the North Pacific Telegraph Expedition*. Westport, CT: Praeger Publishers, 2001.

Engel, Barbara Alpern, *Mothers and Daughters: Women of the Intelligentsia in Nineteenth-Century Russia*. Evanston, Ill.: Northwestern University Press, 2000.

Engel, Barbara Alpern and Clifford N. Rosenthal, *Five Sisters: Women Against the Tsar*. New York: Routledge, 1992.

Fairfield, Francis Gerry, *The Clubs of New York: With an Account of the Origin, Progress, Present Condition and Membership of the Leading Clubs*. New York: Henry L. Hinton, 1873.

Figes, Orlando, *Natasha's Dance: A Cultural History of Russia*. New York: Picador, 2002.

Firelands Historical Society, *The Firelands Pioneer,* vol. ix. Norwalk, OH: The Laning Printing Company, 1896.

Fitzpatrick, Anne Lincoln, *The Great Russian Fair: Nizhnii Novgorod 1840–1890*. New York: Palgrave Macmillan, 1990.

Frank, Joseph, *Dostoevsky: A Writer in His Time*. Princeton: Princeton University Press, 2010.

Frazier, Ian, *Travels in Siberia*. New York: Farrar, Straus and Giroux, 2010. Kindle.

Free Russia: The Organ of the English Society of Friends of Russian Freedom. London: J. Foulger, 1892.

Gaddis, John Lewis, *George F. Kennan: An American Life.* New York: Penguin Press, 2010.

———*Russia, the Soviet Union and the United States: An Interpretive History.* New York: McGraw-Hill, 1990.

Gentes, Andrew A., *Exile, Murder and Madness in Siberia, 1823–61.* London: Palgrave Macmillan, 2010.

———*Russia's Sakhalin Penal Colony, 1849–1917: Imperialism and Exile.* New York: Routledge, 2021. Kindle.

Gilbert, Martin, *The First World War: A Complete History.* New York: Henry Holt, 1994.

Gilder, Rosamond, ed., *Letters of Richard Watson Gilder.* Boston: Houghton Mifflin, 1916.

Gordon, John Steele, *A Thread Across the Ocean: The Heroic Story of the Transatlantic Cable.* New York: Walker & Company, 2002.

Gowing, Lionel F., *Five Thousand Miles in a Sledge: A Mid-Winter Journey Across Siberia.* New York: D. Appleton and Company, 1890.

Greeley, A. W., *Handbook of Arctic Discoveries.* Boston: Roberts Brothers, 1895.

Grosvenor, Edwin S. and Morgan Wesson, *Alexander Graham Bell.* Boston: New Word City, 2016. Kindle.

Harlow, Alvin F., *Brass-Pounders: Young Telegraphers of the Civil War.* Auckland, New Zealand: Pickle Partners Publishing, 2015.

Hartley, Janet M., *Siberia: A History of the People.* New Haven: Yale University Press, 2014. Kindle.

Hartshorn, Peter, *I Have Seen the Future: A Life of Lincoln Steffens.* Berkeley, CA: Counterpoint, 2011.

Hearn, Michael P., ed., *The Annotated Huckleberry Finn.* New York: W. W. Norton, 2001.

Higginson, Thomas Wentworth, *Out-Door Papers.* Boston: Lee and Shephard, 1886.

Jefferson, Robert L., *Roughing it in Siberia: With Some Account of the Trans-Siberian Railway, and the Gold-Mining Industry of Asiatic Russia.* London: Sampson Low, Marston & Company, 1897.

Jepsen, Thomas C., *My Sisters Telegraphic: Women in the Telegraph Office, 1846–1950.* Athens: Ohio University Press, 2000.

John, Arthur, *The Best Years of the Century: Richard Watson Gilder, Scribner's Monthly and Century Magazine, 1870–1909.* Urbana: University of Illinois Press, 1981.

Keesy, Rev. W. A., *War as Viewed from the Ranks: Personal Recollections of the War of Rebellion As Viewed By a Private Soldier.* Norwalk, OH: The Experiment and News Co., 1898.

Kennan, George, *Campaigning in Cuba.* New York: The Century, 1899.

———*A Russian Comedy of Errors: With Other Stories and Sketches of Russian Life.* New York: The Century, 1915.

——*Siberia and the Exile System*, 2 vols. New York: The Century, 1891.

——*Siberia and the Exile System: Abridged from the First Edition of 1891*. University of Chicago Press, 1958.

——*Tent Life in Siberia: A New Account of an Old Undertaking, Adventures among the Koraks and other Tribes in Kamchatka and Northern Asia*. New York: G. P. Putnam's Sons, 1910.

——*The Tragedy of Pelee: A Narrative of Personal Experience and Observation in Martinique*. New York: The Outlook Company, 1902.

Kennan, Thomas Lathrop, *Genealogy of the Kennan Family*. Milwaukee: Cannon Printing, 1907.

Kimmel, Michael, *Manhood in America: A Cultural History*. New York: The Free Press, 1996.

King, Charles, *The Ghost of Freedom: A History of the Caucasus*. New York: Oxford University Press, 2008. Kindle.

Kroll, C. Douglas, *"Friends in Peace and War": The Russian Navy's Landmark Visit to Civil War San Francisco*. Washington, DC: Potomac Books, 2007.

Kropotkine, Petr Alexseevich, *In Russian and French Prisons*. London: Ward and Downey, 1897.

Lincoln, W. Bruce, *The Conquest of a Continent: Siberia and the Russians*. Ithaca: Cornell University Press, 1994.

——*Sunlight at Midnight: St. Petersburg and the Rise of Modern Russia*. New York: Basic Books, 2000.

Lobashkov, A. M., *Istoriia ssyl'nogo kolokola*. Yarolslavl: Upper Volga Publishing House, 1988.

Lubow, Arthur, *The Reporter Who Would Be King: A Biography of Richard Harding Davis*. New York: Charles Scribner's Sons, 1992.

Mackenzie, Catherine, *Alexander Graham Bell: The Man Who Contracted Space*. Boston: Houghton Mifflin, 1928.

Maier, Frith, ed. *Vagabond Life: The Caucasus Journals of George Kennan*. Seattle: University of Washington Press, 2003.

Massie, Robert K., *Peter The Great: His Life and World*. New York: Modern Library, 2012.

Massie, Suzanne, *Land of the Firebird: The Beauty of Old Russia*. New York: Simon and Schuster, 1980.

Munro-Butler-Johnstone, H.A., *A Trip Up the Volga to the Fair of Nijni-Novgorod*. Oxford: James Parker and Co., 1876.

Murrell, Kathleen Berton, *Discovering the Moscow Countryside: A Travel Guide to the Heart of Russia*. London: I. B. Taurus, 2001.

Neering, Rosemary, *Continental Dash: The Russian-American Telegraph*. Ganges, British Columbia: Horsdal and Schubart Publishers, 1989.

Noonan, Mark J., *Reading The Century Illustrated Monthly Magazine: American Literature and Culture, 1870–1893*. Kent, OH: Kent State University Press, 2010.

O'Brien, John Emmet, *Telegraphing in Battle: Reminiscences of the Civil War*. Scranton, PA: The Raeder Press, 1910.

Palmer, O. H., ed., *Statement of the Origin, Organization and Progress of the Russian-American Telegraph*. Rochester: Western Union, 1866.

Perris, G. H., *Russia in Revolution*. London: Chapman & Hall, 1905.

Pipes, Richard, *Russia Under the Old Regime*. London: Penguin Books, 1990.

Plum, William R., *The Military Telegraph During the Civil War in the United States*, 2 vols. Chicago: Jansen, McClurg & Company, 1882.

Pond, James Burton, *Eccentricities of Genius: Memories of Famous Men and Women of the Platform and Stage*. London: Chatto & Windus, 1901.

Prescott, George B., *History, Theory and Practice of the Electric Telegraph*. Boston: Ticknor and Fields, 1860.

Protess, David L., et al., *The Journalism of Outrage: Investigative Reporting and Agenda Building in America*. New York: The Guilford Press, 1991.

Radzinsky, Edvard, *Alexander II: The Last Great Tsar*. New York: Free Press, 2005.

Reeder, Roberta, trans. and ed., *Down Along the Mother Volga*. Philadelphia: University of Pennsylvania Press, 1975.

Reporters of the Associated Press, *Breaking News: How the Associated Press Has Covered War, Peace and Everything Else*. New York: Princeton Architectural Press, 2007.

Ruud, Charles A. and Sergei A. Stepanov, *Fontanka 16: The Tsars' Secret Police*. Montreal: McGill-Queen's University Press, 1999.

Saul, Norman E., *Distant Friends: The United States & Russia, 1763–1867*. Lawrence: University Press of Kansas, 1991.

———*Concord & Conflict: The United States & Russia, 1867–1914*. Lawrence: University Press of Kansas, 1996.

Signor, Isaac Smith and Henry Perry Smith, *Landmarks of Orleans County*. Syracuse: D. Mason & Company, 1894.

Siljak, Ana, *Angel of Vengeance: The "Girl Assassin," the Governor of St. Petersburg, and Russia's Revolutionary World*. New York: St. Martin's Press, 2008.

Slatter, John, ed., *From the Other Shore: Russian Political Immigrants in Britain, 1880–1917*. London: Frank Cass, 1984.

Smith, Harriette Knight, *The History of the Lowell Institute*. Boston: Lamson, Wolffe and Company, 1898.

Spottiswoode, William, *A Tarantasse Journey Through Eastern Russia in the Autumn of 1856*. London: Longman, Brown, Green, Longmans, & Roberts, 1857.

Standage, Tom, *The Victorian Internet: The Remarkable Story of the Telegraph and the Nineteenth Century's Online Pioneers*. New York: Walker and Company, 1998.

Susman, Warren I., *Culture as History: The Transformation of American Society in the Twentieth Century*. New York: Pantheon Books, 1984. Kindle.

Sutherland, Christine, *The Princess of Siberia: The Story of Maria Volkonsky and the Decembrist Exiles*. New York: Farrar Straus Giroux, 1984.

Tayler, Jeffrey, *River of No Reprieve: Descending Siberia's Waterway of Exile, Death, and Destiny*. Boston: Mariner Books, 2007. Kindle.

Tolstoy, Leo, and Louise Maude, trans., *Resurrection*. Hertfordshire, England: Wordsworth Editions Limited, 2014.

Travis, Frederick F., *George Kennan and the Russian-American Relationship, 1865–1924*. Athens: Ohio University Press, 1990.

Turgenev, Ivan S., and C. J. Hogarth, trans. *Fathers and Sons,* London: J. M. Dent & Sons, Ltd., 1921.

Verhoeven, Claudia, *The Odd Man Karakozov: Imperial Russia, Modernity and the Birth of Terrorism*. Ithaca: Cornell University Press, 2009. Kindle.

Ward, H. O., *Sensible Etiquette of the Best Society, Customs, Manners, Morals, and Home Culture*. Philadelphia: Porter & Coates, 1878.

Wells, Ida B., *A Red Record: Tabulated Statistics and Alleged Causes of Lynching in the United States 1892–1893–1894*. Chicago: Donohue & Henneberry Printers, 1894.

Wenyon, Charles, *Across Siberia on the Great Post-road*. London: Charles H. Kelly, 1896.

Wheeler, Tom, *Mr. Lincoln's T-Mails: The Untold Story of How Abraham Lincoln Used the Telegraph to Win the Civil War*. New York: HarperCollins, 2006. Kindle.

Williams, Edward V., *The Bells of Russia: History and Technology*. Princeton: Princeton University Press, 1985.

Williams, W. W., *History of the Fire Lands Comprising Huron and Erie Counties, Ohio*. Cleveland, Ohio: Leader Printing Press, 1879.

Withycombe, Shannon, *Lost: Miscarriage in Nineteenth-Century America*. New Brunswick: Rutgers University Press, 2019.

Wolfe, Bertram D., *Three Who Made a Revolution: A Biographical History of Lenin, Trotsky, and Stalin*. New York: Cooper Square Press, 2001.

Ziegler, Dominic, *Black Dragon River: A Journey Down the Amur River Between Russia and China*. New York: Penguin Books, 2015. Kindle.

Periodicals

Adamia, Shota and G. Zakariadze, et al. (2011). "Geology of the Caucasus: A review." *Turkish Journal of Earth Sciences*. 20. 489–544. 10.3906/yer-1005–11 https://www.researchgate.net/publication/279620884_Geology_of_the _caucasus_A_review.

Ames, Edward. "A Century of Russian Railroad Construction: 1837–1936." *American Slavic and East European Review* 6, no. 3/4 (1947): 57–74. https://doi.org/10.2307/2491700.

Ault, Phillip. "The (almost) Russian-American Telegraph." *American Heritage*, vol. 26, no. 4 (June 1975). https://www.americanheritage.com/almost-russian -american-telegraph.

Badcock, Sarah. "From Villains to Victims: Experiencing Illness in Siberian Exile." *Europe-Asia Studies* 65, no. 9 (2013): 1716–36. http://www.jstor.org /stable/24534182.

Baikalov, Anatole V. "The Conquest and Colonisation of Siberia." *The Slavonic and East European Review* 10, no. 30 (1932): 557–71. http://www.jstor.org /stable/4202706.

Barrett, Thomas M. "The Remaking of the Lion of Dagestan: Shamil in Captivity." *The Russian Review* 53, no. 3 (1994): 353–66. https://doi.org/10.2307 /131191.

Bassin, Mark. "Inventing Siberia: Visions of the Russian East in the Early Nineteenth Century." *The American Historical Review* 96, no. 3 (1991): 763–94. https://doi.org/10.2307/2162430.

Batuman, Elif. "The Bells: How Harvard Helped Preserve a Russian Legacy." *New Yorker* (April 27, 2009), 22–29 https://www.newyorker.com/magazine /2009/04/27/the-bells-6.

Baylen, Joseph O. "Madame Olga Novikov, Propagandist." *American Slavic and East European Review* 10, no. 4 (1951): 255–71. https://doi.org/10.2307 /2492032.

Bernstein, Samuel. "American Labor in the Long Depression, 1873–1878." *Science & Society* 20, no. 1 (1956): 59–83. http://www.jstor.org/stable/40400385.

Bychkov, Oleg V., and Mina A. Jacobs. "Russian Hunters in Eastern Siberia in the Seventeenth Century: Lifestyle and Economy." *Arctic Anthropology* 31, no. 1 (1994): 72–85. http://www.jstor.org/stable/40316350.

Caron, Timothy P. "'How Changeable Are the Events of War': National Reconciliation in the Century Magazine's 'Battles and Leaders of the Civil War.'" *American Periodicals* 16, no. 2 (2006): 151–71. http://www.jstor.org/stable /20770956.

Chatterjee, Choi. "Imperial Incarcerations: Ekaterina Breshko-Breshkovskaia, Vinayak Savarkar, and the Original Sins of Modernity." *Slavic Review* 74, no. 4 (2015): 850–72. https://doi.org/10.5612/slavicreview.74.4.850.

———"Transnational Romance, Terror, and Heroism: Russia in American Popular Fiction, 1860–1917." *Comparative Studies in Society and History* 50, no. 3 (2008): 753–77. http://www.jstor.org/stable/27563697.

Daniloff, Nicholas. "George Kennan and the Challenge of Siberia." *Demokratizatsiya* 7, no. 4 (1999): 601. 07–4_daniloff.pdf (demokratizatsiya.pub).

Davidson, Marshall B. "A Royal Welcome for The Russian Navy," *American Heritage,* vol. 11, issue 4 (June 1960): 1–3. https://www.americanheritage.com /royal-welcome-russian-navy#.

Dawes, Anna Laurens. "George Kennan," *The Century,* vol. 36 (May–October 1888). https://babel.hathitrust.org/cgi/pt?id=mdp.39015010964982&view =1up&seq=631&skin=2021&q1=Dawes.

Ellsworth, William Webster. "George Kennan," *The Outlook,* Vol. 123, 188 (October 1, 1919): 188–89. https://babel.hathitrust.org/cgi/pt?id=msu.3129310 5141539&view=1up&seq=196.

Engel, Barbara Alpern. "The Emergence of Women Revolutionaries in Russia." *Frontiers: A Journal of Women Studies* 2, no. 1 (1977): 92–105. https://doi.org /10.2307/3346112.

Feldstein, Mark. "A Muckraking Model: Investigative Reporting Cycles in American

History." *Harvard International Journal of Press/Politics* 11, no. 2 (April 2006): 105–20. https://doi.org/10.1177/1081180X06286780.

Forde, Kathy Roberts, and Katherine A. Foss. "'The Facts—the Color!—The Facts': The Idea of a Report in American Print Culture, 1885–1910." *Book History* 15 (2012): 123–51. http://www.jstor.org/stable/23315046.

Fromkin, David. "The Great Game in Asia." *Foreign Affairs* 58, no. 4 (1980): 936–51. https://doi.org/10.2307/20040512.

Futrell, Michael. "Dostoyevsky and Islam (And Chokan Valikhanov)." *The Slavonic and East European Review* 57, no. 1 (1979): 16–31. http://www.jstor.org/stable/4207756.

Gentes, Andrew A. "No Kind of Liberal: Alexander II and the Sakhalin Penal Colony." *Jahrbücher Für Geschichte Osteuropas* 54, no. 3 (2006): 321–44. http://www.jstor.org/stable/41051703.

———"Siberian Exile and the 1863 Polish Insurrectionists According to Russian Sources." *Jahrbücher Für Geschichte Osteuropas* 51, no. 2 (2003): 197–217. http://www.jstor.org/stable/41051062.

Gentes, Andrew, Abby M. Schrader, and Leonid Maximenkov. "Letters." *Slavic Review* 67, no. 1 (2008): 269–72. https://doi.org/10.2307/27652837.

Gillespie, Robert. "A Circumference of Emily Dickinson." *The New England Quarterly* 46, no. 2 (1973): 250–71. https://doi.org/10.2307/364117.

Goluboff, Sascha L. "Are They Jews or Asians? A Cautionary Tale about Mountain Jewish Ethnography." *Slavic Review* 63, no. 1 (2004): 113–40. https://doi.org/10.2307/1520272.

Good, Jane E. "America and the Russian Revolutionary Movement, 1888–1905." *The Russian Review* 41, no. 3 (1982): 273–87. https://doi.org/10.2307/129602.

Green, Martin. "Tolstoy as Believer." *The Wilson Quarterly (1976-)* 5, no. 2 (1981): 166–77. http://www.jstor.org/stable/40256117.

Hartley, Janet. "Gizhiga: Military Presence and Social Encounters in Russia's Wild East." *The Slavonic and East European Review* 86, no. 4 (2008): 665–84. http://www.jstor.org/stable/25479267.

Hine, William C. "American Slavery and Russian Serfdom: A Preliminary Comparison." *Phylon (1960-)* 36, no. 4 (1975): 378–84. https://doi.org/10.2307/274636.

Howe, Daniel Walker. "American Victorianism as a Culture." *American Quarterly* 27, no. 5 (1975): 507–32. https://doi.org/10.2307/2712438.

Hundley, Helen, "George Kennan and the Russian Empire: How America's Conscience Became an Enemy of Tsarism." *Woodrow Wilson International Center for Scholars, Kennan Institute Occasional Paper Series, #277* (2000). https://www.wilsoncenter.org/publication/george-kennan-and-the-russian-empire-how-americas-conscience-became-enemy-tsarism-2000.

Jepsen, Thomas C. "Women Telegraphers in the Railroad Depot." *Railroad History*, no. 173 (1995): 142–54. http://www.jstor.org/stable/43523615.

Kennan, George. "Camping Out in Siberia," *Putnam's Magazine*, vol. 2: September 1868: https://babel.hathitrust.org/cgi/pt?id=msu.31293105141539&view=1up&seq=196.

————"The Civil War in Russia: Will the Russian Political I.W.W.s Succeed?" *The Outlook*, vol. 117, November 21, 1917: 455–56. https://babel.hathitrust .org/cgi/pt?id=inu.32000000714784&view=1up&seq=465&skin=2021&q1 =George%20Kennan.

————"A Dog-Sledge Journey in Kamtschatka and North-Eastern Siberia." *Journal of the American Geographical Society of New York* 8 (1876): 96–130. https://doi.org/10.2307/196378.

————"A Few Recollections of Alexander Graham Bell," *The Outlook*, vol.132, September 27, 1922: 146–149. https://babel.hathitrust.org/cgi/pt?id=uc1 .c2620247.

————"Have Reservation Indians Any Vested Rights?" *The Outlook*, vol. 70, March 29, 1902: 759–65. https://babel.hathitrust.org/cgi/pt?id=msu .31293102733064.

————"An Island in the Sea of History: The Highlands of Dagestan," *National Geographic Magazine*, vol. xxiv, no. 10, October 1913: 1087–1140. https:// books.google.com/books?id=ctQKAAAAYAAJ&pg=PA1057&lpg=PA1057 &dq=National+Geographic+Magazine,+vol.+XXIV,+No.+10,+October +1913.%2520%2520%2520&source=bl&ots=sJvRA2zQ4B&sig=ACfU3 U1sKxto_N453Sj8rGN94J-AVxKRlw&hl=en&sa=X&ved=2ahUKEwij9I _D1eH0AhU5q3IEHWO3CHoQ6AF6BAgREAM#v=onepage&q=National %2520Geographic%2520Magazine%252C%2520vol.%2520XXIV%252C% 2520No.%252010%252C%2520October%25201913.&f=false.

————"A Journey through Southeastern Russia." *Journal of the American Geographical Society of New York* 15 (1883): 289–318. https://doi.org/10.2307 /196544.

————"The Mountains and Mountaineers of the Eastern Caucasus." *Journal of the American Geographical Society of New York* 5 (1874): 169–93. https://doi .org/10.2307/196488.

————"Mr. Kennan's Reply to Certain Criticisms," *The Century Magazine*, vol. xlii, October 1891: 958. https://babel.hathitrust.org/cgi/pt?id=mdp .39015007006300.

————"Murder by Adat," *The Outlook*, vol. 113, June 28, 1916: 473–82. https:// babel.hathitrust.org/cgi/pt?id=uc1.b2989256.

————"The New Russian Premier," *The Outlook*, vol. 115, January 24, 1917: 131–32 (unsigned editorial). https://babel.hathitrust.org/cgi/pt?id=umn .31951000709433o&view=1up&seq=115&skin=2021&q1=The%20 New%20Russian%20Premier.

————"Russia After the War III—The Chances of Revolution," *The Outlook*, vol. 109, April 28, 1915: 977–79. https://babel.hathitrust.org/cgi/pt?id=nyp .33433081671541&view=1up&seq=999&skin=2021&q1=George%20 Kennan.

————"Siberia. The Exiles' Abode." *Journal of the American Geographical Society of New York* 14 (1882): 13–68. https://doi.org/10.2307/196467.

————"A Tenth-Century Barbarian," *The Outlook*, vol. 113, May 24, 1916: 201–07. https://babel.hathitrust.org/cgi/pt?id=uc1.b2989256.

————"The Unification of Russia," *The Outlook,* vol. 109, January 13, 1915: 71–74. https://babel.hathitrust.org/cgi/pt?id=uc1.b2989253.

————"The Victory of the Russian People," *The Outlook,* vol.115, March 28, 1917: 546–47. https://babel.hathitrust.org/cgi/pt?id=umn.31951000709433o&view=1up&seq=528&skin=2021&q1=George%20Kennan.

————"A Visit to Count Tolstoi," *The Century Magazine,* vol. xxiv (June 1887): 252–265. https://babel.hathitrust.org/cgi/pt?id=mdp.39015074189708.

Kerensky, Alexandr. "Catherine Breshkovsky (1844–1934)." *The Slavonic and East European Review* 13, no. 38 (1935): 428–31. http://www.jstor.org/stable/4203012.

Kilpatrick, Carroll. "An American in Russia: 1850." *The Virginia Quarterly Review* 28, no. 2 (1952): 183–90. http://www.jstor.org/stable/26439870.

Kucherov, Samuel. "The Case of Vera Zasulich." *The Russian Review* 11, no. 2 (1952): 86–96. https://doi.org/10.2307/125658.

Landale, Nancy S., and Avery M. Guest. "Ideology and Sexuality among Victorian Women." *Social Science History* 10, no. 2 (1986): 147–70. https://doi.org/10.2307/1170861.

Martyn, Henry. "History of the Century Magazine." *The Quarterly Illustrator* 1, no. 2 (1893): 93–96. http://www.jstor.org/stable/25581818.

McCorristine, Shane. "Spiritual Routes and Revelations: The Franklin Mystery Renewed." In *Spectral Arctic: A History of Dreams and Ghosts in Polar Exploration,* 139–69. UCL Press, 2018. https://doi.org/10.2307/j.ctvqhsrj.8.

Menand, Louis. "Getting Real: George F. Kennan's Cold War. *New Yorker,* November 14, 2011, 76–83. https://www.newyorker.com/magazine/2011/11/14/getting-real.

Menke, Richard. "Media in America, 1881: Garfield, Guiteau, Bell, Whitman." *Critical Inquiry* 31, no. 3 (2005): 638–64. https://doi.org/10.1086/430988.

Mironov, Boris. "The Russian Peasant Commune After the Reforms of the 1860s." *Slavic Review* 44, no. 3 (1985): 438–67. https://doi.org/10.2307/2498014.

Naval Historical Foundation. "The Russian Navy Visits the United States." 4–5, 8–16. Library of Congress (September 24, 2019). https://www.loc.gov/item/73151387/

Pedler, Ann. "Going to the People. The Russian Narodniki in 1874–5." *The Slavonic Review* 6, no. 16 (1927): 130–41. http://www.jstor.org/stable/4202141.

Petrova, Maria. "Newspapers and Parties: How Advertising Revenues Created an Independent Press." *The American Political Science Review* 105, no. 4 (2011): 790–808. http://www.jstor.org/stable/23275353.

Phillips, Ben. "'A Nihilist Kohort': Siberian Exile in the Victorian Imagination, c.1830–1890." *The Slavonic and East European Review* 97, no. 3 (2019): 471–500. https://doi.org/10.5699/slaveasteurorev2.97.3.0471.

Pipes, Richard. "The Trial of Vera Z." *Russian History* 37, no. 1 (2010): v–82. http://www.jstor.org/stable/24664570.

Rawson, Donald. "The Death Penalty in Late Tsarist Russia: An Investigation

of Judicial Procedures." *Russian History* 11, no. 1 (1984): 29–52. http://www
.jstor.org/stable/24652643.

Renner, Andreas. "Defining a Russian Nation: Mikhail Katkov and the 'Invention' of National Politics." *The Slavonic and East European Review* 81, no. 4 (2003): 659–82. http://www.jstor.org/stable/4213793.

Richards, John F. "Chapter 2. The Hunt for Furs in Siberia" in *The World Hunt: An Environmental History of the Commodification of Animals*, 55–84. Berkeley: University of California Press, 2014. https://doi.org/10.1525 /9780520958470–005.

Ruane, Christine. "Clothes Make the Comrade: A History of The Russian Fashion Industry." *Russian History* 23, no. 1/4 (1996): 311–43. http://www.jstor .org/stable/24660930.

Sabol, Steven. "Assimilation and Identity." In *"The Touch of Civilization": Comparing American and Russian Internal Colonization*, 205–34. University Press of Colorado, 2017. https://doi.org/10.2307/j.ctt1mtz7g6.10.

Sahni, Kalpana. "Oriental Phantoms: F. Dostoevsky's Views on the East." *Social Scientist* 14, no. 7 (1986): 36–45. https://doi.org/10.2307/3517249.

Schuman, Michael. "History of Child Labor in the United States—Part 1: Little Children Working." *Monthly Labor Review,* 2017. http://www.jstor.org/stable /90001351.

Scott, Arthur L. "The Century Magazine Edits Huckleberry Finn, 1884–1885." *American Literature* 27, no. 3 (1955): 356–62. https://doi.org/10.2307 /2922156.

Stenton, Douglas R. "A Most Inhospitable Coast: The Report of Lieutenant William Hobson's 1859 Search for the Franklin Expedition on King William Island." *Arctic* 67, no. 4 (2014): 511–22. http://www.jstor.org/stable /24363813.

Stults, Taylor. "George Kennan: Russian Specialist of the 1890s." *The Russian Review* 29, no. 3 (1970): 275–85. https://doi.org/10.2307/127536.

Vasil'evskii, R. S., and Chester S. Chard. "The Origin of the Ancient Koryak Culture on the Northern Okhotsk Coast." *Arctic Anthropology* 6, no. 1 (1969): 150–64. http://www.jstor.org/stable/40315694.

Verhoeven, Claudia. "Time of Terror, Terror of Time on the Impatience of Russian Revolutionary Terrorism (Early 1860s–Early 1880s)." *Jahrbücher Für Geschichte Osteuropas* 58, no. 2 (2010): 254–73. http://www.jstor.org/stable /41052430.

Wallach, Glenn. "'A Depraved Taste for Publicity:' The Press and Private Life in the Gilded Age." *American Studies* 39, no. 1 (1998): 31–57. http://www.jstor .org/stable/40642947.

Willerslev, Rane, and Olga Ulturgasheva. "The Sable Frontier: The Siberian Fur Trade as Montage." *Cambridge Anthropology* 26, no. 2 (2006): 79–100. http:// www.jstor.org/stable/23820842.

Willis, James F. "An Arkansan in St. Petersburg: Clifton Rodes Breckinridge, Minister to Russia, 1894–1897." *The Arkansas Historical Quarterly* 38, no. 1 (1979): 3–31. https://doi.org/10.2307/40025947.

Wilson, Charles R. "Cincinnati's Reputation During the Civil War." *The Journal of Southern History* 2, no. 4 (1936): 468–79. https://doi.org/10.2307/2192033.

Worobec C. D. "The Post-Emancipation Russian Peasant Commune in Orel Province, 1861–90." In: Bartlett R. (eds) *Land Commune and Peasant Community in Russia* (1990) Palgrave Macmillan, London. https://doi.org/10.1007/978-1-349-20646-9_7.

Wright, J. K. "British Geography and the American Geographical Society, 1851–1951." *The Geographical Journal* 118, no. 2 (1952): 153–67. https://doi.org/10.2307/1791945.

Wrobel, David. "Considering Frontiers and Empires: George Kennan's Siberia and the U.S. West." *Western Historical Quarterly* 46, no. 3 (2015): 285–309. https://doi.org/10.2307/westhistquar.46.3.0285.

Yarmolinsky, Abraham. "The Kennan Collection." Bulletin of the New York Public Library (February 1921): 1–13, NYPL Box 6.

YMCA of the USA, YMCA of Canada. *Year Book and Official Roster of the Young Men's Christian Associations of Canada and the United States of America.* New York: International Committee, 1896.

Znamenski, Andrei A. "'Vague Sense of Belonging to the Russian Empire': The Reindeer Chukchi's Status in Nineteenth Century Northeastern Siberia." *Arctic Anthropology* 36, no. 1/2 (1999): 19–36. http://www.jstor.org/stable/40316503.

Miscellaneous

Breckinridge, Clifton. Legation of the United States, Russia to Secretary of State Olney, Despatch 191, December 24, 1895, Despatches from Russia, RG 59: General Records of the Department of State, US National Archives. https://catalog.archives.gov/id/188745595.

Gentes, A. "Roads to Oblivion: Siberian Exile and the Struggle Between State and Society in Russia, 1593–1917. A dissertation submitted in partial fulfillment of the requirements for the degree of doctor of philosophy in the department of history at Brown University. Providence, Rhode Island." (2002). https://www.proquest.com/openview/f28e87834902e1ee71ee5541b3128e4f/1?pq-origsite=gscholar&cbl=18750&diss=y.

Stanton, Elizabeth Cady. Elizabeth Cady Stanton Papers: Speeches and Writings,–1902; Speeches; 1870's, extract from a lyceum lecture.–1879, 1870. Manuscript/Mixed Material. https://www.loc.gov/item/mss412100081/.

Wilcockson, S. (1996). Perry Collins's electronic rim around the Pacific : the Russian-American telegraph, 1865 to 1867 (T). University of British Columbia. Retrieved from https://open.library.ubc.ca/collections/ubctheses/831/items/1.0087607.

Notes

"LC" refers to the George Kennan papers at the Library of Congress and "NYPL" refers to the George Kennan papers at the New York Public Library.

Epigraph
1. Beer, *The House of the Dead*, xxi quoting Fyodor Dostoevsky, "Zapiski iz Mertvogo doma," in *Polnoe sobranie sochinenii*, 30 vols. (Leningrad, 1972–90), vol. 4, p. 9.
2. Protess, et al., *The Journalism of Outrage*, 5.

Introduction
3. Kennan, *Siberia and the Exile System* 1:35, 47–57 (Siberia size based on Kennan's calculation), 78. Kennan's description suggests that, at the time of his visit, convicts no longer stopped at the boundary pillar. The practice was to shackle and chain criminals sentenced to hard labor in Siberia. The boundary pillar stood at the border between the province of Perm in European Russia and the Asiatic province of Tobolsk; Siberia, then and now, is not an independent political entity. Convicts lacked both the strength and the funds for the lengthy return journey to European Russia after they finished their sentences, and their home villages and towns frequently denied them permission to come home. Beer, *House of the Dead*, 3, 26–32. Ames, "A Century of Russian Railroad Construction," 67; Lincoln,

The Conquest of a Continent, 198–99; Emiline Kennan, "Notes from My Russian Journal," December 1894, LC Box 68; Notes for uncompleted biography of George Kennan, Jeanette Kennan Hotchkiss, NYPL Box 7 (hereafter "Hotchkiss Notes").

4. Kennan, "The Exiles' Abode," 61.

5. Dawes, "George Kennan," 629; George Kennan to Anna L. Dawes, December 15, 1886, LC Box 10.

6. Unpublished Autobiography of George Kennan (hereafter "*Autobiography*"), 162–63, LC Box 88; Sussman, *Culture as History,* 23–24; Daniloff, "George Kennan," 607, 611; Kennan, *Siberia and the Exile System* 1:347–50; Kennan, *Siberia and the Exile System* (George Frost Kennan introduction to the abridged version), x; Saul, *Distant Friends,* 400.

Prologue: The Bell of Uglich

7. Beer, *The House of the Dead,* 1–2; Williams, *The Bells of Russia,* 47–50; Batuman, "The Bells," 22–24; Lobashkov, *Istoriia ssyl'nogo kolokola,* 32–45.

Chapter 1: The Frozen World from Which Even the Favor of the Creator Had Withdrawn

8. Kennan, 1st Siberian Trip Notebook, September 12, 1865, LC Box 19; Kennan, *Tent Life in Siberia,* 133, 140–47, 308–09; Vasil'evski, and Chard, trans., "The Origin of the Ancient Koryak Culture," 150.

9. *Autobiography,* 76–79, 114–15, 157–58, LC Box 88; George Kennan to Hattie Kennan, February 10, July 2, 1865, LC Box 10; George Kennan to John Kennan, June 29, 1865, LC Box 10; Neering, "Continental Dash," 27–28.

10. Gordon, *A Thread Across the Ocean,* 75, 97–98, 117–20, 131–39, 182–86; Dwyer, *To Wire the World,* 32–33; Palmer, *Statement of the Origin,* 15, 35, 48–53.

11. Palmer, *Statement of the Origin,* 7, 35–36, 104; Kennan, *Tent Life in Siberia,* 1–3; Saul, *Distant Friends,* 344–48, 363–70, 400; Chatterjee, "Transnational Romance," 755–56; Beckert, *The Monied Metropolis,* 157; Travis, *George Kennan,* 10–12; Hine, "American Slavery and Russian Serfdom," 380; "The Great Rebellion," *New York Times,* September 9, 1861, 1.

12. Dwyer, *To Wire the World,* 23–25; Neering, *Continental Dash,* 27–28; "Telegraph," *Wisconsin State Journal,* November 13, 1866, 1; Kennan, *Tent Life in Siberia,* 24, 29–34, 42–45; "Telegraph," *New York Daily Herald,* May 6, 1866, 1.

13. Wilcockson, *Perry Collins' Electronic Rim Around the Pacific,* 118, map 8 & 9; Kennan, *Tent Life in Siberia,* 4, 51–58.

14. Kennan, 1st Siberian Trip Notebook, September 11, 1865; October 3–7, 1865, LC, Box 19; Kennan, *Tent Life in Siberia,* 59–67, 83–87, 95–103, 131–42.

15. Kennan, *Tent Life in Siberia,* 147–50, 163–64; Kennan, 1st Siberian Trip Notebook, October 11, 1865, LC Box 19.

16. Lincoln, *Conquest of a Continent*, 32–37, 54–58, 80–88; Richards, *The Hunt for Furs in Siberia*, 57, 61–62, 70–72, 74–76; Bychkov and Jacobs, trans., "Russian Hunters in Eastern Siberia," 73, 79; Znamenski, "Vague Sense of Belonging to the Russian Empire," 21–22; Hartley, *Siberia*, 3–6, 18, 20, 31–32.

17. Hartley, "Gizhiga: Russia's Wild East," 665–68; Kennan, *Tent Life in Siberia*, 165–67, 176–79, 185–88, 209–10, 230–35. The regime sent Cossacks from European Russia to Siberia in the late sixteenth century. By the time Kennan arrived, they had acquired an identity among Cossacks as "Siberian Cossacks." Hartley, *Siberia*, 43–44.

18. Greeley, *Handbook of Arctic Discoveries*, 72–73; Kennan, *Tent Life in Siberia*, 5–6, 235–44; Dwyer, *To Wire the World*, 23–25. The inland settlement of Anadyrsk, which began in 1649 as a Russian outpost, is not to be confused with the town of Anadyr, which was founded after Kennan's exploration at the mouth of the Anadyr River on the Bering Sea. Only Mahood, a civil engineer, apparently had not served in the Union Army.

19. Kennan, *Tent Life in Siberia*, 245–52.

20. Kennan, 1st Siberian Trip Notebook, January 31, 1866, LC Box 19; Kennan, *Tent Life in Siberia*, 257–59, 261–62, 268–70, 277–79, 292–95; Travis, *George Kennan*, 17. Kennan estimated the distance between his starting point at Gizhiga and the mouth of the Anadyr River at eight hundred Russian "versts," which is around five hundred miles. The settlement of Anadyrsk appears to have been roughly a halfway point in that journey.

21. Kennan, *Tent Life in Siberia*, 298–302.

22. *Autobiography*, 28–30, 123–25, LC Box 88.

23. Kennan, *Tent Life in Siberia*, 300–03; Kennan, "Siberia. The Exiles Abode," 29; George Kennan to Kent Kossuth Kennan, December 25, 1916, NYPL Box 1; George Kennan to Emiline Kennan, January 1, 1899, LC Box 15.

24. Kennan, 1st Siberian Trip Notebook, January 20, 1866, LC, Box 19; George Kennan to Anson Stager, June 2, 1866, NYPL Box 1; Kennan, *Tent Life in Siberia*, 303–09. One historian pointed out that in his account in *Tent Life in Siberia*, but not in his journal recording the search for the buried hut, Kennan described Dodd around the time of the discovery of the stovepipe as having nearly fallen asleep from fatigue and cold. Travis, *George Kennan*, 42–43. But nearly a year later, on a similar rescue mission, Kennan wrote in his journal that the previous year "Dodd gave out [and] wanted to sleep once at the mouth of the Anadyr in a temperature of only -44." Kennan, 1st Siberian Trip Notebook, November 13, 1866, LC Box 19.

Chapter 2: As Miserable as a Young Boy Can Be

25. *Autobiography*, 63–65, LC Box 88; Kimmel, *Manhood in America*, 1–2; Dave Barton, "Sufferers' Land," *Firelands History Website*, Post 50 (February 14, 2018), https://firelands.wordpress.com/2018/02/14/sufferers-land-post-50-norwalk-ohio-life-in-the-1850s/.

26. "Recollections of Northern Ohio," *The Firelands Pioneer*, 81–89, 101–09

(paper prepared by eighty-four-year-old Mary Ann Kennan); Williams, *The History of the Firelands,* 40–43.

27. "Recollections of Northern Ohio," *The Firelands Pioneer,* 83–85, 91; Williams, *History of the Firelands,* 150; Kennan, *Genealogy of the Kennan Family,* 41–42; Travis, *George Kennan,* 4.

28. *Autobiography,* 8–24; Camp, ed., *The Book of Sports and Games,* 3–4.

29. Kennan, *Genealogy of the Kennan Family,* 41–42; Jepsen, *My Sisters Telegraphic,* 2–3, 16–18; *Autobiography,* 4–5, 19–20, LC Box 88; Standage, *The Victorian Internet,* 48–53, 57–59; Prescott, *History, Theory and Practice,* 73–79, 91–93.

30. *Autobiography,* 2, 31, LC Box 88.

31. Schuman, "History of Child Labor," 1–5; Jepsen, *My Sisters Telegraphic,* 13–16; *Autobiography,* 31–33.

32. Mike Mangus, "55th Regiment Ohio Volunteer Infantry (1861–1865)," *The Ohio Civil War Central* (January 17, 2014), https://www.ohiocivilwarcentral.com/entry.php?rec=1183; Keesy, *War,* ix-xiii, 6–7; Kennan, *Autobiography,* 33–39, LC Box 88.

33. *Autobiography,* 37, LC Box 88; Wheeler, *Mr. Lincoln's T-mails,* 1–3, 91–92; Bates, *Lincoln in the Telegraph Office,* 40, 123; Plum, *Military Telegraph* 1:145, 161–65, 190–91, 214–15, 234 & 2:336–37; Harlow, *Brass Pounders,* 195–97; O'Brien, *Telegraphing in Battle,* 142–43; A.W. Greeley, "Military-Telegraph Service," *Signal Corp Association,* no date, http://www.civilwarsignals.org/pages/tele/telegreely/telegreely.html. A relay is a device for amplifying the electrical current in a telegraph line. Prescott, *History, Theory and Practice,* 81.

34. *Autobiography,* 37–49, LC Box 88; George Kennan to Jennie Kennan, September 23, 1862, LC Box 10; Plum, *Military Telegraph* 1:213 & 2:14, 18–19; Prescott, *History, Theory and Practice,* 19–37; George Kennan to Mary Ann Kennan, August 9, 1863, LC Box 10. Stations like Cincinnati were the hubs of the telegraph networks. Lines went from the hub station in a major city to telegraph stations in smaller cities and towns. But since there generally were no lines between the smaller stations, these stations first had to send messages to the hub station to be relayed or distributed to the intended destination. *Autobiography,* 45, LC Box 88.

35. George Kennan to John Kennan, November 30, 1862, January 24, August 15, 1864, LC Box 10; George Kennan to Hattie Kennan, January 2, 1864, LC Box 10; George Kennan to Mary Ann Kennan, August 9, 1863, Undated (likely 1864), LC Box 10; George Kennan to John Kennan and Mary Ann Kennan, October 5, 1862, July 25, 1863, LC Box 10; *Autobiography,* 52–53, 61–63, LC Box 88. "General Craigie as a Telegrapher," *Telegraph Age,* vol. xxiv, no. 23 (December 1, 1906), 609, https://books.google.com/books?id=EoA3AQAAMAAJ&printsec=frontcover&source=gbs_ge_summary_r&cad=0#v=onepage&q&f=false.

36. *Autobiography,* 63–69, LC Box 88; "Thomas Wentworth Higginson," *UNL Libraries and Collections,* no date, http://higginson.unl.edu/introduction

.html; Higginson, *Out-Door Papers,* 49; John Kiesewetter "Civil Unrest Woven Into City's History," *Cincinnati.com* (June 8, 2018), https://www .cincinnati.com/story/news/blogs/our-history/2018/06/08/civil-unrest -woven-into-citys-history/685960002/; Leonard Harding, "The Cincinnati Riots of 1862," *Bulletin of the Cincinnati Historical Society,* 230–39, vol. 25 no. 4 (October 1967), http://library.cincymuseum.org/topics/c /files/civilwar/chsbull-v25-n4-cin-229.pdf; Greg Hand, "From Bucktown to Vanceville: Cincinnati's Lost 19th Century Neighborhoods," *Cincinnati Magazine* (November 20, 2017), https://www.cincinnatimagazine .com/citywiseblog/bucktown-vanceville-cincinnatis-lost-19th-century -neighborhoods/.

37. *Autobiography,* 69–73, LC Box 88.
38. *Autobiography,* 73–76, LC Box 88.

Chapter 3: I Have the Satisfaction of Knowing That I Have Not Failed in Anything

39. Kennan, *Tent Life in Siberia,* 308–10.
40. Dwyer, *To Wire the World,* 140–42; Kennan, *Tent Life in Siberia,* 309–312, 324–27 (emphasis in the original); Gillespie, "Circumference of Emily Dickinson," 259; Kennan, 1st Siberian Trip Notebook, January 23, 1866 (misdated as 1865), LC Box 19; Bush, *Reindeer Dogs,* 340–42.
41. Kennan, *Tent Life in Siberia,* 329–33.
42. Kennan, *Tent Life in Siberia,* 335–37; George Kennan to Dr. Morrill, July 4–16, 1866, NYPL Box 1.
43. George Kennan to Hattie Kennan, July 9, 1866, NYPL Box 1; Kennan, *Tent Life in Siberia,* 335–39, 352–62, 369–70.
44. Kennan, 1st Siberian Trip Notebook, November 2, 3, 5, 15, 29, December 5, 1866, LC Box 19; Kennan, *Tent Life in Siberia,* 369–88; *Autobiography,* 219–22, LC Box 88; Kennan, "Have Reservation Indians Any Vested Rights?" 759–65; Dwyer, *To Wire the World,* 143–49.
45. George Kennan to Serge Abaza, February 17, 1866, Smithsonian Institution Archives, https://transcription.si.edu/view/11130/SIA-SIA2017–046898; Kennan, *Tent Life in Siberia,* 389, 392, 411–12.
46. Kennan, *Tent Life in Siberia,* 413–18; George Kennan to John Kennan, February 22, 1867, NYPL Box 1; Travis, *George Kennan,* 14; "The Russo-American Telegraph," *Buffalo Commercial,* April 6, 1867, 2; "Mr. Seward and the Atlantic Telegraph," *Sydney Morning Herald* (Sydney, Australia), June 21, 1867, 3.
47. Gordon, *A Thread Across the Atlantic,* 190–203.
48. Kennan, *Tent Life in Siberia,* 419–26, 443–44; Kennan, 1st Siberian Trip Notebook, 1866 otherwise undated, LC Box 19; Travis, *George Kennan,* 14; "The Russo-American Telegraph," *Buffalo Commercial,* April 6, 1867, 2.
49. Kennan, *Tent Life in Siberia,* 427–29, 443–52; *Autobiography,* 236–40, LC Box 88.

50.   Tayler, *River of No Reprieve*, 12; *Autobiography*, 248–58, LC Box 88; Kennan, *Tent Life in Siberia*, 453–59; Gowing, *Five Thousand Miles in a Sledge*, 70–73, 100–02; Anna Sorokina, "10 facts about the Russian troika," *Russia Beyond* (July 18, 2020), https://www.rbth.com/history /332458-russian-troika-facts.

51.   *Autobiography*, 279–82, LC Box 88; Massie, *Land of the Firebird*, 248–49, 253, 262–63; Kennan, *Tent Life in Siberia*, 459–73; Kennan, *Siberia and the Exile System*, 1:49.

52.   Lincoln, *Sunlight at Midnight*, 7–8, 108–09, 134–35; Massie, *Land of the Firebird*, 99; Massie, *Peter the Great*, 441.

53.   Crankshaw, *The Shadow of the Winter Palace*, 231; Gentes, "No Kind of Liberal," 326 (arguing that Alexander II had always pursued an autocratic strategy); Figes, *Natasha's Dance*, 145–46; Rudd and Stepanov, *Fontanka 16*, 31–32; Radzinsky, *Alexander II*, 39–46. It's worth noting that the tsar and the serfs had different definitions of freedom. Alexander was irate when the serfs insisted on real liberty and not simply exchanging their ownership by the nobles for the paternalist hegemony of the village communes and local bureaucracies. Mironov, "The Russian Peasant Commune," 438–44; Worobec, "The Post-Emancipation Russian Peasant Commune," 86; Massie, *Land of the Firebird*, 280; Verhoeven, *The Odd Man Karakov*, 7–8, 27, 164.

54.   Barrett, "The Remaking of the Lion of Dagestan," 353–54; Maier, *Vagabond Life*, 37–38; King, *The Ghost of Freedom*, 31; *Autobiography*, 282, 326–27, LC Box 88; Michael A. Reynolds, "The Brawl of Civilization," *Foreign Policy Research Institute* (January 2, 2019), https://www.fpri.org/article/2019 /01/the-brawl-of-civilizations-a-tale-of-a-mixed-martial-arts-fighter-from -dagestan/.

55.   *Autobiography*, 71–72, LC Box 88; Travis, *George Kennan*, 18; "The Cession of Russian America," *New York Herald*, April 29, 1867, 6.

Chapter 4: The Mountaineers of the Caucasus

56.   *Autobiography*, 283–301, LC Box 88; Travis, *George Kennan*, 36; Kennan, "Camping Out in Siberia," 257–67; John Kennan to George Kennan, November 25, 1867, NYPL Box 1.

57.   *Autobiography*, 291–96, 301–06, LC Box 88; Hotchkiss Notes, NYPL Box 7; Mark Feeney, "Still Ruskin after all these years," *Boston Globe*, March 24, 2019, N1-N4.

58.   *Autobiography*, 306–24, LC Box 88; Mehmet Samuk, "The American Lyceums," *SMU Research Scholars* (November 15, 2016), https:// stmuhistorymedia.org/the-american-lyceums/; "Extract from a Lyceum Lecture," Elizabeth Cady Stanton Papers, LC Box 5; "Adventures in Northern Asia," *Cincinnati Enquirer*, January 22, 1870, 8; "Young Men's Association Lecture Course," *Daily Milwaukee News*, December 14, 1869, 5, quoting from *Louisville Democrat*; "Lieut. Kennan's Lecture," *Daily Ohio Statesman* (Columbus, Ohio) January 29, 1869, 3; "Synopsis

of Lecture of Geo. Kennan," *Hancock Courier* (Findlay, Ohio), December 23, 1869, 2; "Our Life in Siberia and Kamtschatka," *Cincinnati Daily Enquirer,* January 11, 1870, 8; Hotchkiss Notes, NYPL Box 7; Travis, *George Kennan,* 37–40.

59. Maier, ed., *Vagabond Life,* 7, 24–29, 84–88, 93–101; *Autobiography,* 324–30, 358–59, LC Box 88; George Kennan to Kennan family, September 12, 1870, LC Box 13; King, *The Ghost of Freedom,* xiv, 9–10, 22; Michael Reynolds, "The Brawl of Civilization," *Foreign Policy Research Institute* (January 2, 2019), https://www.fpri.org/article/2019/01/the-brawl-of -civilizations-a-tale-of-a-mixed-martial-arts-fighter-from-dagestan/.

60. Sarah Marcus, "Mountain Jews," Tabletmag.com, August 26, 2010, http: //www.tabletmag.com/Jewish-news-and-politics/42649/mountain-jews; Goluboff, "Are They Asians or Jews?" 113; Kennan, "The Mountains and Mountaineers of the Eastern Caucasus," 171, 181–82; Maier, *Vagabond Life,* 7, 44, 85–87, 93–99, 102 n.13, 103–04, 106–117; George Kennan to Kennan family, September 12, 1870, LC Box 13; Chronology of George Kennan's Life Prepared by Emiline Weld Kennan (hereafter EWK Chronology), NYPL Box 7; Kennan, "An Island in the Sea of History," 1090.

61. de Waal, *The Caucasus,* 6, 9–10; Kennan, "An Island in the Sea of History," 1104; Meier, ed., *Vagabond Life,* 40–41 n. 95; 121–23. Another, less admirable, example of Dagestan hospitality was the custom of mountaineers to provide a young virgin girl for their overnight guests to sleep with, although as Kennan wrote in his journal, "no serious connection is permitted. Resembles the American custom of bundling." Id. 115–16.

62. Maier, ed., *Vagabond Life,* 95 (from Kennan's description of typical Dagestan mountaineer), 123–26 (based on Kennan Handwritten Lecture Notes, LC Box 64); Kennan, "An Island in the Sea of History," 1104–05, 1107.

63. Kennan, "The Mountains and Mountaineers of the Eastern Caucasus," 174, 177–79; Maier, ed., *Vagabond Life,* 18–19, 41, 92–93, 129–40, 236; "Kennan's Thrilling Tale," *Daily Inter Ocean* (Chicago), February 7, 1890, 2.

64. Maier, ed. *Vagabond Life,* 148–50, 235–37.

65. Kennan, "The Mountains and Mountaineers of the Eastern Caucasus," 187–88; Maier, ed. *Vagabond Life,* 150; Sahni, "Oriental Phantoms," 43.

66. Maier, ed., *Vagabond Life,* 41–42, 157–61.

67. Kennan, "A Tenth-Century Barbarian," 201–06; Maier, ed., *Vagabond Life,* 182–85, 242.

68. Kennan, "Murder by Adat," 479–82; Kennan, "A Tenth-Century Barbarian," 202–06; Maier, ed., *Vagabond Life,* 176–217; Michael Reynolds, "The Brawl of Civilization," *Foreign Policy Research Institute* (January 2, 2019), https://www.fpri.org/article/2019/01/the-brawl-of-civilizations-a-tale-of-a -mixed-martial-arts-fighter-from-dagestan/.

69. Maier, ed., *Vagabond Life,* 217–23; "Kennan's Vagabond Life," *Brooklyn Times Union,* April 15, 1890, 4.

Chapter 5: The Making of a Journalist

70. Landale and Guest, "Ideology and Sexuality," 149 (reflecting disagreement among sociologists over nineteenth-century women's attitude toward sexual relations); Signor and Smith, *Landmarks of Orleans County,* 367–68; Cutter, *Genealogical and Family History,* 761; "Mrs. Emaline [*sic*] Kennan," *Chicago Tribune,* May 28, 1940, 16; Untitled, *Norwalk Daily Reflector,* January 23, 1888, 3; Daniloff, "George Kennan," 607; two undated letters from George Kennan to Emiline Rathbone Weld, written in the mid-1870s, LC Box 15; EWK Chronology 1872, NYPL Box 7 ("first references to ERW in letters to his family"); George Kennan to Mary Ann Kennan, October 1, 1871, LC Box 13; Travis, *George Kennan,* 48–49 quoting George Kennan to Jennie Kennan, approximately early 1872, LC Box 13.

71. "New Publications," *New York Times,* October 10, 1870, 2; "Kamchatka," *Nation,* August 31, 1871, 145–46; "Literature," *New York Herald,* December 10, 1870, 2; "Recent Literature," *Atlantic Monthly,* January 1871, 140; "Review of New Books," *Philadelphia Inquirer,* October 24, 1870, 3; "Tent Life in Siberia," *Pall Mall Gazette,* November 24, 1870, 12; George Kennan to Emiline Rathbone Weld, November 13, 1875, LC Box 15; Travis, *George Kennan,* 41–42, 48, 74. Kennan never wrote a book about his Caucasus travels, in part because his editor George Putnam died in 1872. Id.

72. George Kennan to Kossuth Kent Kennan, December 25, 1916, NYPL Box 1; George Kennan to Mary Hinman, June 2, 1873 (emphasis in the original), LC Box 6; Undated typewritten manuscript, LC Box 60; Travis, *George Kennan,* 50.

73. Signor and Smith, *Landmarks of Orleans County,* 358; Anderson, Barry, and Sanderson, *Mark Twain's Notebooks & Journals* I, 302; Wright, "British Geography and the American Geographical Society," 1–2; McCorristine, "Spiritual Routes," 139–40; "About the American Geographical Society: History," *American Geographical Society,* no date, https://americangeo.org/about/; Hotchkiss Notes, NYPL Box 7; George Kennan to Mary Ann Kennan, November 27, 1883 (emphasis in the original), LC Box 60.

74. Kennan, "A Dog-Sledge Journey," 96–130; George Kennan to Emiline Rathbone Weld, June 5, 1876, LC Box 15; Bernstein, "American Labor in the Long Depression," 60–61; Ward, *Sensible Etiquette of the Best Society,* 142, 254; Beckert, *The Monied Metropolis,* 58, 208–09.

75. Fairfield, *The Clubs of New York,* 31–32, 215–21; George Kennan to Emiline Rathbone Weld, May 1877, LC Box 15; George Kennan to Mary Ann Kennan, July 23, 1877, LC Box 13.

76. George Kennan to Mary Ann Kennan, July 23, 1877, LC Box 13; Travis, *George Kennan,* 51; "Cooper Union Free Saturday Night Lectures," *New York Tribune,* February 25, 1875, 12; "Young Men's Christian Association," *New York Times,* January 11, 1878, 7; George Kennan to Emiline Rathbone Weld, July 24, 1876, May 1877 (no date), LC Box 15.

77. "Central Asia," *New York Daily Tribune,* February 22, 1873, 3, 6. The phrase "the Great Game" was later found in the British officer's papers,

although the term was only first made popular in Rudyard Kipling's *Kim*. Fromkin, "The Great Game in Asia," 936, 947–48. Kennan's other letters to the *Tribune* were less measured. He defended the Russian suppression of a Chechen uprising and even suggested that Russian expansion in the Caucasus was due, at least in part, to the necessity of defending Christians from enslavement, although his defense was probably inspired less by religious bias than by his reflexive Russophilia. It's unclear whether Kennan knew that the slave trade went both ways: Russians sent their Muslim captives to Siberia as slave laborers. "A Defense of Russia," *New York Daily Tribune*, January 31, 1877, 5; "Letters from the People," *New York Daily Tribune*, July 7, 1877, 3; King, *The Ghost of Freedom*, 61–62; Travis, *George Kennan*, 77–78.

78. *Autobiography*, 1–25 (chapter at the end titled "Jerry McCauley's Prayer-Meeting"), LC Box 88. Kennan even wrote many years later that "And yet, the emotions that lived and died in that Water Street mission more mightily stir my heart, even now, than any royal tragedy ever represented on the stage, or recorded in the history of mankind." Id. 25. "Jerry McCauley's Mission," *Chicago Tribune*, February 18, 1877 (reprinting an article from the *New York Sun*), 13; George Kennan to Emiline Rathbone Weld, September 13, 1876 and 1877 (no date), LC Box 15.

79. Reporters of the Associated Press, *Breaking News*, 18–19, 39–40 (the wire service was originally called the New York Associated Press); Lauren Easton, "What is AP? CEO explains in Op Ed," *Associated Press* (May 29, 2019), https://blog.ap.org/behind-the-news/what-is-ap-ceo-explains-in-op-ed; "George Kennan and the Phillips Code," *Telegraph and Telephone Age* (February 16, 1917), 83, https://books.google.com/books/about/Telegraph_and_Telephone_Age.html?id=JZc2AQAAMAAJ; "Old Senate Chamber," *Architect of the Capitol*, no date, https://www.aoc.gov/capitol-buildings/old-senate-chamber; George Kennan to Emiline Rathbone Weld, undated, November (no date), 5, 12, 1878, LC Box 15.

80. George Kennan to Emiline Rathbone Weld, November 5, 1878, LC Box 15; Joe-Stanley Brown to Anna L. Dawes, March 25, 1886, NYPL Box 6; Travis, *George Kennan*, 57–60; Kenneth D. Ackerman, "The Garfield Assassination Altered American History," Smithsonian.com (November 19, 2018), https://www.smithsonianmag.com/history/garfield-assassination-altered-american-history-woefully-forgotten-today-180968319/. The Associated Press and newspapers depended on White House bulletins on the president's condition that historians have since shown were misleadingly optimistic. Menke, "Media in America," 646; EWK Chronology, July–December 1882, NYPL Box 7; "The Literary Society," *Evening Star* (Washington, DC), August 8, 1885, 12.

81. Withycombe, *Lost*, 4; Hotchkiss Notes, NYPL Box 7; George Kennan to John Kennan, March 20, May 13, 1883, LC Box 13; Jennie Kennan to George Kennan, March 4, 1883, NYPL Box 1; George Kennan to Kennan family, March 30, 1883, LC Box 13; Travis, *George Kennan*, 107 n. 76.

82. Hotchkiss Notes, NYPL Box 7; Mary Ann Kennan to George Kennan, November 15, 1883, NYPL Box 1; George Kennan to Mary Ann Kennan, November 27, 1883, LC Box 60; Undated typewritten manuscript, LC Box 60 (emphasis in the original).

Chapter 6: It Will Really Be a Magnificent Trip

83. Saul, *Concord & Conflict*, 131–32, 200, 233–34, 271–72.
84. Siljak, *Angel of Vengeance*, 1–7, 11–12, 139–44, 149, 180–81, 205–13; Perris, *Russia in Revolution*, 230; Pedler, "Going to the People," 133–34; Figes, *Natasha's Dance*, 222, 227–28; Pipes, "The Trial of Vera Z.," 5–6, 11, 14–23, 34–35; Engel, "The Emergence of Women Revolutionaries in Russia," 98; Engel and Rosenthal, *Five Sisters*, xi, 12–13; Pipes, *Russia Under the Old Regime*, 165–66.
85. Ruud and Stepanov, *Fontanka 16*, 38–43; Pipes, "The Trial of Vera Z.," 1, 15, 33–39, 55–61, 66–67; Siljak, *Angel of Vengeance*, 1–3, 5–12, 154–55, 211–12; Engel and Rosenthal, *Five Sisters*, xxi–xxii. Between 1873 and 1877 approximately 15 percent of the more than fifteen hundred individuals arrested for political crimes were women. Engel, "The Emergence of Women Revolutionaries in Russia," 92; Wolfe, *Three Who Made a Revolution*, 167. Other historians describe Trepov as the chief of police. Crankshaw, *The Shadow of the Winter Palace*, 296.
86. Radzinsky, *Alexander II*, 406–17; Ruud and Stepanov, *Fontanka 16*, 50–51; Engel, "The Emergence of Women Revolutionaries in Russia," 92, 100; Pipes, "The Trial of Vera Z.," 73.
87. Crankshaw, *The Shadow of the Winter Palace*, 317–19; "Avenged," *Boston Weekly Globe*, April 20, 1881, 1; "Emperor and Nihilists," *New York Times*, April 9, 1881, 1; "Foreign News," *New Ulm Review* (New Ulm, Minnesota), May 4, 1881, 2; "The Assassins of the Czar and their Accomplices Strangled in Public," *Pantagraph* (Bloomington, Illinois) April 16, 1881, 1; "The Execution of the Czar's Assassins," *Cheshire Observer* (Chester, England), April 23, 1881, 8; Eva Sohlman, "Overlooked No More: The Russian Icon Who Was Hanged for Killing a Czar," *New York Times*, May 30, 2018, D12; Pipes, "The Trial of Vera Z.," 5–6; Radzinsky, *Alexander II*, 424; Engel, "The Emergence of Women Revolutionaries in Russia," 100.
88. Saul, *Concord & Conflict*, 236–49; Crankshaw, *The Shadow of the Winter Palace*, 326–27, 332–33; Ruud and Stepanov, *Fontanka 16*, 51–55 n. 42; "Russia's Rulers," *Boston Globe*, April 19, 1881, 3; "The Hebrews in Russia," *New York Times*, February 2, 1882, 8; "Expressions of Sympathy," *New York Times*, March 15, 1881, 2; "The King-Killers," *Chicago Tribune*, April 30, 1881, 5; Pipes, *Russia under the Old Regime*, 305–13; Beer, *The House of the Dead*, 295–98; Untitled, *Times* (Philadelphia), March 5, 1882, 4; George Kennan to J. A. MacGahan, February 28, 1882, LC Box 6, quoted in Travis, *George Kennan*, 85, see id., 81–82; Kennan, "Siberia. The Exiles Abode," 61–68; Kennan, *Siberia and the Exile System* 1:242.

89. George Kennan to George Frost, April 17, 1885, NYPL Box 6; Armstrong, *Siberia and the Nihilists,* 15–24, 46–47, 64–65, 80, 87–151; Travis, *George Kennan,* 48, 86–88; Hundley, "George Kennan and the Russian Empire," 2–3; Kennan, "Siberia. The Exiles Abode," 61–68; "The Land of the Exiled," *New York Times,* February 25, 1882, 8; "Siberia Not a Desert," *Boston Evening Transcript,* August 12, 1882, 6; "George Kennan," *Chicago Tribune,* May 6, 1882, 3.

90. John, *The Best Years of the Century,* ix, 1–3, 94–95, 108, 126–30, 140; Noonan, *Reading the Century Illustrated Monthly Magazine,* 155; Rosamond Gilder, ed., *Letters of Richard Watson Gilder,* viii, 66; Caron, "How Changeable Are the Events of War," 154–57; Hearn, *The Annotated Huckleberry Finn,* Introduction, xxxi-xxxii.

91. Feldstein, "A Muckraking Model," 1–5; Forde and Foss, "The Facts—The Color!—The Facts," 127–35; Baldasty, *The Commercialization of News in the 19th Century,* 16–35; Wallach, "A Depraved Taste For Publicity," 34; Petrova, "Newspapers and Parties," 792–93; Bly, *Ten Days in a Mad-House,* 91–93; Wells, *A Red Record,* 1–35.

92. George Kennan to Emiline Kennan, September 5, 9–10, 1884, LC Box 15; Travis, *George Kennan,* 91–92, quoting George Kennan to David R. McKee (the manager of the Associated Press's office in Washington), September 6, 1884, LC Box 6.

93. George Kennan to Richard Gilder, March 10, 1885, LC, Box 6; Bassin, "Inventing Siberia," 792–93; Lubow, *The Reporter Who Would be King,* 67; John, *The Best Years of the Century,* 130–31; Travis, *George Kennan,* 95; George Kennan to Emiline Kennan, July 24, 1885, LC Box 15; Jefferson, *Roughing it in Siberia,* 23.

94. Martyn, "History of the Century Magazine," 93–96; "Soldier And Artist," *Boston Globe,* January 15, 1893, 23; John J. Henderson and Roger E. Belson, "George Albert Frost (1843–1907)," *White Mountain Art and Artists,* no date, http://whitemountainart.com/about-3/artists/george-albert-frost-1843–1907/; Frederick A. Hunnewell to George F. Kennan, November 28, 1948, NYPL Box 6; George Kennan to George Frost, April 16 & 17, 1885, NYPL Box 6; John, *The Best Years of the Century,* 127–31; Kennan, 2nd Siberian Trip Notebook, December 23, 1885, LC Box 20.

95. George Kennan to George Frost, April 17, 27, 28, 1885, NYPL, Box 6; George Kennan to Roswell Smith, May 30, 1885, LC Box 6.

96. Kennan, *Siberia and the Exile System* 1:1–2; George Kennan to Roswell Smith, May 30, 1885, LC Box 6; EWK Chronology, NYPL Box 7.

97. The term "nihilism," derived from the Latin word *nihil,* or nothing, may have been introduced in Russia in Ivan Turgenev's novel *Fathers and Children* (also translated as *Fathers and Sons*) in the character Yevgeny Bazarov. The novel's setting was the Russian student demands for change in the 1860s, which brought a younger activist generation into conflict with older liberals content to criticize the existing order only passively. Figes, *Natasha's Dance,* 222; Kennan, *Siberia and the Exile System* 1:iii (preface), 3, 302–03 n. 1.

98. George Kennan to Roswell Smith, May 30, 1885 (emphasis in the original), LC Box 6; Hundley, "George Kennan and the Russian Empire," 3–6; Travis, *George Kennan,* 113.

99. Renner, "Defining a Russian Nation," 659–60; Massie, *Land of the Firebird,* 300–06; Munro, Butler and Johnstone, *A Trip Up the Volga,* 70–73; Fitzpatrick, *The Great Russian Fair,* 27–28; Maier, ed., *Vagabond Life,* 70–78; Kennan, *Siberia and the Exile System,* 1:5–9; Williams, *The Bells of Russia,* 62.

100. Reeder, trans., *Down Along the Mother Volga,* 35; Kennan, *Siberia and the Exile System* 1:6–9, 15–24, 353; Kennan, 2nd Siberian Trip Notebook, June 9, 1885, LC Box 19.

101. Kennan, *Siberia and the Exile System* 1:25–31, 47–48; Pipes, *Russia under the Old Regime,* 290–302; Ruud and Stepanov, *Fontanka 16,* 18–19, 32–34; George Kennan to Richard Watson Gilder, June 19, 1885, LC Box 6; David Filipov, "The Search for Siberia: even Russians in dark," *The Windsor Star* (Windsor, Ontario), January 7, 2017, 56; Spottiswoode, *A Tarantasse Journey Through Eastern Russia,* 26–28.

102. Wenyon, *Across Siberia on the Great Post-road,* 34–43; Spottiswoode, *A Tarantasse Journey Through Eastern Russia,* 33; *Autobiography,* 241–42; Kennan, *Siberia and the Exile System* 1:47–49; Kennan, *Tent Life in Siberia,* 453–54; Chekhov, *Sakhalin Island,* 31.

103. Kennan, *Siberia and the Exile System* 1:49–54.

Chapter 7: Every Respiration Seemed to Pollute Me to the Very Soul

104. Kennan, *Siberia and the Exile System* 1:63–68; Hartley, *Siberia,* 46–47.

105. Kennan, *Siberia and the Exile System* 1:70–74.

106. Kennan, *Siberia and the Exile System* 1:83–95, 306 & 2:264 n.1; Beer, *The House of the Dead,* 314; "Extract from a Letter From Victor Casturin," presumably written to George Kennan, May 25, 1886, 8, NYPL Box 1; George Kennan to Roswell Smith, June 28, 1885, LC Box 6.

107. Kennan, *Siberia and the Exile System* 1:107–10, 375; Beer, *The House of the Dead,* 38 (exiles were permitted to bring with them a maximum of twenty-five pounds).

108. Kennan, *Siberia and the Exile System* 1:110–19, 296–97, 370, 398; Kennan, 2nd Siberian Trip Notebook, June 20, 1885, LC Box 19.

109. Kennan, *Siberia and the Exile System* 1:363–64; George Kennan to Roswell Smith, June 28, 1885, LC, Box 6; Kropotkine, *In Russian and French Prisons,* 138–39 (mortality during the journey was as high as 8 to 10 percent by one calculation).

110. Beer, *The House of the Dead,* 4, 16; Gentes, *Roads to Oblivion,* 10, 13; Kennan, *Siberia and the Exile System* 1:74–75; Rawson, "The Death Penalty in Late Tsarist Russia," 31–33.

111. Beer, *The House of the Dead,* 14–17, 22–24, 30–38; Kennan, *Siberia and the Exile System,* 1:74–77; Murrell, *Discovering the Moscow Countryside,*

172; Badcock, "From Villains to Victims," 1720; Spottiswoode, *A Tarantasse Journey Through Eastern Russia,* 37.

112. Lincoln, *The Conquest of a Continent,* xix; Kropotkine, *In Russian and French Prisons,* 181–82; Beer, *The House of the Dead,* 22–23, 34–35, 45–46, 216–21, 230–31, 272, 282–83; Kennan, *Siberia and the Exile System* 1:76–77, 382, 398–99; Kennan, 2nd Siberian Trip Notebook, September 2, 1885, LC Box 20; Chekhov, *Sakhalin Island,* 293–94.

113. Kennan, *Siberia and the Exile System* 1:390–94, 400–02; Beer, *The House of the Dead,* 46–48, 179–80; Hartley, *Siberia,* 126–27.

114. Hartley, *Siberia,* 107–09; Gentes, *Exile, Murder and Madness,* 22–27, 66–70; Kennan, *Siberia and the Exile System* 1:77–78 n.1, 80 n.1; Beer, *The House of the Dead,* 36–41.

115. Pipes, *Russia Under the Old Regime,* 310; Ziegler, *Black Dragon River,* 67 (Turkish derivation); Gentes, *Exile, Murder and Madness,* 35; Beer, *The House of the Dead,* 25, 227; Kennan, *Siberia and the Exile System* 1:79–80, 242–43, 271.

116. Beer, *The House of the Dead,* 34–35, 42–45, 241–47, 253–55; Kennan, *Siberia and the Exile System* 1:78–83, 370–71.

117. Beer, *The House of the Dead,* 52–80; Sutherland, *The Princess of Siberia,* 101–02, 107–09, 116–20, 124–25, 135–40.

118. Kennan, *Siberia and the Exile System* 1:242–46, 370; Beer, *The House of the Dead,* 297–99.

119. Kennan, *Siberia and the Exile System* 1:81–82, 276–77, quoting Juridical Messenger (the journalistic organ of the Moscow Juridical Society), October 1883, 332 & 2:34–50, quoting in part from the "Rules Relating to Police Surveillance" which governed the life of administratively banished exiles after 1882; Beer, *The House of the Dead,* 298–99, 306.

Chapter 8: The Exile System Is Worse Than I Believed It to Be

120. Kennan, *Siberia and the Exile System* 1:130–34.

121. George Kennan to Emiline Kennan, June 23, July 7, 1885, LC Box 15; Kennan, *Siberia and the Exile System* 1:134–43.

122. Beer, *The House of the Dead,* 160–70, 183; Frank, *Dostoevsky,* 166–75, 188–89. The novels included *Crime and Punishment, The Idiot,* and *The Brothers Karamazov*; Kennan, "Siberia: The Exiles Abode," 40.

123. Chekhov, *The Steppe,* 3; George Kennan to Roswell Smith, June 28, 1885, LC Box 6; Kennan, *Siberia and the Exile System* 1:120–23.

124. George Frost to James W. Hunnewell, August 20, 1885, NYPL Box 6; Kennan, *Siberia and the Exile System* 1:150–58.

125. Kennan, *Siberia and the Exile System* 1:158–69; Kennan, 2nd Siberian Trip Notebook, July 15, 1885, LC Box 20. The name Pavlovsky was invented by Kennan to protect the official, whose real name was P. E. Makovetsky, a local justice of the peace. Travis, *George Kennan,* 163.

126. Kennan, *Siberia and the Exile System* 1:170–74; Turgenev, *Fathers and Sons,* 67.

127. Kennan, *Siberia and the Exile System* 1:174–78.

128. George Kennan to Roswell Smith, July 16, 1885, LC Box 6; Kennan, *Siberia and the Exile System* 1:179–87.

129. Kennan, *Siberia and the Exile System* 1:188–228; Kennan, 2nd Siberian Trip Notebook, August 2, 1885, LC Box 19.

130. Kennan, *Siberia and the Exile System* 1:229–37, 278–85, 308–12; Kennan, 2nd Siberian Trip Notebook, August 18, 1885, LC Box 19.

131. Tolstoy, *Resurrection*, 431; Kennan, *Siberia and the Exile System* 1:312–21; Kennan, "Siberia: The Exiles Abode," 61.

132. Slatter, ed., *From the Other Shore*, 67–69; Perris, *Russia in Revolution*, 226–30; Kennan, *Siberia and the Exile System* 1:333–34. Another Tomsk exile, Prince Alexander Kropotkin, also impressed Kennan. The brother of a well-known author and anarchist, Kropotkin had been sent into exile on a charge of "political untrustworthiness." Once a wealthy landowner, his exile had impoverished him and left him despondent, and not long after Kennan returned to the United States, he committed suicide. Id. 325–33; "Life in Russian Prisons," *New York Times*, November 23, 1890, 17; Felix Volkhovsky, "George Kennan in Tomsk," *Free Russia*, vol. v, no. 1, January 1, 1894, 7. https://books.google.com/books/about/Free_Russia.html?id =7-A5AQAAMAAJ&printsec=frontcover&newbks=1&newbks_redir=0 &source=gb_mobile_entity.

133. Kennan, *Siberia and the Exile System* 1: 348–50.

Chapter 9: A *Telega* Will Simply Jolt a Man's Soul Out in Twenty-Four Hours

134. Kennan, *Siberia and the Exile System* 1:369–87; Deutsch, *Sixteen Years in Siberia*, 200–01.

135. Kennan, *Siberia and the Exile System* 1:351–54.

136. Kennan, *Siberia and the Exile System* 1:354–60.

137. George Kennan to Frank Scott, September 14, 1885, LC Box 6; Kennan, *Siberia and the Exile System*, 1:362–68; Kennan, *Tent Life in Siberia*, 464. The distance from St. Petersburg on the sign in the post station was not a straight-line calculation.

138. Sutherland, *The Princess of Siberia*, 138–39, 148–54.

139. Kennan, *Siberia and the Exile System*, 1:302–05 & 2:1–8; Kennan, 2nd Siberian Trip Notebook, September 13–15, 1885, LC Box 20.

140. Lincoln, *The Conquest of a Continent*, 246–48; Kennan, *Siberia and the Exile System* 2:60–71; Kennan, 2nd Siberian Trip Notebook, September 24–26, 1885, LC Box 20; Wenyon, *Across Siberia on the Great Post-road*, 119–20.

141. Lincoln, *The Conquest of a Continent*, 51–53; Wenyon, *Across Siberia on the Great Post-road*, 139–41; Kennan, *Siberia and the Exile System*, 2:60–62, 72–97 (emphasis in the original), 107–09, 116–17; Kennan, 2nd Siberian Trip Notebook, September 29, 1885, LC Box 20; Ziegler, *Black Dragon River*, 108–10.

142. Her full name was Ekaterina Constantinovna Breshko-Breshkovskaya. Blackwell, ed., *The Little Grandmother of the Russian Revolution*, 1–10, 39–42, 79–101; Pipes, "The Trial of Vera Z.," 34; Kennan, *Siberia and the Exile System*, 2:117–18.
143. Kennan, *Siberia and the Exile System*, 2:121–22; Kennan, 2nd Siberian Trip Notebook, September 29, October 16–17, 1885, LC Box 20.
144. Kennan, *Siberia and the Exile System*, 2:128–29, 131–37.

Chapter 10: The Mines of Kara

145. Lincoln, *The Conquest of a Continent*, 164–65, 185–86; Beer, *The House of the Dead*, 81–82; Kennan, *Siberia and the Exile System*, 2:138, 142 & n.1, 206–07, 279–80.
146. Kennan, *Siberia and the Exile System*, 2:139–42.
147. Kennan, *Siberia and the Exile System*, 2:168–69, 199–200.
148. Kennan, *Siberia and the Exile System*, 2:124, 142–46, 157–58.
149. Beer, *The House of the Dead*, 48–51; Kennan, *Siberia and the Exile System*, 1:290–91, 395–96 & 2:149–50 (emphasis in the original), 207–08, 220–21, 260.
150. George Kennan to George Frost, August 18, 1886, NYPL Box 6; Kennan confirmed four cases of convicts punished by being chained to wheelbarrows. The last occurred in 1884, the year before he went to Siberia. Kennan, *Siberia and the Exile System*, 2:143–44, 160–74, 207 n.1, 227–28, 544–55.
151. Deutsch, *Sixteen Years in Siberia*, 238, 246; Kennan, *Siberia and the Exile System*, 2:170–83; Kennan, 2nd Siberian Trip Notebook, November 6, 1885, LC Box 20.
152. Kennan, *Siberia and the Exile System*, 2: 183–87 (emphasis in the original), 227–28; Kennan, 2nd Siberian Trip Notebook, November 6, 1885, LC Box 20; Breshkovsky, *A Message to the American People*, 2 (Introduction by George Kennan).
153. Kennan, *Siberia and the Exile System*, 2:183–87; Tolstoy, *Resurrection*, 384–85.
154. Engel, *Mothers and Daughters*, 201; Kennan, *Siberia and the Exile System*, 2:187–90, 192–93. In *Siberia and the Exile System* Kennan erroneously described Vera Zasulich's target as "General Mezentsef," the St. Petersburg chief of police.
155. Kennan, *Siberia and the Exile System*, 2:189–95.
156. Kennan, *Siberia and the Exile System*, 2:195–200, 275; George Kennan to George Frost, January 10, 1888, NYPL Box 6.

Chapter 11: There Are People Who Intend to Murder Us

157. Kennan, *Siberia and the Exile System*, 2:278–82.
158. Gentes, "Siberian Exile and the 1863 Polish Insurrectionists," 212–13; Kennan, *Siberia and the Exile System*, 2:279–80; Beer, *The House of the Dead*, 81–82, 85–87.

159. George Frost to James W. Hunnewell, December 9, 1885, NYPL Box 6; Kennan, *Siberia and the Exile System,* 2:282–301; Kennan, 2nd Siberian Trip Notebook, November 19, 1885, LC Box 20.

160. Kennan, *Siberia and the Exile System* 2:288, 300–16; Kennan, 2nd Siberian Trip Notebook, November 22–23, 1885, LC Box 20.

161. Beer, *The House of the Dead,* 82–84; Sutherland, *The Princess of Siberia,* 157–58.

162. Kennan, *Siberia and the Exile System* 2:128–29, 319–39, 342 (emphasis in the original); Kennan, 2nd Siberian Trip Notebook, December 1, 1885, LC Box 20.

163. Beer, *The House of the Dead,* 92–94, 104–06, 111–12; Sutherland, *The Princess of Siberia,* 198–99, 204–18, 233.

164. Kennan, *Siberia and the Exile System* 2:336–38, Frost illustration. Kennan earlier described the ordeals of these exiles without providing a source, id. 212–16, and later wrote that he had heard the stories from the Chita exiles, id. 338. Alexandra Guzeva, "What's Behind the Traditional Russian Shirt's Design," *Russia Beyond* (September 29, 2020), https://www.rbth .com/arts/332778-kosovorotka-russian-shirt.

165. Kennan, *Siberia and the Exile System* 2:338–41; Kennan, 2nd Siberian Trip Notebook, December 6, 23, 1885, LC Box 20.

166. Kennan, *Siberia and the Exile System* 2:342–44; Emiline Kennan to Jennie Kennan, January 24, 1886, LC Box 13.

167. Sutherland, *The Princess of Siberia,* 7, 214, 235–36, 269–303; Beer, *The House of the Dead,* 131.

168. Kennan, *Siberia and the Exile System,* 2:344–54; Kennan, 2nd Siberian Trip Notebook, January 8–10, 1886, LC Box 20.

169. George Frost to James W. Hunnewell, February 10, 1886, NYPL Box 6; Kennan, *Siberia and the Exile System,* 1:399–402 & 2:355–62, Frost illustration.

170. Hotchkiss Notes, NYPL Box 7; Kennan, *Siberia and the Exile System* 2:361–65; Kennan, 2nd Siberian Trip Notebook, January 15–17, March 5–7, 1886, LC Box 20.

171. Kennan, *Siberia and the Exile System* 2:365, 381–85, 405–07, 413–15.

172. Kennan, *Siberia and the Exile System* 2:415–18; Kennan, *A Russian Comedy of Errors,* 140; George Kennan to Emiline Kennan, February 15, 1886, LC Box 15 (emphasis in the original).

173. Kennan, *Siberia and the Exile System* 2:418–22; Kennan, 2nd Siberian Trip Notebook, January 10, March 1–4. 1886, LC Box 20; George Kennan to George Frost, December 10, 1887, NYPL Box 6; George Kennan to David McKee, May 11, 1886, NYPL Box 1.

174. George Kennan to Emiline Kennan, March 3, 1886, LC Box 15; George Kennan to George Frost, December 10, 1887, January 10, 1888, NYPL Box 6; Kennan, *Siberia and the Exile System* 2:422–24; Kennan, 2nd Siberian Trip Notebook, March 2, 4–5, 7–18, 1886, LC Box 20.

175. Emiline Kennan, "Notes From My Russian Journal," December 1891, LC

Box 68; Hotchkiss Notes, NYPL Box 7; Emiline Kennan to Jessie [last name unknown], April 2, 13, 1886, LC Box 13; George Kennan to Emiline Kennan, July 24, 1885, LC Box 15; Emiline Kennan to Mary Ann Kennan, January 1, 3, 16, February 17, 1886, LC Box 13; Emiline Kennan to Jennie Kennan, January 24, 1886, LC Box 13; George Kennan to David McKee, May 11, 1886, NYPL Box 1; "Soldier And Artist," *The Boston Globe,* January 15, 1893, 23; George Kennan to Richard Gilder, November 22, 1886, reprinted in NYPL Digital Collection, https://digitalcollections .nypl.org/items/71a1bf80–7faa-0135–073e-1161a3f9f8b0/book#page/7 /mode/; Emiline Kennan to her mother, March 29, 1886, LC Box 13.

176. George Kennan to George Frost, August 18, 1886, NYPL Box 6; Kennan, *Siberia and the Exile System* 2:544–55; Travis, *Kennan,* 140–42; Emiline Kennan, "Notes From My Russian Journal," December 1891, LC Box 68; "Her Experiences in Russia," *The News and Observer* (Raleigh, North Carolina), March 28, 1895, 5 (for this later lecture Emiline wore the "holiday dress" of a Russian peasant); YMCA of the USA, *Yearbook and Official Roster,* ii (advertisement listing Emiline Kennan among the lecturers of the Redpath Lyceum Bureau of Boston and Chicago for the 1896–97 season); "Their Life in Russia," *Democrat and Chronicle* (Rochester, New York), April 16, 1895, 7.

177. Kennan, "A Visit to Count Tolstoi," 252–65; Travis, *Kennan,* 143–44; Kennan, *Siberia and the Exile System* 2:194 n. 1; George Kennan to William Dudley Foulke, February 4, 1888, NYPL Box 1.

Chapter 12: *Siberia and the Exile System*

178. Barbara Schmidt, "Mark Twain on Czars, Siberia and the Russian Revolution," www.twainquotes.com, 10–11 no date, http://www.twainquotes .com/Revolution/revolution.html (Mark Twain scholar Howard Baetzhold suggested that Twain's depiction of enslaved people in *A Connecticut Yankee in King Arthur's Court* may have been inspired by Kennan's writings and lectures on the exile system); "When Mark Twain Wept," *Nebraska State Journal* (Lincoln, Nebraska), April 13, 1888, 1 (filed by the Washington correspondent for the *Philadelphia Record*); "The Literary Society," *Evening Star* (Washington, DC), August 8, 1885, 2; Travis, *George Kennan,* 178.

179. George Kennan to William Dudley Foulke, February 4, 1888, NYPL Box 1; Travis, *George Kennan,* 154, quoting George Kennan to Hartwell Osborn, November 26, 1887, LC Box 10 and Roswell Smith to George Kennan, October 13, 1887, LC Box 57; George Kennan to Richard Gilder, January 16, 1886 (misdated, likely 1887), LC Box 6; "Siberia and the Exiles," *Brooklyn Times Union,* September 24, 1887, 7; Stults, "George Kennan," 276, 283–84; George Kennan to Alfred J. P. McClure, March 15, 1891, LC Box 11.

180. Kennan, *Siberia and the Exile System* 1:402 & 2:98–99; Ellsworth, "George Kennan," *The Outlook,* 188 (October 1, 1919); Henry Sandham to William Carey, April 11, 1889, NYPL Century Magazine Records

Digital Collection, Henry Sandham file http://archives.nypl.org/mss/504 #c1149910 ; Travis, *George Kennan*, 156; John, *The Best Years of the Century*, 131.

181. "Cruel Russia," *New York Times*, December 27, 1891, 19; "Literature," *San Francisco Chronicle*, November 29, 1891, 7; Saul, *Concord & Conflict*, 282; "Kennan's Siberia," *New York Tribune*, December 9, 1891, 8; Salisbury, "Journey into the Interior of a Nightmare," *New York Times*, February 2, 1958, 3.

182. Stults, "George Kennan," 280–81; "Through Siberian Wastes," *Kansas City Times*, March 25, 1890, 2; Pond, *Eccentricities of Genius*, 144, 231, 290, 497; "The Kennan Lecture," *Chattanooga Daily Times*, February 23, 1890, 4; Hundley, "George Kennan," 8; "From the Grave of Freedom," *Omaha Daily Bee*, October 28, 1891, 2; Travis, *George Kennan*, 177–78; Good, "America and the Russian Revolutionary Movement," 274; Andrew Gentes, "George Kennan and the Russian Nihilists: A Sojourn into the Dialectics of Friendship," *Library of Congress*, Video (August 5, 2010), https://www.loc.gov/item/webcast-5048; Caceres, "Advocacy Journalism," Oxford University Press, June 25, 2019, https://doi.org/10.1093/acrefore /9780190228613.013.776;.

183. "Russian Exiles," *San Francisco Chronicle*, December 3, 1891, 4; "A Thrilling Recital," *Salt Lake Herald*, March 1, 1895, 3; "With Siberian Convicts," *San Francisco Examiner*, November 27, 1891, 3; "Autocratic Russia," *Boston Globe*, February 26, 1889, 8; "Experiences in Siberia," *Chicago Tribune*, April 19, 1889, 6; "Tales of Suffering," *St. Paul Globe*, March 11, 1890, 3; "Kennan's Tale of Woe, *Journal* (Meriden, Connecticut), December 10, 1889, 6; "Horrors of Siberia," *Philadelphia Inquirer*, November 14, 1889, 2; "George Kennan Interviewed," *Stentor* (Lake Forest, Illinois) February 16, 1891, 99–100; "The Kennan Lecture," *Chattanooga Daily Times*, February 23, 1890, 4; Good, "America and the Russian Revolutionary Movement," 274; Beer, *The House of the Dead*, 315–23 (the highly publicized flogging incident occurred after Kennan's investigation). The exiles, who had barricaded themselves in a building to protest their coming march in lethally cold temperatures to settlements in the Russian Arctic, were killed in a clash that also cost the lives of a soldier and a police officer. Id. Frederick Travis suggests that Kennan's use of the costume may have left the impression that the political exiles were also put in chains, which was generally not the case. But Kennan certainly had no need to embellish the ordeal of the political exiles and as Travis also points out, while Kennan's lectures were indeed dramatic, he did not resort to "rhetorical ranting," and in fact spoke with the "force of calm persuasiveness." Travis, *George Kennan*, 178, 180–181.

184. "Autocratic Russia," *Boston Globe*, February 26, 1889, 8; Smith, *The History of the Lowell Institute*, 48–76; Travis, *George Kennan*, 58, 178.

185. "Russian Exiles," *San Francisco Chronicle*, December 3, 1891, 4; Travis, *George Kennan*, 178; "The Kennan Lecture," *Hartford Courant*, November

2, 1889, 5; "The Russian Exiles," *Pittsburgh Dispatch,* February 20, 1890, 4; "Why the Czar Trembles," *Chicago Tribune,* February 14, 1890, 3.

186. "In the Mines at Kara," *Daily Inter Ocean* (Chicago, Illinois), January 22, 1891, 6; "Horrors of Siberia," *Philadelphia Inquirer,* November 14, 1889, 2; "From Hell's Depths," *Cincinnati Enquirer,* February 25, 1890, 4; "A Million Signers," *Topeka State Journal,* October 25, 1891, 1. Philadelphia activists alone gathered three hundred thousand signatures, which filled a good-size room to a height of six feet. "A Petition to the Czar," *Baltimore Sun,* June 22, 1891, 1; Travis, *George Kennan,* 197–98; "The Siberian Exile Petition," *Evening Journal* (Wilmington, Delaware), October 27, 1891, 1; Yarmolensky, "The Kennan Collection," 13.

187. "Through Siberian Wastes," *Kansas City Times,* March 25, 1890, 2; "Mrs. George Kennan," *Boston Weekly Globe,* January 8, 1890, 7; "A Helpful Wife," *Wyoming Democrat* (Tunkhannock, Pennsylvania), May 30, 1890, 1; Travis, *George Kennan,* 225, quoting from George Kennan to Alfred J. P. McClure, November 18, 1890, LC Box 11; Pond, *Eccentricities of Genius,* 289–90; Kennan, "A Few Recollections of Alexander Graham Bell," 146–49; Hotchkiss Notes, NYPL Box 7; George Kennan to J. B. Pond, October 1, 1894, LC Box 58; "Baddeck's Lace Makers," *Rochester Democrat and Chronicle,* September 8, 1895, 8; Mackenzie, *Alexander Graham Bell,* 278–79 (the friendship between the Kennans and the Bells was "perhaps the one really close one that Graham Bell and his wife ever had"); See generally, Grosvenor and Wesson, *Alexander Graham Bell.*

188. "George Kennan Breaks Down," *Chicago Tribune,* November 28, 1891, 1; Untitled, *Times Democrat* (New Orleans), November 30, 1891, 4; "Lectures by George Kennan," *Chicago Tribune,* February 8, 1892, 3; George Kennan to J. B. Pond, October 1, 1894, LC Box 58; Travis, *George Kennan,* 199–206, 213, 224–28, 286, 311 n.111; "Our London Correspondence," *Guardian,* June 12, 1893, 5.

189. "Tales of Suffering," *St. Paul Globe,* March 11, 1890, 3; "The Kennan Lecture," *Chattanooga Daily Times,* February 23, 1890, 4; "Kennan's Tale of Woe, *Journal* (Meriden, Connecticut), December 10, 1889, 6; "A Sad Story," *Oakland Tribune* (Oakland, California), November 24, 1891, 8; Kennan, *Siberia and the Exile System* (George Frost Kennan introduction to the abridged version), xiii–xiv; Menand, "Getting Real," *New Yorker,* November 14, 2011, 76. The younger Kennan was referring to Kennan's book, but his observation was equally true, if not more so, of the lectures. Kennan, 2nd Siberian Trip Notebook, November 6, 1885, LC Box 20.

190. Slatter, ed., *From the Other Shore,* 69–70; Kennan, *Siberia and the Exile System* 1:343–44; Travis, *George Kennan,* 216–20; "George Kennan Interviewed," *Stentor* (Lake Forest, Illinois) February 16, 1891, 99–100; Hundley, "George Kennan," 11–12; Stults, "George Kennan," 277.

191. Beer, *House of the Dead,* 347; Gentes, *Russia's Sakhalin Penal Colony,* 225–26. In an early draft of *Resurrection* Tolstoy included as a character an Englishman who was a Russophile and was writing a book to repudiate

George Kennan. The Englishman, according to Frederick Travis, was clearly the real-life Harry de Windt, who did just that. Travis, *George Kennan,* 232–34.

192. Gentes, *Russia's Sakhalin Penal Colony,* 13, 446–48; Hundley, "George Kennan," 11–12 citing George Kennan to Felix Volkhovsky, March 17, 1889, LC Box 1; Travis, *George Kennan,* 175–76, 228–29; Baylen, "Madame Olga Novikov," 256–57; Kennan, *Siberia and the Exile System* 2:514–17; Pipes, *Russia Under the Old Regime,* 301.

193. Kennan, *Siberia and the Exile System* 1: Preface, vi–vii & 2:515–17, 523; Kennan, "Mr. Kennan's Reply to Certain Criticisms," 958; Travis, *George Kennan,* 172–75; Gaddis, *Russia,* 30–31.

194. "Tales of Suffering," *St. Paul Globe,* March 11, 1890, 3; "Facts About Nihilism," *San Francisco Examiner,* December 16, 1888, 1 (a Russian-born American citizen and former Union Army officer accused Kennan of defending Russian nihilists who had committed murder); "About the City," *Star Tribune* (Minneapolis, Minnesota), March 15, 1890, 5; Kennan, *Siberia and the Exile System* 2:455–56.

195. George Kennan to Roswell Smith, October 15, 1888, enclosing J. G. Paxton to George Kennan, October 8, 1888, NYPL Digital Collections, https://digitalcollections.nypl.org/items/71a1bf80–7faa–0135–073e -1161a3f9f8b0/book?page_start=left#page/357/mode/2up; Kennan, *Siberia and the Exile System,* 1:98–102. Kennan divided the average daily Tiumen prison population by the annual number of inmate deaths, even though he had rejected that methodology in the 1885 letter to Roswell Smith, which Kennan had written while he was in Tiumen. In the letter Kennan explained that in the forwarding prison, where thousands of exiles pass through the prison between May and September alone, annual mortality cannot be calculated as though the prison population remained "fixed and stationary" throughout the year. George Kennan to Roswell Smith, June 28, 1885, LC Box 6; Travis, *George Kennan,* 167–69 & n. 51.

196. Beer, *The House of the Dead,* 348–50; Stults, "George Kennan," 275–82; George Kennan to Mary Ann Kennan, November 11, 1893, LC Box 68; "Kennan on the Jews," *Daily Inter Ocean* (Chicago, Illinois), October 15, 1891, 5; Kennan, *Siberia and the Exile System* 1:Preface, x.

197. Stults, "George Kennan," 284–85; Travis, *George Kennan,* 254–56, quoting Ida Tarbell to Emiline Kennan, July 25, 1901, LC Box 57; Daniloff, "George Kennan," 610; George Kennan to Robert Underwood Johnson, March 20, 1910, NYPL Digital Collections, https://digitalcollections.nypl .org/items/71a1bf80–7faa–0135–073e-1161a3f9f8b0/book?page_start =left#page/357/mode/2up.

198. Kennan, *Campaigning in Cuba,* 99–100, 141–47; George Kennan to Robert Underwood Johnson, December 4, 1903, April 3, June 11, 1910, NYPL Digital Collections, https://digitalcollections.nypl.org/items /71a1bf80–7faa–0135–073e-1161a3f9f8b0/book?page_start=left#page /357/mode/2up; George Kennan to Emiline Kennan, June 27, 1898, May

26, 1902, LC Box 15; Kennan, *The Tragedy of Pelee,* 100; Travis, *George Kennan,* 257–64, 277–80, 285, 289–91, 365–66.

199. Kennan, "A Few Recollections of Alexander Graham Bell," 146–49; George Kennan to George Frost Kennan, November 18, 1916, NYPL Box 1; Hotchkiss Notes, NYPL Box 7.

200. Travis, *George Kennan,* 301; Kennan, "The Unification of Russia," 71–74; Kennan, "The New Russian Premier," 131–32 (unsigned editorial); Kennan, "Russia After the War," 977–78; Kennan, "The Victory of the Russian People," 546; Gilbert, *First World War,* 313–15, 373–74.

201. "Ruination is Bolshevists' Motto," *Billings Gazette* (Billings, Montana), January 20, 1919, 2; "The Little Russian Grandmother," *Palladium-Item* (Richmond, Indiana), March 1, 1919, 19; Beer, *The House of the Dead,* 351; Blackwell, ed., *The Little Grandmother of the Russian Revolution,* 111–12, 119, 311–12. Before the revolution, between interludes of Siberian exile, she also spoke abroad to raise money for revolutionary causes. Chatterjee, "Imperial Incarcerations," 854–58; "Gallery Bolshevists Hiss M. Breshkovsky," *St. Louis Globe-Democrat,* May 19, 1919, 11; "Meets Explorer After 35 Years," *Asbury Park Press* (Asbury, New Jersey), February 11, 1919, 6; Kennan, *Siberia and the Exile System* (George Frost Kennan introduction to the abridged version), xvi, describing a conversation with a former Bolshevik, Mikhail Kalinin, now the chairman of the Presidium of the Supreme Soviet of the USSR; Kennan, "The Civil War in Russia," 455–56.

202. Beer, *The House of the Dead,* 383–85; Beer, "How Russia Wields Prisons as a Weapon Against its Political Opponents," *Globe and Mail,* December 21, 2017 https://www.theglobeandmail.com/opinion/how-russia-wields-prisons-as-a-weapon-against-its-political-opponents/article37411231/; Lincoln, *The Conquest of a Continent,* 164; Andrew E. Kramer, "What Awaits Navalny in Russia's Brutal Penal Colony System," *New York Times,* February 5, 2021, A10; Hartshorn, *I Have Seen the Future,* 315. Kennan and Emiline had been living in Medina since 1920. George Kennan, "The Leopard's Spots," *Medina Tribune,* July 12, 1923, 4. His commentary was picked up by a number of newspapers, e.g., "New Constitution of Russia Only a Farce," *Press Democrat,* (Santa Rosa, California), July 29, 1923, 10; Chatterjee, "Imperial Incarcerations," 857.

Epilogue: The Changing of the Guard

203. Williams, *The Bells of Russia,* 50; Beer, *The House of the Dead,* 1; Lobashkov, *Istoriia ssyl'nogo kolokola,* 32–45; "A Russian Bell," *Kansas City Age,* September 16, 1892, 5. The bell hangs today in the Uglich Museum of History and Art.

204. "Our Relations Toward Russia," *Argus Leader* (Sioux Falls, South Dakota), March 25, 1890, 2, quoting *New York Evening Post*; Good, "America and the Russian Revolutionary Movement," 273–79; Saul, *Concord & Conflict,* 468–69; Clifton Breckinridge to Secretary of State Richard Olney,

December 24, 1895, Despatch 191, Despatches From Russia, RG 59. The reference to the flogging of women may have been to Natalya Sigida, an imprisoned member of the People's Will, who was viciously flogged in 1889 for slapping the commander of the Kara women's prison and afterward committed suicide by taking poison. Beer, *House of the Dead*, 319–22.

205. George Kennan to George Frost Kennan, November 18, 1916, NYPL Box 1; George Kennan to Kossuth Kent Kennan, December 30, 1912, December 25, 1916, NYPL Box 1; Hotchkiss Notes, NYPL Box 7; Gaddis, *George F. Kennan*, 12; Frazier, *Travels in Siberia*, 59; Daniloff, "George Kennan," 607; Menand, "Getting Real," 76–83. The middle name "Frost" had nothing to do with the artist George Frost, but was on account of the friendship between George Frost Kennan's parents and a couple whose last name was Frost. Gaddis, *George F. Kennan*, 9.

206. *Autobiography*, 6–8, LC Box 88; George Kennan to Horace Morse, December 27, 1923, LC Box 14; "Mrs. Emaline [*sic*] Kennan," *Chicago Tribune*, May 28, 1940, 16; Hotchkiss Notes, NYPL Box 7.

Index